Motor Torpedo Boat Manual
February 1943

U.S. Navy

Motor Torpedo Boat Manual

February 1943

U.S. NAVY

UNITED STATES
GOVERNMENT PRINTING OFFICE
WASHINGTON: 1943

This manual must be burned or sunk, before it is possible for it to fall into the hands of an enemy.

~~RESTRICTED~~
[DECLASSIFIED]

COMMANDER IN CHIEF UNITED STATES FLEET,

NAVY DEPARTMENT,

Washington, D.C., February 1, 1943.

1. This Motor Torpedo Boat Manual (short title--Motorprons Two) is approved and issued to the service for use. This manual is RESTRICTED, may be issued to officers and petty officers of the Navy, and for instruction of naval personnel. It shall not be carried in aircraft for use therein.

2. Although motor torpedo boats are a relatively new weapon, considerable operating experience has been accumulated. Peacetime operation promoted valuable experimental work and the development of tactical, administrative, and operative procedures. Wartime operation against the enemy in the Pacific, to date, has already greatly added to the total experience

gained. As new squadrons are commissioned and sent to outlying bases, the importance of passing on the benefits of operating experience to new personnel needs no elaboration.

3. Each commanding officer shall keep a record of issue of this manual within his command. When no longer required or when its destruction is ordered, it shall be destroyed by burning. No report of destruction is required.

R.S. EDWARDS,
Chief of Staff.

Contents

Transcribed and formatted for HTML by Larry Jewell & Patrick Clancey, Hyperwar Foundation

Motor Torpedo Boat Manual

February 1943

⚓

U.S. Navy

PART I. MOTOR TORPEDO BOAT SQUADRONS, REGULATIONS AND INSTRUCTIONS (REVISED SEPTEMBER 1942)

Chapter 1. SQUADRON AND BOAT ORGANIZATION

SQUADRON ORGANIZATION

General.--The organization of the motor torpedo boat squadron is similar to that of an aircraft squadron in that the squadron, rather than the individual boat, is the commissioned unit. However, each motor torpedo boat functions as a commissioned vessel when acting singly.

For operations and tactics, the squadron is organized into several divisions of two or three vessels each which usually are the basis for task assignments. For administration and maintenance, the squadron is organized into departments.

An officer of suitable rank and experience will command each division. He will exercise tactical command at all times and

administrative command only when absent from the squadron commander. He will be responsible for the training and fighting efficiency of his division.

An officer assigned as boat captain will command each boat. Boat captains are directly responsible to the squadron commander for the preservation and operation of material in their charge, and for the training, efficiency and safety of personnel under their command. They will keep their boats in readiness for action at all times unless otherwise directed by the squadron commander for reasons of making overhaul and repairs.

Boat captains may be assigned additional duties as heads of departments or be required to perform other squadron duties.

Junior officers will be assigned duties as executive officers on individual boats in addition to collateral duties as assistant department heads. Such officers will be responsible to the respective heads of their departments for the proper performance of their collateral duties and responsible to their respective boat captains for their duties as executive officers.

Each boat captain and head of department will properly instruct an assistant (enlisted man if no officer assistant is available) so that the department or boat will function normally in his absence.

The duties of the squadron commander are, in general, those prescribed in Navy Regulations for the commanding officer of a ship.

The squadron executive officer will normally be the officer next in rank to the squadron commander. His duties are, in general, those prescribed in Navy Regulations for the executive officer of a ship, i. e., he will coordinate and supervise the interior administration of the squadron. He will be regarded as the representative of the squadron commander in issu:ng all orders and instructions. In the absence of the squadron commander he will take command of the squadron and carry out the orders and policies of the squadron commander.

The squadron shall be organized into the following administrative departments: Gunnery, navigation, communications, engineering, personnel, stores, commissary.

The senior officer in each department will be the head of department with other officers in that department as his assistants. In some cases, one officer may have more than one of the duties listed above.

Department heads will, in their relations to the squadron commander, bear responsibilities as laid down in Navy Regulations for department heads aboard ship. Each head of department will initiate the required action on all routine or other matters within the cognizance of his department.

BOAT ORGANIZATION

Complement.--Each boat shall normally consist of a crew of nine enlisted men and two officers. Each boat shall be under the command of an officer of suitable rank and ability, assigned as boat captain. The executive officer on each boat shall assist the boat captain in every way and he should strive to qualify in all respects for the position of boat captain.

The enlisted ratings on each boat will normally be:

> 1 TM, 1 GM, 1 QM, 1 RM, 3 engineers, 1 seaman, 1 SC.

Duties of a boat captain.--Each boat captain is responsible for the fighting efficiency of his boat and for the training and discipline of his crew. He is responsible also for its proper material upkeep and for the submission of all necessary records and reports. He must be prepared, when acting independently, to carry out his duties as commanding officer in accordance with Navy Regulations.

Each boat captain will make out a Watch, Quarter, and Station Bill for his crew which will be kept posted (a sample bill is included in the appendix). This bill is, in effect, the basis for the efficient organization and operation of the boat under the specific situations provided for and therefore it is of great importance that all hands familiarize themselves and carry out its provisions promptly and intelligently.

In addition, he will maintain on board a complete file of squadron orders, notices, and memorandums and insure that they

are understood by his crew. The following standard orders will be posted conspicuously as indicated:

Chart room:

> Deviation table.
> Speed, RPM, table.
> Fuel consumption table.

Near conn:

> Torpedo firing procedure.
> Below deck compartments:
> No smoking signs.

Engine room:

> Main engine starting and securing instructions.
> Engine safety precautions.

Guns:

> Operating instructions, safety precautions.

Magazines:

> Safety precautions.

Crew's compartment:

> Watch, Quarter, and Station Bill.
> Boat's orders.
> MTB safety precautions.
> Articles for the Government of the Navy.

Cleanliness and appearance.--The cleanliness and appearance of a boat should never be sought at the expense of the care and upkeep of its equipment; however, unless particularly heavy operating schedules have been maintained, boat personnel should be able to keep top side and below compartment spaces clean and shipshape. Boats' crews should take a pride in the cleanliness and appearance of their individual boats. A clean and smart looking boat reflects on the efficiency and ability of the officers and men on board.

The following are examples of a few specific practices to be observed in keeping a boat clean and shipshape:

Top side

Decks should be washed down daily with fresh water when available.

Lines and fenders should be stowed neatly and fenders never left hanging after getting under way.

Bunting should be kept two blocked and clean.

Colors should be made promptly and smartly by men in uniform.

Irish pennants should be eliminated.

Mats should be placed on top of torpedo tubes or on the parts of the boat where there is the most traffic to catch mud and to save the paint work.

Painted areas should be conspicuously marked and roped off.

Below decks

Bright work should be covered with a light oil and never polished unless so ordered by the boat captain.

Mats and decks should be swept down daily and washed twice a week or when otherwise required.

Bedding should be aired weekly.

Galleys should be kept scrupulously clean. Food should never be left exposed without reason and should always be removed from the ice box whenever the refrigeration system is secured. The cook should wash the ice box weekly with hot water and soda. All mess gear and silver should be kept clean and dry.

Heads should be kept clean and orderly. Towel racks and compartments for toilet articles should be provided for all hands. Toilet bowls should be emptied after use and drained before getting under way. The valve should always be secured after using the toilet under way.

Bulletin boards should be rid of old notices and a minimum of old reading material should be kept aboard.

Oilskins should not be stowed after a cruise until they are washed down with fresh water and dried.

Broken light bulbs and damaged equipment should be repaired or replaced promptly.

When moored to docks, boat captains will see that their crews are indoctrinated in proper methods of garbage disposal and also that dock areas used by their boats are kept clean.

Security in port.--All hands are in a duty status when on board and are responsible for the safety of the boat. The senior man or officer will take charge in case of an emergency.

An armed heel and toe sentry watch will be set outside of working hours on each boat or group of boats.

Whenever a boat is alone, at least two men will be aboard at all times and one of the two men should be an engineer.

Safety precautions.--Boat captains will take the steps necessary to insure that all members of his crew understand the Squadron Safety Regulations and Orders (see part III) and that same are conspicuously posted. Frequent fire drills should be held to promote a complete understanding of the location and use of all fire apparatus. Boat captains should insist on regular inspections for gas fumes and leaks.

Watertight integrity.--Watertight integrity measures will vary with the type of boat used; however, practical drills and demonstrations should be held to familiarize all hands with this subject. A boat expecting action with the enemy should establish maximum watertight integrity in advance of such action.

Inspections and reports.--When not under way (or if under way, on returning) the senior engineer and deck force ratings will thoroughly inspect their assigned spaces every Friday and report any material defects to the boat captain (faulty gaskets, supplies or parts needed, faulty drains, missing or broken fittings, broken or cracked planking, etc.). In conjunction with this inspection, self-bailers and drains will be cleaned.

While under way the boat captain will have all bilges inspected once each watch.

Stowage plan.--A standard stowage plan for each squadron, designed for the type boats used, should be promulgated and adhered to. Proper stowage is important for the following reasons:

1. Increases speed.

2. Facilitates keeping the boat clean and shipshape.

3. Expedites getting at equipment, bilges, lines, and hull damages when necessary.

4. Facilitates familiarization with location of equipment on board. When gas masks and life jackets are needed no time can afford to be lost searching for them.

It is the individual responsibility of each boat captain to see that unnecessary gear does not accumulate on his boat.

Wake effects.--Boat captains will make sure that their boats do not use excessive speeds in restricted waters and harbors. When passing the following close aboard, speed should be reduced to "Ahead" on one engine:

1. Diving or special operations.

2. Dredging.

3. Vessels flying Baker.

4. Small boats.

5. Pile drivers in operation.

6. Barges in tow.

7. Vessels alongside one another.

Good judgment in every case must govern. Justified complaints against boat captains on this account, will result in disciplinary action.

Change of Command

Relieving another of command.--In the case of an officer relieving another of command the boat captain about to be relieved will, before the transfer is effected, make a thorough examination of the boat and its equipment in company with his successor and cause the crew to be exercised at their emergency stations. He will point out any defects and account for them and explain fully any peculiarities of construction or arrangement of the boat. The officer about to be relieved will deliver to his successor the originals or authenticated copies of all general regulations and orders that are in force aboard, all documents received for his guidance in command, and other publications belonging to the boat. The officer being relieved will have all records and reports up to date and he shall sign all of them (including the deck log) before he is relieved. Under no circumstances will he remove the original records of his official correspondence, original letters, documents, or papers concerning, the boat. He will show his relief the location and conditions of all Title B and Title C equipment; whereupon, the relief will sign all the original custody cards accepting custody of all equipment. A statement in triplicate of the inspection and the relief will be drawn up, signed by the officer being relieved and, if satisfactory, signed by the officer relieving him. If the boat equipment, records, reports, or personnel are not satisfactory in

any respect, the officer relieving will so state with full details, and the officer being relieved will make such explanations as he may deem necessary, each over his own signature. One copy of this statement is to be forwarded to the squadron commander, and one retained by each of the officers between whom the transfer of command takes place.

Succession to command.--Should the officer regularly assigned to command a boat be absent, disabled, relieved from duty or detached without relief, the command will devolve upon the executive officer (or if there is no executive officer, on the senior man in crew) until relieved by competent authority, or Until the regular boat captain returns. This officer or man succeeding temporarily to command has the same authority and responsibilities as the regular boat captain, but he will make no change in the existing general orders, organization, or other permanent dispositions and will endeavor to have the routine and other affairs of the boat carried on the same as usual. An officer or man who succeeds to command as provided above acquires no increase of rank nor change in title.

Assuming command.--If assuming command of a new boat receipt for the boat should not be made and the boat not accepted until the boat has been inspected, its condition found satisfactory, and its equipment inventoried and noted in full on the receipt.

Chapter 2. Squadron Administration

A. GUNNERY DEPARTMENT

The duties of the gunnery officer shall be those of both a gunnery and a torpedo officer. His duties shall include the following:

1. Take charge generally of the procurement, care, and maintenance of all ordnance material (including blueprints and instruction books) of the squadron.

2. Supervise the issue and installation of all ordnance and pyrotechnic equipment.

3. Supervise the gunnery exercises of the squadron (including small arms practice).

4. Instruct boat captains and crews in the operation and care of all ordnance and pyrotechnic equipment.

5. Prepare and publish safety precautions relative to ordnance equipment and instruct personnel therein.

6. Check regularly to see that the routine upkeep and overhaul of ordnance equipment is being made on all boats.

7. Maintain all torpedoes and guns in a ready condition.

8. Frequently inspect for proper stowage and the condition of all squadron ammunition, explosives, and pyrotechnics whether on the boats, the base, or the tender.

9. Be responsible for required records and reports.

10. Take steps to replace all expended ordnance equipment.

11. Experimental work of a technical nature.

Care of ammunition and equipment.--The gunner's mate and torpedoman on each boat should each keep a rough log containing pertinent information on all ordnance equipment.

Too much stress cannot be laid on the importance of having all guns, torpedoes, depth charges, and ammunition in good serviceable working condition at all times. This goal can be achieved only if the gunner's mate and torpedoman on each boat give constant attention to their equipment.

--9--

In many cases certain standard practices exist for the care of ordnance equipment. These should always be used in preference to individualized or haphazard methods. For example, when making routine checks and inspections, the following check-off lists should be used:

Routine upkeep of torpedo tubes.
Routine upkeep of torpedoes.
Routine upkeep of .50-caliber MGs.
Routine upkeep of 20-mm. Oerlikon.
Routine upkeep of the Mark VI depth charges.
Routine upkeep of the smoke screen generator.

Copies of these check-off lists are given in the appendix of part II. Each boat should keep a supply on hand.

Incorrectly stowed ammunition may cause a disaster. Standard stowage of ammunition and pyrotechnics should always be observed. The following is a suggested stowage plan for the various types of boats:

--10--

Normal ammunition stowage

	Detonators	.50 cal.	20 mm.	Boosters	Impulse charges	Very's cartridges
Elco 77'	Cork-lined can fastened to starboard side of cockpit in wheel-house.	Tank room under turrets.	Ready boxes.	In boxes in sound room.	Cork-lined metal box after end tank room.	In belt on rack on port side of wheel house.
Elco 80'	Cork-lined can fastened to overhead in radio and chartroom.	Small arms locker near officers' stateroom.	do	In boxes in rack on bulkhead compartment aft of officers' breakfast nook.	Cork-lined cases under seat in officers' breakfast nook.	In belt stowed in rack in chartroom on after bulkhead.

Huckins	Cork-lined cans fastened to ledge on starboard side of ladder to small gear locker.	In .50 cal. lockers or just abaft guns.	do	In racks on starboard bulkhead of officers' stateroom.	In small locker on starboard side of cockpit.	In belt in rack on starboard side of cockpit.
Higgins	Cork-lined boxes on starboard side of after chartroom bulkhead near overhead.	At guns or in ready boxes.	do	In boxes in small locker outboard starboard side of superstructure.	None	In belt in rack on chartroom after bulkhead.

Inspection and care of .30, .45 and .50 caliber ammunition.--

1. Protect ammunition against dirt, moisture, or blows which might injure ammunition.

2. Make a thorough visual examination of new ammunition to eliminate defective rounds.

3. Keep ammunition covered and out of direct rays of the sun.

4. Remove any trace of rust with kerosene periodically.

5. Do not polish or grease cartridges.

6. Stow belts (.50 cal.) properly in boxes.

7. While firing (.50 cal.) maintain alignment of the cartridges in the belts to insure uninterrupted fire. Load with loading machine and handle carefully to avoid misalignments.

8. Do not stow black powder, detonators, or boosters with small arms ammunition.

9. When possible after firing, the boat captain will take steps, at the first opportunity, to have all empty cartridge cases, clips, and packing boxes shipped to the nearest Naval Ammunition Depot. Precaution should be taken to see that no live cartridges are boxed with the empty cartridge cases. Each box containing empty cartridge cases should have a tag with the inspecting officer's name attached.

Care and handling of 20 mm. ammunition.--

1. Ammunition should be kept cleaned and greased.

2. Ammunition should be loaded with a tracer ratio of one tracer to three nontracers.

3. Tension should be left off the magazine spring of all but two magazines until reasonably

sure action is imminent, i. e. within a few hours.

4. Two magazines with tension should be kept available at all times.

5. Rotate the above magazines.

6. When tension is on, it should be kept fully on.

7. Magazines should be stowed in ready boxes except when loaded on the gun.

Torpedo tubes.--Due to the necessity for keeping torpedoes ready for firing at a moment's notice, tube covers are no longer kept on the tubes. Therefore, in order to insure against stop pins shearing and a torpedo unexpectedly slipping out, all Mark 18-1 tubes should be equipped with 1/4-inch steel-wire bridles to secure over the war head. This bridle has a tripping

latch which can be tripped in a second once action is expected.

To replace the watertight features of a tube cover, a heavy axle grease packed liberally in the seam between the tube and the warhead will prove very satisfactory.

Tubes should be dove once a month and slushed. Kerosene or paint thinner can be used to clean tubes. A good slush is a mixture of heavy grease and hot-running torpedo oil. Care must be taken to prevent grit, etc., from getting into the tube as a small amount of grit will cause a long deep scratch oh the air flask.

Torpedoes.--Since torpedoes are the most important piece of equipment on a boat, no effort should be spared in caring for them.

New squadrons getting torpedoes should inspect them immediately for defects. One defect was discovered in the starting lever of a torpedo which was too long. The torpedo was loaded in the tube without difficulty but a small amount of friction tripped the lever and started a hot run.

War heads.--War heads hit by .50 caliber bullets are not apt to explode on impact; however, they will probably start burning and explode shortly; therefore, war heads ignited in this way should be disposed of by firing the torpedo or otherwise jettisoning it.

Depth charges.--The gunnery officer should require boat captains to have white depth index lines painted on depth charges to facilitate reading settings at night without the aid of light.

Machine guns.--To forestall rust action in the case of the 20 mm. Oerlikon and the .50 cal machine guns, it will be necessary to break down and clean the guns at least weekly if they have not been directly exposed to salt spray or sea water. When the latter is the case, the guns should be cleaned and oilea at the first opportunity. A great deal of unnecessary cleaning work can be avoided by keeping the guns covered when action is not expected; however, good judgment must always govern in this regard; readiness for action must never be sacrificed to keep equipment dry. In the case of the .50 cal. machine guns, keeping small covers over the stabilizers at the end of the barrels will keep moisture from getting down the barrels and, in an emergency, the guns can be fired without removing these covers.

Machine gun links.--From considerable experience it has been noted that the M-1 links cause considerable jamming. It is recommended that the M-2 should be the only type accepted in commissioning allowances. This type is considerably more reliable.

20 mm. Oerlikon.--Difficulty sometimes arises in clearing a jammed 20 mm. projectile from the barrel. It is not safe to hit the ejector tool with a hammer.

One method of clearing the barrel is to cut small grooves with a rat-tail file in the cup of the ejector tool and then press on the handle until the fuse can be backed off.

Another method is to place the barrel in a vise, insert the ejector, and place a jack (with suitable backing) so that pressure can be put on the ejector handle to back out the projectile.

Torpedo impulse charges.--In connection with preservation of torpedo impulse charges, the wadding should be shellacked to prevent entrance of moisture, even though the wadding has originally been treated with acetone to produce a seal.

Smoke screen generator.--Care should be taken not to paint over working parts. They should be kept cleaned and greased,

Rust.--A commercial compound named "Oakite" will produce marked results in removing rust; however, an ounce of prevention is worth a pound of cure, particularly with regard to rust.

The above suggestions for caring for and handling ammunition and equipment are only a few samples of the sort of care and> attention the ordnance equipment should receive.

B. NAVIGATION DEPARTMENT

The duties of the squadron navigator, in general, shall be as follows:

1. See that squadron and boats' deck logs contain correct entries and are up to date.

2. Be responsible for procurement of firing notices and corrections to all charts and navigational publications used by the squadron.

3. Collect and prepare all navigation and weather reports and submit same to boat captains or quartermasters.

4. See that each boat has a record of intended courses to be steered and rendezvous points on extended operations.

5. Submit estimated dates and mileage of proposed operations to stores and commissary officer to facilitate their ordering of stores, fuel, oil, provisions, etc.

6. See that all compasses are properly calibrated and deviation tables prepared and posted on each boat.

7. Experimental work of a technical nature.

Chronometers and Chronometer Record Books

The squadron navigator should have custody of all squadron chronometers and chronometer record books. He should see that the chronometers are wound regularly, that "ticks" are gotten daily, and entries made in the record books.

The quartermaster of any boat undertaking an extended operation or taking up a patrol or readiness station or duty should draw the boat's chronometer and record book from the squadron navigator and report this fact to the boat captain before getting under way.

Charts and navigational publications.--Perhaps the most important single duty of a squadron navigator is to see that boat captains have their charts and navigational publications kept corrected to date. It is also his duty to check the security of all registered charts.

Log writing.--In Part A, Records, samples are given of writing the ship's log. The squadron navigator should indoctrinate squadron quartermasters in correct log writing procedures in order to achieve uniformity, accuracy and completeness.

Charts.--Charts should be kept clean and corrected to date. They should also be filed in an orderly manner to permit quick, ready reference.

Compasses.--The boat's compass must be kept accurately calibrated and a deviation table posted in the chart room.

Fuel consumption, RPM versus speed table.--These tables must be kept posted in the chart room.

Publications.--The following navigation publication should be kept on board each boat: Coast Pilot, Tide and Current Tables, Nautical Almanac, Chart List, Bowditch, HO 205, HO 206. HO 211.

Clocks.--All boats' clocks should be kept wound regularly and synchronized daily with the squadron timepiece.

Chartroom lights.--It has been determined that the brilliance of a normal white chart room light has an adverse effect on vision for as long as 30 minutes after exposure and that certain colored, lights adversely affect vision to a much lesser degree; red, for instance, impairs the vision for only 10 minutes after exposure. Boat captains would do well to experiment to get the most satisfactory lighting arrangements possible for their chartrooms. Red battle lights are now part of standard equipment.

Lookouts.--Boat captains must indoctrinate their crews in the vital importance of standing taut lookout watches and in the prescribed method of reporting objects sighted. When practicable, lookouts should always use binoculars and keep dark glasses on hand. Lookouts should be relieved frequently and. should be notified of objects the boat captain expects to sight.

Care of equipment.--Navigation equipment must be kept in a first class, orderly condition at all times. The following are a few examples of "good practice" for the quartermaster:

1. Keep charts corrected to date, clean, and neatly filed.

2. Keep navigation publications corrected to date, neatly stowed, and readily available.

3. Keep all Title B equipment such as binoculars, clocks, stop watches, etc., carefully accounted for, clean, and neatly stowed when not in use.

4. Keep bunting in good repair and neatly stowed.

5. See that lines are well dried before stowing and are stowed neatly.

6. See that oilskins are dried and clean before hanging up.

7. If available, keep a small supply of towelling on hand for wear around the neck under oilskins.

8. Keep an adequate supply of sharpened pencils, scratch paper, lens paper, thumb tacks, etc., so that laying out a course will not be delayed by last minute searches for these items.

C. COMMUNICATION DEPARTMENT

The squadron communication officer is responsible for efficient and rapid communications between units of the squadron and between the squadron and other activities and units of the fleet and armed forces. The more specific responsibilities of the communications officer will include:

1. The proper safeguarding of registered and classified publications and change and corrections thereto.

2. The upkeep, repair, and overhaul of radio and electrical equipment.

3. Instruction of officers and boats' crews in communication discipline, practice and procedure.

4. The dissemination of recognition signals to the boats and their destruction after use.

5. Establishing of a coding board when necessary to have one.

6. Censorship.

7. Familiarization of all squadron personnel with the principles of security and informing them of the subjects which must never be discussed outside the squadron.

8. Collection and dissemination of intelligence information and reports. Duties as squadron intelligence officer.

9. Investigating and developing methods for efficient communication in emergencies with other units of the fleet and armed forces, including predetermined frequency and call arrangement, plans, etc.

10. Supervising proper calibration of all radio direction finders.

11. The proper routing of dispatches, for information or action, to members of the squadron.

The communication officer should thoroughly familiarize himself with the following publications:

a. Communications Instructions, U.S. Navy.

b. MTB Doctrine and Standard Procedure Part V, Ch. 2.

c. U.S. Navy Call Sign Book Part I and II.

d. Operators Manual.

e. Berne List.

f. Communication Procedure Signals.

g. Coding System(s) in use for the squadron and on the boats.

He should see that (c) through (f) inclusive are carried on the boats. The boats should carry only those codes on board which are absolutely necessary for contact reports and minimum communication of confidential and secret information. For this latter purpose MTBs are currently using aircraft codes.

Security.--The communications officer will see that all hands are notified that the following subjects, particularly, should never be discussed outside the squadron:

a. The design, armament, construction, power, and and speed of the boats.

b. The type of equipment used, fuel or fresh water capacity, cruising radius.

c. The disposition of the boats and their tactical use or employment.

d. Their movements, how transported, and casualties to the boats or to the squadron personnel.

e. Other ships present in harbors, their movements. Arrival or departure of supplies or equipment.

f. In addition to the above, all hands must be indoctrinated in the principles of security to be observed with regard to the operation of the radio.

Dispatches.--The communication officer will see that all officers in the squadron are familiar with the degrees of urgency assigned to dispatches, how to determine same, and the correct procedure for handling all dispatches.

Care of equipment.--In carrying out his duties in caring for radio and electrical equipment, the communications officer should see that the boat captains have the following general practices carried out on all boats:

Radio

1. Protection of radio equipment from the weather, with immediate steps to dry and clean equipment which has been accidentally exposed.

2. Keep manufacturer's instruction book and operating instructions for the set near the radio.

3. Keep calibration cards on equipment properly filled out.

4. Operation of transmitter and receiver at least 15 minutes daily, testing all phones and microphones at this time.

5. Keep all antennae connections tight and insulators clean and free of paint.

6. Keep all dials and controls in good working order.

7. Have all vacuum tubes tested monthly.

8. Keep 100 percent spare tubes and 300 percent spare fuses on board.

9. Keep motor generators greased in accordance with instructions in TCS instruction book.

10. Immediately report erratic performance of the equipment to the squadron repairman,

Direction Finder

1. Protection of equipment from exposure to the weather.

2. Keep RDF battery fully charged and properly watered.

3. Operation of equipment at least 15 minutes daily.

4. Keep all insulators clean and free of paint.

5. Have vacuum tubes tested monthly.

6. Have collector rings cleaned and greased lightly, monthly.

7. Keep 100 percent spare vacuum tubes and 300 percent spare fuses aboard.

8. Check mechanical alignment of loop weekly.

M. P. Light

1. If exposed to the weather, clean and dry the light immediately after use.

2. If light is battery operated, check condition of batteries weekly.

3. Operate light daily.

4. Keep one spare bulb and one spare battery aboard.

5. NEVER stow light unless dry and clean.

Searchlight

1. Operate light daily.

2. Keep switches and controls in good working order at all times.

3. Keep one spare bulb and 300 percent spare fuses aboard.

4. Immediately replace any cracked or broken lens.

5. Keep light trained down when not in use.

Blinker tube

1. Operate daily, moving iris through its scope.

2. Keep tube free of corrosion.

3. Keep one spare bulb and one set of batteries aboard.

4. NEVER stow tube unless dry and clean.

Except for the wiring in the engine room instrument panel, radioman will not be held responsible for electrical equipment in the engine room. This equipment will be cared for and checked by engineers.

D. ENGINEERING DEPARTMENT

The duties of the engineering officer shall also include those of hull officer (first lieutenant) on a ship. He should familiarize himself with engineering practices contained in Motor Torpedo Boat Squadrons Doctrine and Standard Procedures, the Packard instruction book, and the Manual of Engineering Instructions, U.S. Navy. His duties will include:

1. The maintenance of engines, power plant instruments, fuel systems, oil systems, engine accessories, and auxiliary power plants and their installations.

2. The maintenance and repair of the structural parts of boats, including surfaces, hull, ship-control instruments, and torpedo tube, machine gun turret, and engine foundations.

3. The conduct of suitable inspections of work being done on equipment under his cognizance. Experimental work of a technical nature pertaining to power plants and their accessories and to structural features of the boats.

4. The maintenance of hull and machinery histories, engine logs, and auxiliary power unit logs, and the recording of all

necessary data pertaining to the operation of power plants and their installations. The execution of frequent inspections to see that individual boat engineering records are properly kept and up to date.

5. The compilation of reports relative to engineering required by the Bureau of Ships (Engineering).

6. The instruction of boat captains and engineers in the best methods of operation of power plants and their accessories arid the posting of proper and adequate instructions and safety precautions in each boat relative to operating same.

7. The publication of MTB Engineering bulletins publicizing sound engineering practices and procedures.

8. Obtaining and maintaining supply of essential engineering and hull spare parts.

9. The weekly weighing and recharging, as necessary, of all fire extinguishers. These should be recharged if the weight is less than the weight stamped on the data plate.

Care of Equipment

New engines.--When a new engine is installed, a short "break in" period is desirable before the engine is subjected to normal operating conditions. The following schedule should be followed:

Time	R.P.M.
30 minutes	800
30 minutes	1,000
1 hour	1,200
1 hour	1,400
1 hour	1,600
1 hour	1,800
1 hour	2,000
30 minutes	2,200

Overhauls.--The engines of a PT boat must be kept in good condition regardless of operating schedules. Prescribed 25-, 50-, and 100-hour checks, as outlined in the Packard instruction book, must be made.

Major repairs.--Salt-water corrosion seriously damages engines and increases the cost of overhaul by several thousand dollars per engine. The extent of the damage done may be greatly reduced and in some cases eliminated by the proper application of a thin film of Rust Preventative Compound, Grade III, (Tectyl 511). This material is a thin liquid consisting of preservative compounds of the so-called polar type dissolved in naphtha. When applied to metal, it spreads over the surfaces and after evaporation of its volatiles, leaves a tenacious moisture-resisting film. This compound also has the property of displacing water from contact with metal surfaces.

As soon as possible after an engine has been immersed it should be treated as follows:

1. The lubricating oil tank should be filled with compound and it should be circulated through the lubricating oil system by turning the engine over, either with the starter or by hand.

2. The spark plugs should be removed and the cylinders slushed with compound. The engines should be turned over to aid in spreading the compound.

3. The valve-housing covers should be removed and the valve gear and camshaft slushed.

4. The flame arrester should be removed and the carburetor and supercharger slushed.

5. The crankcase should be filled with compound and then drained.

6. The hand-hole inspection plate on top of reverse gear housing should be removed, the housing filled with compound and then drained.

7. All accessories and exterior surfaces should be sprayed or painted with compound.

8. If practicable the engine should be dried with low pressure air. The compound should never be allowed to stand on electric coils because it has a tendency to cause the insulation to swell.

Tectyl 511 may be obtained from Navy Yard, New York, Norfolk, or Mare Island.

If an excess of water comes in contact with a surface treated with this compound, the surface must be re-treated as the compound is soluble in water.

Until regular base facilities for repair and overhaul become available, it is preferable to have major repairs on engines performed at the factory, if possible, especially during the guarantee period of 90 days after delivery. Minor repairs may be accomplished

by the ship's force or present naval shore establishment units.

When an engine is returned to the factory for overhaul or repair, the following procedure applies:

1. Exhaust stacks, flanges, and salt water cross-connections are left on the boat.

2. On wing engines, remove exhaust manifold and plate and install one without a petcock.

3. Pipes leading from the salt-water manifold are removed and left on the boat.

4. Temperature units for "oil in," "oil out," and "water out" are removed and left on the boat.

5. All fresh water piping above fresh water stacks on valve housing are removed and left on the boat.

6. All piping on fresh water suction is left on the boat.

7. All of tachometer sending unit except the outside flange remains with the boat.

8. Booster-coil connecting-wire remains with the boat.

9. (Elco) Starter solenoid may be taken off new engine and returned with old one (solenoid not used).

   (Higgins) Junction box on top of starter is removed and left on boat.

   (Huckins) Solenoid is used on starter, old one should be removed with engine and a new one installed.

10. Reverse gear, starter, and generator are returned with old engine.

11. Oil primer and vacuum lines of copper and elbow on vacuum oil reducer bushing remain on the boat.

12. Shifting lever remains on the boat.

13. As rust preventative measures, the following steps are taken using Tectyl 511:

    A. The spark plugs are removed and each cylinder slushed with compound and sprayed with a spray gun. The engine should be jacked over during the operation.

    B. The supercharger shaft vent plug is removed and the compound poured over the supercharger impeller shaft; oil-seal ring-housing assembly.

    C. The valve housing covers are removed and the valve-gear camshaft slushed.

    D. Spray crankshaft and rods through breather ports on starboard side of engine.

E. Remove cover plate on reverse-gear housing and spray with compound. Jack engine over several times during operation.

F. Spray tectyl on all external bare neutral parts.

Broken parts should be labelled and wrapped and secured to the engine. The engine, with engine log attached, is returned in the box in which it was originally shipped from the Packard Motor Co., Detroit, Mich., or a similar box. This shipping is taken care of through the nearest naval supply officer.

The above routine also applies to engines which are to be laid up for any length of time. It applies particularly to Packard 4M-2500 engines, but will also apply to other engines as much as is practicable.

Hull.--In connection with caring for the hull the following points should be observed:

a. Self bailers should be checked weekly. Bilge bailers should be checked three times a week to see that intake strainers are clean, fittings are tight, the valve works freely, and the anti-siphon hole is open.

b. Care must be taken not to fall into the habit of painting over instead of cleaning. A complete coat of paint weighs over two hundred pounds and will affect the boat's speed. No painting other than that authorized by the hull officer will be permitted. Bilges should not be painted grey, as this color prevents detection of gas stains which indicate the presence of gas fumes.

c. All structural casualties, cracks, fractures, etc., should be reported immediately to the hull officer to permit repair before a condition becomes aggravated.

Casualties.--Whenever a machinery casualty occurs, the boat captain will enter details as casualty and repairs effected in deck log N. nav. 140, and engineering log. He will also see that the casualty is entered on machinery history cards and, if main engines, entered also in the main engine log book. He will

submit immediately to squadron commander, via squadron engineer, a complete report on Report of Machinery Derangement form (see chapter on Reports and Records). He will take all possible steps to repair the casualty as soon as possible.

The squadron engineer will assist the boat captain in the above step and will take all possible steps to see that the casualty does not occur again in the squadron.

Engineering bulletins.--From time to time as engineering developments occur, certain practices will be seen to be advisable in the care and handling of the engines, such practices, precautions, information, and orders as become apparent will be published periodically in

MTB Engineering Bulletins. A complete file of these will be kept on each boat and will be read and complied with by the boat captain and all engineering ratings. Engineering routine upkeep and check-off lists will be available to, and frequently checked by, the squadron engineering officer.

E. PERSONNEL DEPARTMENT

The personnel officer shall also be welfare and recreation officer and shall act as assistant to the executive officer. He shall make a continuous effort to familiarize himself with all important official matter on subjects pertaining to personnel.

He shall keep himself informed, insofar as practicable, of the physical capacity, service record, and experience of each man assigned to the squadron, and he will carry out the following duties:

1. Keep a record of names, rates, special qualifications, and assignments to boats, of all men attached to the squadron, and of particular duties assigned each man.

2. Prepare and maintain personnel reports and records, and be in charge of the squadron office personnel and files.

3. Make recommendations regarding the assignment of men for various duties in the squadron.

4. Receive and prepare recommendations relative to all personnel requests and record and investigate all reports against men in the squadron.

5. Receive muster reports.

6. Interest himself in the general health, welfare, recreation, and contentment of the enlisted personnel; take charge of general educational courses and courses for advancement in rating; advise men as to military, civil, and social rights and privileges.

7. Have charge of berthing and messing of enlisted personnel.

8. Be responsible for establishing and maintaining security watches in accordance with the orders of the squadron commander.

The personnel officer will see that orders and regulations regarding the following are publicized and enforced:

a. Alcoholic beverages.
b. Cameras.
c. Discipline.

    d. Emergency drills.

    e. Uniform.

    f. Gambling.

    g. Leave.

    h. Liberty.

    i. Squadron duty lists and watches.

    j. Squadron vehicles.

Depending on the wishes of the squadron commander concerned and the particular circumstances surrounding the squadron, the exact nature of the above orders and regulations are publicized and carried out.

The personnel officer will provide for and supervise the following:

Training.--As in the other specialized branches of the Navy, the proper training of personnel is of great importance in MTB duty. It is likely that the majority of all MTB squadron personnel will be graduates of the MTB Training Center; however, it is important that all personnel who are not graduates, be qualified at the earliest possible date. To qualify new personnel, the personnel officer should arrange a period and course of instruction for the new men, supplying them with adequate instructional material and arranging for qualified PT men to give them practical instruction in the boats.

After a reasonable period of training (4 weeks at least) the personnel officer should have the candidate given a written and practical examination by each department. The examinations

will be based on the requirements approved by the Bureau of Naval Personnel (a copy of these is included in the appendix). When the candidate(s) pass the examination and are recommended by the squadron commander, they may be considered qualified. The personnel officer should then have an entry made in each man's service record to this effect. No unqualified man should be permitted to wear the MTB insignia until duly qualified. The personnel officer should see that this order is publicized.

Advancement in rating.--One of the most important subjects affecting enlisted morale is advancement in rating. Personnel officers and boat captains should thoroughly familiarize themselves with this subject. In this regard they should study:

    Bureau of Naval Personnel Manual--Part D.

    Bureau of Naval Personnel Circular Letters.

    Yearbook of Enlisted Training.

Squadron personnel officers should write the Training Division of the Bureau for an adequate supply of course books, progress tests, and general training courses. The course books should be made available to men wishing to study for advancement. They should be taken up, however, during progress test examinations.

In view of the close working relationship of boat captains and their crews, boat captains, as well as the personnel officer, should interest themselves in the details of advancement in rating. Only by knowing the details will they be able to guide and counsel their crews in this important matter.

Athletics.--When operating schedules are not too severe and facilities are available, squadron personnel should be encouraged to participate in voluntary athletics. Good physical condition in PT duty is essential although this fact is not always apparent to those who have never experienced long hours on board a PT in rough weather.

The personnel officer should make the necessary arrangements and provide the facilities for a successful athletic program.

Welfare and recreation fund.--When money becomes available from Ship's Service receipts or from the sale of soft drinks, etc., a welfare and recreation fund should be established. Money in this fund may be used only for the comfort and recreation of the

enlisted personnel and for no other purpose. This fund should be audited by the stores officer or the disbursing officer if one is attached to the squadron.

Morale

The commanding officer of a ship is explicitly charged with the promotion of a healthy morale. The executive officer is responsible for the efficient administration of all details relating to personnel. The personnel officer of a squadron can greatly assist the squadron commander and executive officer in promoting good morale by keeping the training, health, comfort, and contentment of the enlisted personnel at heart and by efficient administration of personnel problems.

Personnel administration.--Officers with little or no experience in personnel administration should familiarize themselves at the first opportunity with the following specific subjects as they are of recurring importance (the source of information is also given; in each case the publication is the Bureau of Naval Personnel Manual):

a. The Terms of Reenlistment and Extension of Enlistment (D-1002, 1005, 1006, 1007).

b. Preparation of Identification Tags (D-2005).

c. Service Records--Care, Description and Custody of (D-4001, 4002, 4003, 4004).

d. Continuous Service Certificates--Description of (D-4005).

e. Report of Personnel (D-4007).

f. Personnel Accounting (D-4012), the Transfer Book (D-4014), the Ration Book (D-4015).

g. Service Record---Detailed Instructions--be familiar with but do not commit to memory (D--1021, 4022).

h. Ratings and Their Abbreviations--memorize (D-5101).

i. Precedence of Ratings (D-5102).

j. Distribution of Ratings by Pay Grades--memorize (D-5103).

k. Advancement in Rating--General (D-5104)--peruse (D-5105, 5304).

l. Navy Mail Clerk--peruse (D-5305).

m. Permanent and Temporary Additions to Pay (D-5326).

n. Appointments and Promotions--peruse (D-6101, 6225).

o. Transfers and Details--peruse (D-7001).

p. Transmittal of Records and List of Records Accompanying Transfers (D-7009).

q. Pay Accounts--During Transportation, Not Received (D-7012, 7013).

r. Leave and Liberty (D-7027, 7028).

s. Unauthorized Absence; Stragglers; Desertion (D-8001, 8002, 8003, 8004).

t. Marks; Standards Established (D-8020).

u. Classification of Discharges (D-9101).

v. Small Stores (consult senior yeoman or storekeeper).

F. STORES DEPARTMENT

The stores officer has the following duties:

1. He will have cognizance over matters relating to supply and will act as squadron supply officer unless a regular supply officer is attached.

2. He will be charged with the procurement of all material and will sign all custody receipts to the supply officer to whom supply and storekeeping activities of the squadron are regularly assigned.

3. He will at all times have information available concerning the amount of unexpended and unobligated portion of allotments .

4. He will act as representative for the squadron commander in all supply details.

5. He will order fuel and oil and supervise delivery of the same.

6. He will maintain, on the duplicate copy of Title B custody records, signed sub-custody receipts for equipage in use in the squadron.

7. He will survey parts worn out. in .use which are no longer suitable for use as spares. (Requests for survey will be.submitted through him.)

8. He will be responsible for the cleanliness.and preservation, of MTB storage spaces on the tender and storerooms ashore,

9. He will not be relieved from his duties as such or detached.

Until the squadron supply officer has indicated in writing that all material for which he is held responsible has been signed for by his successor, or otherwise properly accounted for.

10. He will collect monthly lists of stores and spare parts not on hand and required by the boats for the next three months. These lists will be approved by heads of departments. These lists should permit the stores officer to procure stores in a normal manner and avoid last-minute rushes. It is impossible to obtain many spares and stores on a few days' notice.

11. He will prepare job orders for repair and overhaul of boats.

12. He will maintain account of and make reports on status of repair funds.

13. He will administer and keep account of welfare and recreation fund.

G. COMMISSARY DEPARTMENT

The mission of the commissary department is the efficient administration of the general mess for the health and contentment of the personnel subsisted therein.

The following are the duties and responsibilities of the commissary officer:

1. The commissary officer is directly responsible to the commanding officer concerning the condition of the mess.

2. The commissary officer will make all reports to Bureau of Supplies and Accounts, quarterly.

3. He will keep an accurate file on all reports, orders, provisions ordered and received.

4. He will approve all orders for provisions (Form No. 48) and sign same before they are mailed to contractors.

5. He will keep a record of all purchases including name of contractor, contract number, items purchased, amount, and unit cost. This record will be used to check against bills received at the end of each month.

6. He will require all boat captains operating independently to keep a record of all provisions purchased and received from supply officers afloat and ashore, and submit same to commissary officer at the end of each month. He will also require boat captains to report number of rations claimed for the month including rations furnished officers. Where supplies are secured

--30--

from a supply officer at a Navy Yard he will require: the boat captains to get an invoice before leaving port.

Whenever possible provisions should be obtained from supply officers. Open purchases are allowed only where no contracts are in force. The consent of the commanding officer is necessary to make open purchases. When they are made, the following signed certificate will be made on dealers bills:

Awarded after competition to the lowest responsible bidder.

Received, inspected, passed. Prices hereon are correct.

Delivered at_____   Date_____

_____
Commanding

An inventory should be taken monthly and upon change of commanding officers. The following statement should be placed on each inventory:

I certify that this inventory covers all provisions actually on board this date and that I hold myself accountable for them.

_____

The following is an inclusive list of commissary forms to be submitted with the quarterly ration record to the Bureau of Supplies and Accounts:

Record	*Form*
(*a*) Monthly Ration Record	S&A No. 45
(*b*) Order and Inspection Report	S&A No. 48
(*c*) Receipt, Expenditure Invoice	S&A No. 71
(*d*) Statement of Sales to Mess	S&A No. 332
(*e*) Survey Request, Report, and Expenditure	S&A No. 154
(*f*) Monthly Ration Memorandum	S&A No. 27
(*g*) Certified Inventory of Provisions	S&A No. 143

The commissary officer should get copies of these forms and familiarize himself with them. The Chief Commissary Stewards Training Course Book, Assignment No. 10, gives complete information on these forms and should be studied.

--31--

In addition to the duties and responsibilities outlined above, the commissary officer should also see that:

a. Commissary personnel wear clean, white uniforms and are personally clean.

b. Refrigeration and storage spaces, galley equipment, and mess gear are clean and orderly. (Cleanliness of mess gear in the Navy is normally the responsibility of the first lieutenant but in operating MTB squadrons it is customary for the commissary officer to assume this

c. Satisfactory seating and "chow line" arrangements are made after consultation with the personnel and executive officers.

d. Hot coffee and sandwiches are available to boats returning from late operations and to men on late working parties.

e. Watertight, abandon ship rations are issued to the boats.

The commissary department of a motor torpedo boat squadron must be of the highest standard. Unavoidable circumstances such as inadequate base facilities, continual change of bases, irregular hours of operation of boats, etc., require unusual patience and resourcefulness on the part of the commissary department if all hands are to get appetizing and nourishing rations.

--32--

Chapter 3. Safety Precautions and Regulations

It is of vital importance that all hands attached to motor torpedo boat squadrons realize and appreciate the importance of observing all safety precautions and regulations. One careless step may result in the loss of life and the destruction of millions of dollars' worth of fighting equipment. The following safety measures must be rigidly observed and enforced:

1. **Smoking.**--

    a. There shall be no smoking on any boat while in a nest or while moored in a harbor.

    b. There shall be no smoking at anytime below decks. The smoking lamp shall be lit only with the boat captain's permission.

    c. There will be no smoking on boats in the war zone at night.

    d. Lighted cigarettes will never be thrown over the side.

    e. Smoking shall not be permitted within 25 feet of a nest of boats.

2. **Fueling.**--During fueling, the following precautions shall be observed:

    a. Hoist Baker.

    b. Secure the master load switch.

    c. Two CO_2 extinguishers topside near the fuel inlet.

    d. All hands (other than those actually fueling) must be off the boat.

    e. A three-way grounding between the nozzle of the hose and the boat and the truck or fuel pipe.

    f. Fire truck at scene.

    g. Notify all hands in the vicinity that fueling is in progress and post a member of the crew to keep people away from boat during operation.

    h. Avoid filling tanks to overflow point. If tanks overflow the engines should not be lighted off until the wind or tide has carried the gas clear of the hull.

i. Avoid any actions generally that might cause sparks.

j. Do not fuel at night unless absolutely necessary.

k. Have fire extinguishers permanently available on dock.

Safety precautions for fueling under way from tender.--

a. The routine safety precautions always observed in fueling.

b. No one is permitted on deck except those necessary for fueling.

c. The personnel actually engaged in fueling the boat must wear life preservers.

d. Damage to the boat must be prevented by the use of fenders and under no conditions should boat personnel attempt to fend the boat off by hand.

e. If there are more MTB's which have completed fueling or are standing by to fuel, one should proceed astern of the tender and be prepared to pick up any one who may fall off the boat which is fueling. The others should patrol off the bow of the tender as an antisubmarine screen.

3. **Bonding.--**

a. All broken bonding must be reported to the boat captain promptly and repairs effected immediately.

b. Bonding is the main safeguard against sparks due to static electricity and therefore the bonding system should be inspected regularly at frequent intervals.

4. **Tetraethyl fumes.--**These fumes are highly poisonous and if present in the air in sufficient volume will poison personnel quickly. These fumes are most likely to be present during operation of the mufflers. Therefore, no person will be permitted to sleep in the lazarette of a boat or in any other part that the boat captain may determine to be unsafe from fumes.

5. **Hydrogen gases.--**Storage batteries must be properly ventilated to permit normal escape of hydrogen gas. Poorly ventilated batteries cause dangerous gas pressures to develop which may cause a serious explosion.

6. **Firing circuits.--**Torpedo-firing circuits must be tested daily before getting under way and a report made to the boat captain to this effect. They should never be tested with a live impulse charge in the chamber.

7. **Testing gears.--**Before making a landing, the helmsman will signal engines in neutral to

test for proper functioning of gears. This must be done sufficiently in advance of making a landing to allow time to correct for a "stuck" gear.

8. **Early fueling**.--All boats will adhere to a policy of fueling at the earliest possible moment on returning from operations and whenever the boat's fuel supply drops below five-sixths of capacity. Emergencies cannot be met instantly if time has to be taken out for fueling.

9. **Ammunition stowage**.--The prescribed stowage plan for ammunition set forth in each squadron must be adhered to. This applies particularly to the stowage of pyrotechnics, detonators, impulse charges, and 20 mm. ammunition. (See Stowage of Ammunition.)

10. **Armament on safe**.--When in confined or restricted friendly waters and harbors, boat captains shall see that armament is restored to a "safe" condition. Impulse charges should be removed from chambers; depth charges put on safe; 20 mm. and .50 cal. unloaded. Of course, if attack by enemy aircraft is anticipated, antiaircraft batteries should be kept ready.

11. **Oily rags and cleaning fluids**.--Due to the danger of spontaneous combustion, greasy or oily rags will not be stored aboard. This order also applies to inflammable cleaning fluids which should be left at the base.

12. **Dangerous voltages**.--The radio transmitter during operation generates dangerous voltages which can produce a severe shock to personnel that may come in contact with the antenna. Personnel should be instructed to keep clear for this reason.

13. **Explosive ammunition**.--Before going into action radio antennas and masts should be lowered to prevent detonating 20 mm. shells.

14. **War heads**.--If war heads have been hit and ignited by machine gun or other fire the torpedo affected should be, fired or jettisoned instantly.

Chapter 4. SPARE PARTS

The success of MTBs depends on keeping the boats, guns, and torpedoes all in working condition. Spare parts play a vital role in the achievement of this objective.

Before sailing for outlying bases, new squadrons should see that they have their commissioning allowances filled and, in addition, have any spares or extra equipment that are considered necessary. Commissioning allowances are apt to be inadequate in many respects, and shortages or incomplete items are not likely to be noticed unless particularly careful attention is given this matter by department heads. Every effort should be made to anticipate what spares will be needed over and above allowance lists. In brief, a complete and carefully considered supply of spares should be on hand before sailing. The fortunes of war may very likely make acquisition of spares impossible once a squadron leaves a main source of supply. At best, delivery of spares to distant bases involves considerable time and delay.

When a squadron becomes settled at its new base, one complete set of spares should be made up for each boat and boxed separately in one or two boxes. The advantage of this is that if a squadron or a part of one is suddenly required to move, each boat can load its own spares aboard quickly and expeditiously. Moreover, where concentrated bombing attacks are anticipated there is an obvious advantage to having spares broken down into small compact units that can be easily scattered.

After each boat has gotten its own complete supply of spares segregated, the boat captain should consult department heads and members of his crew as to what spares should be carried on board. The guiding rule should be to take aboard only those spares that can be quickly and easily used under way and that are likely to be needed. Limitations of space and requirements of speed demand that careful judgment and thought be exercised in this matter.

The following is a suggested list of spares that is considered practical and advisable to carry on board:

Gunnery

1. One complete set of 20 mm. tools.

2. Screwdrivers, pliers, mallet.

3. Torpedo tools nos. 13-14, 227, 141, propeller lock for each tube.

4. 1 spare Oerlikon barrel.

5. 1 spare .50 cal. barrel.

6. Spares for .50 cal.:
   1 driving spring.
   3 firing pins.
   1 firing pin spring.
   1 extractor.

7. 20 mm. spares:
   1 hammer.
   2 recoil springs.
   1 striker pin.
   1 face plate for breech.

8. Heavy grease, paint thinner, oil for oil buffer .50 cal., Tectyl, light oil in small amounts.

9. 100 percent spare shear screws, charging extension.

Engineering

1. 2 cam-rocker lever-tappet assembly.

2. 1 fuel pump and gasket.

3. 1 magneto rubber coupling.

4. 2 valve springs, inner and outer.

5. 1 salt-water pump and drive shaft.

6. 2 exhaust manifold gaskets.

7. 1 thermal unit.

8. 1 temperature gage 30°-230°.

9. 6 spark plugs and gaskets.

10. 12 nuts, 1/4-28, plain and regular.

11. 12 nuts, 5/16-24, plain and regular.

12. 12 nuts, 3/8-24, plain and regular.

13. 6 nuts, 1/2-20, plain and regular.

14. 2 pairs valve spring collar key.

15. 2 valve spring collar, upper.

16. 2 valve spring collar, lower.

17. 1 30" x 36" sheet velumoid gasket material.

18. 12 universal hose clamps.

19. 6 shims (for 3836 forward tension reverse gear).

20. Assortment of lockwashers and flat washers.

21. 1 roll sponge rubber for water leaks of cylinders.

22. 2 magneto breaker points.

23. 1 roll of friction tape.

24. 1 roll of rubber tape.

25. 1 coil locking wire.

26. 2 each size Rayboult sealing rings.

27. 1 oil pressure gauge.

28. 2 generator spark plugs.

29. 1 set generator magneto points.

Radio and Electrical

1. 300 percent spare fuses.

2. 100 percent spare vacuum tubes.

3. 1 spare headphone.

4. 1 spare microphone.

5. 4 flashlights.

6. 200 percent spares of the following bulbs:

    a. Searchlight.

    b. Navigation lights.

    c. Tachometer lights.

    d. Compass lights.

    e. Engineroom panel lights.

7. Small electrical repair kit.

8. Emergency antennae.

Chapter 5. RECORDS AND REPORTS

A. RECORDS

Squadron log.--The squadron log should be kept by the squadron duty officers and checked periodically by the navigation officer. The log should include entries of the following nature:

1. Weather data (in prescribed place).

2. Boats present; arrival and departure of same with times.

3. Results of fire and security inspections.

4. Air raid alarms, air raids, and all events, of an unusual or significant nature.

5. Men or officers reporting for duty or transferred to other duty.

6. Arrival of provisions or stores with statement as to quantity and quality.

7. Reports of, and times of relief of, sentry watch.

8. Record of all courts and boards, masts, etc.

9. Any special information.

Boat logs.--Boat captains are responsible for keeping their logs correct and up to. date. (The navigation officer is required to check logs monthly.) The quartermaster on each boat should keep a rough log notebook so that all entries: can be noted briefly as they occur and then be entered in the regular log at a later time. The following subjects should be entered in each boat's log:

1. Officers and crew on board and changes in same.

2. Matériel and personnel casualties.

3. Emergency drills; air raids; engagements with the enemy; events of unusual significance with times and places.

4. When under way, a record of major changes of courses, speeds, navigational aids sighted and passed; also a record of other ships and planes sighted and passed with times of same.

5. Particulars as to injuries or accidents to personnel.

The following are samples of correct phraseology and entries:

A. "Moored port side to PT-22 alongside USS Niagara at pier #1 Naval Torpedo Station, Newport, R. I. 0800 Mustered crew on stations, no absentees. 0830 DOOR, W. T., TM1c, USN, left the ship on 5 days' leave. 0905 Under way in company with PT's 24, 36, and 28 for type tactics at sea. 1130 Moored port side to USS Niagara at pier #1, Naval Torpedo Station, Newport, R. I. 1310 Doe, J., QM1c, USN, returned from 6 days' leave. 1330 Commenced fueling. 1425 Completed fueling, received 1,900 gallons 100-octane gasoline from the Shell Oil Co. of New England. 1510 Pursuant to verbal orders. COM MTB RON TWO shifted his Flag from PT-20 to PT-25."

B. "0830 Commenced replacement of center engine, serial number 777 with spare engine from Packard Motor Car Co. serial number 888."

C. "DOOR, W. T., QM1c, USN, was sent to sick bay of USS Niagara for treatment of abrasions to right leg suffered as a result of his slipping between the dock and the boat's side. Injury not due to his own misconduct."
Note---When medical officer has determined full extent of injury, the exact information should be entered in the log.

D. "1000 Exercised at fire quarters. 1015 Secured from fire quarters."

E. "1633 Fuel pump on starboard engine broke down. Started hand pump. 1640 Received orders from squadron commander to drop out of formation and replace defective pump. 1715 Repairs effected. Rejoined formation. Breakdown of pump found to have been caused by fractured drive shaft due to misaligned bearing."

F. "0830 Held quarters for muster followed by squadron commander's inspection of personnel and boats."

File of Notices to Mariners.--A complete file of "Notices to Mariners" will be kept as a quick check as to whether or not the charts are corrected to date. The corrections will be checked in the file as they are made. It is essential to safe navigation that the charts and publications be corrected as soon as the Notices are received.

Chronometer watch error.--The chronometer-watch used on motor torpedo boats cannot be expected to be as accurate as the chronometer of a large ship.

Nevertheless chronometer record books must be kept up and chronometers kept wound by the squadron quartermaster under the supervision of the navigation officer.

PT boats will, from time to time, be required to use celestial navigation, and it is imperative that chronometers be available for extended missions.

Ordnance and ammunition logs.--Each boat captain will maintain an ordnance log divided into four sections: Torpedo, machine guns, smoke generators, and depth charges.

Under the appropriate part, all pertinent equipment with mark, model, and serial numbers will be listed.

Each part of the log will also list (with dates) repairs made to pertinent equipment, data on torpedoes fired, rounds of ammunition fired from machine guns, smoke screens generated, and parts broken and replaced.

Boat captains will also maintain ammunition logs in which they will show the amount of ammunition received or expended, its caliber, lot number, price, invoice number, date, and from whom it has been received. They will forward to the gunnery officer copies of all receipts and credits invoices on ammunition as soon as they are received.

Torpedo record book.--The torpedo record book bears the same relation to the torpedo as the engine log to the main engines. It is an individual record and remains with the torpedo until the latter is lost or expended.

The boat captain is responsible for a full entry of all adjustments, repairs, firing data, and other information as required by the instructions in the torpedo record book.

Engineering log.--The engineering log for each boat consists of a standard journal-size notebook and engineering log sheets. Entries are made in the log sheets every half hour when under way, or with any major speed change.

The notebook is divided into three sections. The first is a record of hours operated by auxiliaries. The center section (machinery history) is similar to the rough log kept in the engine room of larger ships. It is a running report of all adjustments, repairs, replacements, etc. to - auxiliaries and main engines. The third section lists amounts of fuel and oil received, the dealer, and its octane rating or Navy symbol.

Engineering logs will be kept up to date and available for reference by squadron engineering officer at any time.

Main engine log.--Each main engine will have a log which will remain with it from time of installation until it is declared unfit for further use. All repairs, replacements, and adjustments will be carefully entered.

If engine is removed from the boat for any reason, the log will be wired to it. The factory, navy yard, ship's force, or any other activity which makes repairs, overhauls, or does any

work on the engines will enter the details of same in his engine log.

MTB engineering bulletins.--A complete file of MTB engineering bulletins will be kept on each boat.

Hull repair records.--Each boat captain will keep a hull repair record. This record will list casualties to, or deficiencies in, the hull of the boat on the left hand half of each page and the corresponding repairs or alterations on the right hand half of the page opposite the proper casualty or deficiency. All items will be properly dated.

Material casualty reports.--When a material casualty occurs it will be reported immediately to the squadron Commander via head of department concerned. Forms for these reports will be made up by the heads of department concerned. In general they will contain the following information:

> Squadron.
> Boat.
> Date of report.
> Time and date of casualty.
> Time and date remedied.
> Whether or not similar casualty has occurred during current fiscal year.
> Position of boat at time of casualty.
> Main engine RPM.
> Major unit deranged (engine, torpedo tube, etc.), manufacturer's name and designation or mark and modification, serial or register numbers.
> Unit broken, injured, or otherwise causing casualty (exhaust-valve rocker arm, torpedo-tube training worm, etc.), manufacturer's designation, ordnance piece No., drawing No., serial No., etc.
> Description of casualty.
> Cause of casualty.
> Method of remedy.

When any major casualty occurs, details will be entered in deck or engine room log and in machinery history, hull repair record, or ordnance log.

If a major casualty occurs while the boat is on detached duty, the squadron commander will if practicable be notified by despatch.

Health records.--When facts and circumstances of an injury, disease, or sickness are not entered in the health record of a man, due to absence of a medical officer, a responsible witness (officer, if present) will make a brief but comprehensive report, including responsibility for injury, to the Bureau of Medicine and Surgery, via the squadron commander. The boat captain will comment on, and endorse this report, and data from it will be entered in the health record of the injured.

Post battle reports.--After combat, a full report will be made to the squadron commander as soon as possible concerning:

1. Conduct of personnel.

2. Ship's movements--illustrate with diagrams.

3. Condition of wind and sea.

4. Bearing, distance, and outline of any land in sight.

5. Efficiency of ship and amount of munitions before and after battle.

6. Action of enemy and damage sustained by him.

7. Number, disposition, speed, course, and location of enemy after the battle.

8. Casualties, personnel and material, sustained.

File of squadron orders.--A complete file of all orders to the squadron will be kept on each boat.

Title B custody cards.--Each boat captain will keep a file of Title B custody cards covering all Title B items and signed by members of the crew.

Reports.--The following reports are required as indicated:

--43--

Report	By	To	When made	Form
Gunnery department				
Ammunition	Boat captain	Gunnery officer	When received or expended, transferred and on hand July 1.	Memorandum.
Annual report small arms target practice	Gunnery officer	CNO	Annually	
Service record of torpedo	do	Receiver	When torpedo is transferred	N. Ord. 52.
Ordnance derangement report	do	BuOrd	When occurring	Letter.
Navigation department				
Patrol boat log	Boat captain	BuPers	Quarterly	N. Nav. 410.

List of confidential charts and other confidential publications of the Hydrographic Office.	Naval officer	Hydrographic office.	Annually	N. H. O. 698a.
Census report	Personnel officer	BuPers	1 Jan	Letter.
Dates of receipt orders, travel and reporting in obedience thereto.	do	do	When occuring	N. Nav. 17, B Slips.
Leave of absence	do	BuPers (Copy to officer carrying pay accts.).	do	N. Nav. 296.
Officers reports, detached or ordered	do	BuPers	do	N. Nav. 64.
Stores department				
Fuel report	Stores office	BuS&A	Monthly	S&A Form 115.
Welfare and recreation report	do	do	Quarterly	N. Nav. 539.
Title "B" inventory	Boat captain	Stores officer	do	Memorandum.
Requisition Afloat				S&A Form 44 and 44a.
Commissary department				
Bill, receipts, invoices	Boat captains (when operating singly).	Commanding officer.	On receipt	Signed receipts.
Number of rations credited for month	Commanding officer.	BuS&A	Quarterly with S&A 45	S&A Form 27.
Ration record	do	do	Quarterly	S&A Form 45.
Communications department				
Quarterly or transfer report	do	District RPS library.	Quarterly or on transfer	RPS1.
Registered publications	do	CNO	Quarterly	RPSH3.
Movement reports	Boat captains and commanding officer.	Duty officer and Captain of Yard.	When occurring	Either orally or by telephone or by Regular Confidential Movement Report-- as the case requires.

			do	BuShips.
Engineering department				
Condition of machinery	Engineering officer.	BuShips	Monthly	NBS 110.
Engineering performance record	do	do	do	NBS 171.
Report on engine auxiliary generator and reverse gear.	do	do	do	NBS 172.
Machinery shipment report	do	Packard Motor Car Co.	When occurring	NBS 173.
Machinery and hull derangment	do	BuShips	do	NBS 174.
Personnel department				
Casualties to personnel	Boat captain	Squadron commander.	When occurring	Memorandum.
Roster of officers	Personnel officer	BuPers	Monthly	N. Nav. 37.
Report of changes	do	do	Monthly and prior to sailing.	N. Nav. 5b.
Report of enlisted personnel	do	do	Monthly (submitted 1st of of month).	N. Nav. 25.
Statement of allotment T. E. W.	do	do	Quarterly	N. Nav. 539.

Routine check off lists.--In addition to the above reports the maintenance of the following routine check off lists by boat captains is required as indicated below. Copies of the gunnery forms are appended to Part 2, Gunnery Instructions.

Gunnery Department:

    Routine Upkeep of Tubes.
    Routine Upkeep of Torpedoes.
    Routine Upkeep of Machine Guns and Small Arms.
    Routine Upkeep of Depth Charges.
    Routine Upkeep of 20 mm.
    Routine Upkeep of Smoke Screen Generator.
    Torpedo Preliminary Adjustment Check-off List.

Torpedo Final Adjustment Check-off List.
Check-off List for .50 cal. Machine Gun Firing.

Engineering:

Engineering Maintenance Record (see Hull, Part 5).
Routine Upkeep of Hull (see Packard Manual).
25-, 50-, 100-, 200-hour Check-off Lists (engines) (see Packard Manual).

Chapter 6. STORES

MTB officers, in the course of routine duties, are principally concerned with Title B articles. The expression "nonexpendable" articles for which accountability by individual items is required, means that every item on the allowance list of Title B equipage must have a custodian. This custodian is held responsible for the retention and proper condition of the article. He is, in effect, the guardian of that piece of Government property.

The system of accounting for Title B is based on the Title B card. On this card are spaces to list each article, its index or serial number, other pertinent data as shown, the location when stowed or fixed, and the signature of the custodian.

Upon taking over a boat, or when receiving the allowance list items for a new boat, an MTB officer personally inspects every item and sees that it is in good condition and properly stowed. Then, and only then, should he sign the original card as the custodian of any article. Copies of the cards are retained on board, the originals being kept in files of the squadron stores officer. Thus all such equipment is accounted for at all times. When being relieved, the officer concerned should make certain that his relief signs for all articles on board. The last signature appearing on the original of the card is the one used in fixing responsibility, whether or not the officer is present. It is therefore imperative that a boat captain exercise care in maintaining custody of Title B articles on his boat.

After the original cards have been signed, the officer custodian may then use the copies retained on board to turn over custody to appropriate members of his crew. For example, the quartermaster should take custody of the sextant, chronometers, and navigational instruments. The men who take custody sign the copy of the card in the provided space, and are then responsible to the officer custodian.

In PT boats, an inventory of all Title B equipment will be made by each boat captain once each quarter (within 10 days of the first day of quarter) and entered in the deck log (N. Nav 410). A report, in writing, of this inspection and of any articles found to be missing or in unsatisfactory condition, is made to the stores officer by the tenth day after the end of the quarter.

The custody of Title B equipage does not stop with mere prevention of loss. Keeping the articles in proper condition and properly disposing of them when rendered unfit for use are just as important.

The matter of maintenance requires a working knowledge of the procedure for effecting repairs. Should a Title B article be broken or otherwise in need of repair incident to normal use aboard ship, the ship's force should repair it if possible; otherwise it will be necessary to have a work request made up and repair done in the navy yard.

A. NAVY ACCOUNTING SYSTEM (TITLES OF STORES)

In accounting for Government property, the Navy uses certain classifications called Titles. The following is a brief explanation of their meanings as defined in Navy Regulations and in the Bureau of Supplies and Accounts Manual. In addition, since the definitions in Navy Regulations are quite condensed, it is highly advisable to consult the Navy Classification Index and Bureau of Supplies and Accounts Manual when questions arise. Thus the proper title can be ascertained.

Title A includes the original cost or appraised valuation of the ship's hull, machinery and fittings are included, and, in the case of a new ship, every expenditure that may properly be made a direct charge during its original construction. This means that engines, generators, stoves, ice boxes, and other items originally furnished with or built into the vessel are Title A. However, there are some departures from this definition as explained under Title B.

Title B represents the value of those nonexpendable articles of equipage (furniture, guns, equipment which makes a ship serviceable and habitable) on board ship for which accountability by individual items is required. To enlarge upon this definition, these are articles used for ship equipment which are separately furnished after building the ship. For example, one example of Title A is the stove or range furnished. If further stoves of a

different type are obtained later, they will probably be accounted for as Title B.

Title C covers the operating expenses and cost of maintenance of ships in commission. Among the items included are supplies used in ordinary maintenance, fuel, paints, lumber, cleaning gear, small spare parts, etc. In other words, the money spent in running and maintaining the vessel is usually spent under Title C, except as shown later.

Title D charges may be defined as those incurred in repairs to Title A and B material.

Title K includes all expenditures on Titles A and B for changes and alterations, which are in the nature of improvements to hull and permanent fittings.

Title X embraces all supplies and material (including equipage required for construction, maintenance, and operation of the Naval Establishment) ashore or afloat, which are awaiting issue for use and are not charged to some other title.

Title Z, with which MTB officers are frequently concerned during fitting out or overhaul at yards, includes all articles in process of manufacture. It is, like Title X, a suspense title, used until a final one is assigned. For example, if a Title B item is to be repaired, charges are under Title D. If it is to be made up entirely new as a replacement, Title Z covers the expense while under manufacture. Quite often, new bolts, engine parts, and the like are manufactured under Title Z to effect repairs and then charged to Title D after repairs have been made.

B. ALLOWANCES AND ALLOTMENTS

The following Title B and Title C allowance lists exist for each boat:

> Bureau of Ships--Engineering; 2. Bureau of Ships-- Hull; 3. Bureau of Ships--Navigation; 4. Bureau of Ordnance--(A) Torpedo, (B) Small Arms, (C) Ammunition, (D) Smoke Generators; 5. Bureau of Supplies and Accounts.

Boat captains should have a copy of each of these allowance lists on hand and should requisition any Title B or C equipment in which the boat might be deficient.

If a Title B article which is on the allowance list is lost, broken, stolen, worn out by usage, or otherwise not serviceable, it must

be surveyed as outlined in the section below under "Surveys" before a replacement can be obtained.

C. REQUISITIONS

When materials are required, a requisition (S & A Form 44) is used. When prepared by the stores officer and approved by the squadron commander and head of department it becomes the authority for the supply department to procure and issue the material. Some material such as ammunition, is procured by letter but only as specifically directed by the cognizant Bureau.

The preparation of requisitions in general is as follows:

1. Requisitions are numbered serially throughout the fiscal year commencing with one, on the 1st of July each year. A separate series for each squadron is maintained for the Bureau of Ships (NSA Quarterly Allotment) and for the Bureau of Ordnance. The

number is usually followed by the year, as 4-43 for the fourth requisition of the fiscal year 1943. Each boat, before going on detached duty, will be assigned a group of requisition numbers in order to avoid duplication of numbers.

2. One requisition shall embrace material under only one appropriation and one title. That is, Title B and Title 0 should not be on the same requisition, nor should Title B under the Bureau of Ordnance and Title B under the Bureau of Ships be on the same requisition.

3. The following data are to be indicated on all requisitions:

   A. Bureau.

   B. Accounting number and name of appropriation.

   C. Title of material.
      Title C--Operating expenses of boat (expendable stores).
      Title D--All repairs to Title A material.
      Title K--All alterations.
      Title B--Nonexpendable articles of equipage.

   D. Name of squadron.

   E. Purpose for which, material is required.

   F. Arrangement of items:

      1. By dates of desired delivery.

      2. Under each date group, alphabetically by classes.

      3. Number items consecutively without regard to classes, in left hand margin.

   G. Complete description (refer to standard Navy specifications where possible). If no standard specifications are available, use most complete description possible to insure procurement of exactly what is needed.

   H. Whether the requisition is "in excess" or "not in excess":

      1. All nonstandard material (not in Federal Standard Stock Catalogue) is "in excess."

      2. Standard material not on the allowance list, or a greater amount than is on allowance list, is also "in excess."

I. Estimated cost.

J. Time and place of delivery.

4. Requisitions will not be prepared unless funds are available to cover the expenditure, nor will they be prepared by other than the squadron stores officer when the squadron is together. If a boat is on detached duty, the boat captain is authorized to prepare, sign for, and draw material that is absolutely essential. In this case, a copy of the requisition showing amount expended should be sent to the squadron stores officer immediately.

Care must always be taken not to over-expend the allotment. In emergencies, if allotments are exhausted, additional allotments may be requested from the next senior in the chain of command above the squadron commander.

D. SURVEYS

Whenever the condemnation, appraisal, disposition, or expenditure of naval property becomes necessary, a survey shall be held.

1. A formal survey shall be made for:

   A. Lost or missing articles of ship's equipage when the value of the articles or total of identical articles exceeds $100.

   B. Certain special items designated by the various bureaus.

   C. When specifically ordered by the squadron commander.

   An informal survey will be made in all other cases.

2. When it becomes necessary to survey an article on a PT boat, the boat captain shall prepare a Survey Request on Bu. S&A Form 154 which shall be forwarded to the head of the department concerned.

3. If a formal survey is not required, the head of department shall himself make the survey in the same manner as a surveying officer whose duties are shown below. If a formal survey is required, the head of department shall appoint some officer other than the head of department or the officer on whose books the article is carried, to act as surveying officer. Whenever circumstances warrant such action, and in all cases where the value of the missing or damaged articles exceeds $100, a board of three officers shall be appointed.

4. In cases where the boat is detached from the squadron, the boat captain shall not send the survey request to the head of department but shall himself survey the article and send

the report for review to the squadron commander via the head of department, unless a formal survey is necessary, in which case action shall be delayed until the boat joins the squadron.

5. The surveying officer(s) or head of department (if it is not a formal survey) shall make a thorough inspection of the articles to determine their conditions at time of survey, or, if missing, a thorough examination of the circumstances attending the loss, and he (they) shall, if possible, fix the cause and responsibility for the damaged condition or loss. He (they) shall appraise the value of articles when the invoice price is unobtainable or when the invoice price is not present value. Specific recommendation as to disposition shall always be made. Disposition may be: repair, burn, expend, throw overboard, salvage usable parts, turn into store, or exchange in part payment for new equipment.

   Upon being signed by the head of department in informal surveys, the Bu. S&A Form 154 becomes a survey report, and the original and all copies are sent to squadron commander for review.

6. If the reviewing officer does not approve of certain recommendations made by the surveying officer, he shall eliminate such articles from the report. These items shall be covered by a new form prepared in the same manner as if on an original request.

7. In the following eases, the approval of the cognizant Bureau must be obtained before any further action is taken:

   A. When the reviewing officer does not approve the recommendation of the surveying officer.

   B. When major items have been recommended by the commanding officer of repair ship to be used in making repairs afloat.

   C. When sale has been recommended.

   In these cases, disposition will be carried out only when approval or specific orders are received from the Bureau concerned. In all other cases, the officer on whose books the article is carried may proceed with the disposition upon receiving the original approved report from the squadron commander. The survey is used as the transfer or expenditure invoice.

8. Procedure.

   A. The boat captain shall prepare the original and seven copies of the survey request on Bu. S&A Form 154 and shall retain one copy as will the head of department. The original and remaining copies shall be used by the surveying officer in making the survey report, and all shall be sent to the squadron commander for review.

    B. When the approval of the Bureau is required, it shall be supplied with the original and one copy. When sale has been recommended, the original and two copies are necessary. When the Bureau has returned the report with its approval, the officer who will make the expenditure will be given the original and at least three copies.

    C. The remaining copies shall be distributed according to the local custom in the district and yard in which the survey is held.

Requisitioning fuel.--Under normal conditions, when all boats are assembled in one locality, the purchase of fuel will be handled by the squadron stores officer. However, when a boat is operating independently it may be necessary for a boat captain to place the order himself.

Gasoline is supplied to the Navy by the lowest bidder in a given locality. The Bureau of Supplies and Accounts publishes a quarterly bulletin showing the various successful bidders.

PT boats require 100 octane gasoline for maximum power output, although 92 octane may be used successfully if 100 octane is not obtainable. Gasoline with an octane rating of less than 87 should never be used in the main engines. One gasoline company may hold a contract for 100 octane gasoline while another may hold the contract for 92 octane.

High-test gasoline cannot be obtained in all ports. Therefore arrangements should be made well in advance for the accumulation of the required fuel at ports where refueling will be necessary. 100 octane gasoline can usually be obtained upon short notice in ports where Government air activities are located.

Upon arrival in a port where gasoline is to be obtained, the commercial firm holding a Government contract should be contacted and the order placed in the name of the squadron. If at a navy yard, the order should be placed through the supply officer.

When delivery has been completed, a copy of the delivery receipt should be obtained and forwarded immediately to the squadron stores officer.

After an order has been placed for delivery at a given time and a given place, every endeavor should be made to be prepared to receive it as ordered. If unforeseen circumstances arise which will not permit the reception of the fuel, the contractor should be notified immediately, so that he may not unnecessarily tie up his equipment.

Lubrication oil is furnished the Navy by contractors who hold the contract for the period of one year. Usually the required oil may be obtained direct from the supply officer of a navy yard or the supply officer attached to another naval activity. However, the contractor will furnish the oil promptly when ordered.

Letting of bids.--There is no authority for purchasing without a contract, except in the case of a military emergency. In that case, when no naval activities or supply officers are near enough to be available and no contract bulletins are in effect in the locality, open purchase may be resorted to. This is an emergency measure only and is not to be used to circumvent the usual procurement methods.

--54--

Chapter 7. REFERENCE MATERIAL

Although it is virtually impossible to remember all of the detailed orders and instructions of the various bureaus of the Navy, an officer can efficiently carry out his administrative duties if he knows which publications and letters are available for ready reference and how to use them; therefore, it is essential that he should learn where the desired information may be obtained.

United States Nary Regulations

All naval personnel should be familiar with and must comply with the United States Navy Regulations. These regulations set forth the duties, responsibilities, authority, distinctions, and relationship to each other of the various bureaus, offices, and individual officers. In general, Navy Regulations cover matters pertaining to the Navy as a whole, coordinating the efforts of officers or persons in the naval establishment, and coordinating the Navy's transactions with other Government or private agencies.

All officers should read Chapter 22 of U.S. Navy Regulations and become familiar with the duties of a commanding officer as set forth therein. Chapter 52 of U.S. Navy Regulations should be referred to for all matters pertaining to correspondence, and all officers and radiomen (who act as yeomen on boats on detached duty) should be especially familiar with the procedure and forms outlined therein. Official letters from any officer in the squadron to an outside officer or activity should be sent via the squadron commander.

The Navy Department Publications

Each Bureau of the Navy has its own manual which contains information about requirements of that Bureau, inspection of material finder its cognizance, and other information concerning that Bureau.

--55--

General Orders include all orders of permanent or temporary-application addressed to the naval service: ceremonial orders, commendation of persons in the service, and similar matters not affecting the Navy Regulations.

Uniform Regulations include all regulations and instructions relative to the uniforms of all persons in the Navy and Marine Corps.

Filing Manual describes and provides for a standardized filing system for the Navy and is of particular value in learning how to look up correspondence.

Communication Instructions, published by the Chief of Naval Operations (Director of Naval Communications), contains the general orders and information necessary for intelligent operation and understanding of the Navy's communication system and procedures. The Movement Report System is explained fully in the Communication Instructions.

A few of the headings of the chapters in the Communication Instructions will serve to give an idea of its contents.

1. Duties of Communications Officers.
2. Security.
3. Messages and drafting.
4. Direction-finder service.
5. Procedure.
6. Call signs.
7. Semaphore and wig-wag.
8. Flag hoists.
9. Tolls.
10. Abbreviations.
11. Radio telegraph and telephone.
12. Flashing light.

This is not a complete list.

Communication Circular Letters contain all special temporary instructions for handling communications, communication personnel, reports, etc. Communication Circular Letter 6-41 contains the allowance of nonregistered (restricted) publications of a PT boat (radio signals, flag signals, international codes Berne lists, etc.) These should be requested and kept corrected, up to date.

Registered Publications are issued by the Registered Publications

Section under the classification of Secret or Confidential, depending upon the nature of the material contained therein (see Communication chapter). These publications must be kept in a safe when not in use.

The communication officer is the custodian of all these publications and never issues one unless he receives, in return, a signed custody receipt. Loss or divulgence of secret or confidential material is punishable as a General Court Martial may direct. All officers attached to the motor torpedo boat squadrons should familiarize themselves with Article 75 1/2 U.S. Navy Regulations which deals with the proper handling of classified matter.

Bureau of Naval Personnel Manual covers matters pertaining to personnel, both Regular and Reserve, advancements in rating, promotions, general training, Naval Observatory, libraries, and navigational equipment and publications.

Bureau of Naval Personnel Circular Letters are temporary orders and instructions concerning Navy personnel. They are listed in letter form. The Bureau compiles these letters into a pamphlet, at which time superseded letters are canceled or revised.

Bureau of Naval Personnel Bulletins are pamphlets, published monthly, containing personnel items which might be of interest to naval personnel. To quote the Bureau these are-- "Published for the purpose of disseminating general information of probable interest to the service."

The Year Book of Enlisted Training is concerned with the training of men for advancement in rating. The training courses available are listed therein.

The Navy Register is a list of the commissioned and warrant officers of the Navy and Marine Corps, both active and retired. It is in book form and includes the signal number of officer.

The Navy Directory (Confidential) lists the place of duty of all officers (Regulars and Reserves on active duty) of the Navy and Marine Corps and the place of residence of all retired Regular Officers of the Navy and Marine Corps. It lists active officers in groups in the same ship or at the same station.

Naval Reserve Register gives information regarding all commissioned Reserve officers, particularly date of rank, class of commission, etc.

The Bureau of Ordnance Manual contains the following: general ordnance information and information on: reports and returns, guns and attachments, machine guns, small arms, fire control and optics, explosives, ammunition, turrets, broadside mounts, antiaircraft mounts, handling and stowage of ammunition and explosives, torpedoes and torpedo equipment, torpedo tubes, mines, depth charges, nets, and ordnance safety precautions.

Bureau of Ordnance Circular Letters contain special instructions and temporary orders on the subjects listed above under the Bureau of Ordnance Manual.

Bureau of Ordnance Pamphlets contain detailed instructions and drawings for operation, dismantling, assembling, and adjustment of the individual pieces of material and equipment. These and Bureau of Ordnance Circular Letters and indexes for all of them may be secured upon request from the Naval Gun Factory, Washington, D. C.

The Bureau of Construction and Repair Manual describes the following: care and preservation of vessels, experiments, towage, and handling of inflammable materials, gas warfare, rescue breathing apparatus, fire-fighting apparatus, boat instructions, ground tackle, and painting instructions. This manual is concerned mainly with the hull of the ship and its fittings.

The Manual of Engineering Instructions is a comprehensive publication covering all matters pertaining to marine engineering plants and good engineering practice. It is divided into sections which thoroughly describe one phase of engineering such as boilers, fuels, power boat engines, or main engines (turbines, steam reciprocating engines, diesels, and lubricating systems). The precautions for safe operation of all equipment and machinery under cognizance of the Bureau of Ships (Engineering) may be found in M. E. I., and all officers responsible for the operation of machinery should familiarize themselves with this publication.

The Bureau of Aeronautics Manual contains detailed instructions for operation of aircraft and aircraft machinery and equipment, and handling and reporting of material casualties to aircraft.

The Bureau of Supplies and Accounts Manual gives detailed instructions concerning the methods of procuring and accounting

--58--

for stores, money, and equipment under all titles. It also gives detailed method, of making surveys and handling general mess accounts. This manual is highly technical and therefore the most difficult one from which to obtain the desired information. If unable to interpret it, consult an officer of the Supply Corps.

The Bureau of Supplies and Accounts Memoranda includes temporary orders and special interpretations of the SandA Manual. They include examples of purchasing and finance which have arisen in the past, giving the Comptroller General's decisions in each example.

The Manual of the Medical Department deals with promotions of medical personnel, duties of medical personnel ashore and afloat, physical examinations, hospitals, health records, sanitation, quarantine reports and all other matters relating to the personnel and material of the Medical and Dental Corps.

The Bureau of Yards and Docks Manual deals with operations, internal organization, construction, operating expenses, etc., of navy yards and bases.

Naval Courts and Boards includes the instructions governing the procedure of naval courts and boards. This publication is the principal reference book for a summary court martial recorder and a deck court officer and should be studied by all young officers.

Court Martial Orders are published frequently for the information of the naval service. They give a summary of the various courts held and record decisions made by various legal authorities in the Navy. These records serve as a guide for subsequent courts-martial. In connection with these orders an index-digest of the orders of the year is published annually. C. M. O. are the secondary reference for S. C. M. recorders.

In addition to the numerous publications, letters, manuals distributed by the Navy Department and its bureaus, commanders of units afloat issue regulations, orders, instructions, and so forth, which must be carried out. For training purposes, all vessels of the Navy not attached to a naval district are subject to the orders of the Commander in Chief, U.S. Fleet.

All the above publications may be obtained from the various bureaus on request. General Orders, Uniform Regulations and the Filing Manual are obtained from the Bureau of Personnel.

APPENDIX 1

EXAMINATION FOR QUALIFICATION FOR MOTOR TORPEDO BOAT DUTY

I. Gunnery

A. *Practical factors.--*

    1. Field strip and make adjustments to:

        a. 20-mm. machine gun.

        b. 50-cal. machine gun.

        c. Thompson submachine gun.

        d. Springfield rifle.

        e. 45-cal. pistol.

    2. a. Point, train, load, and fire above weapons.

b. Demonstrate knowledge of correct positions for firing.

3. Estimate target angle and speed, either from actual ship or model and set up the MTB's torpedo director.

4. Demonstrate, with an actual depth charge, knowledge of how to prepare it for firing and launching.

5. Demonstrate working knowledge of a smoke screen generator.

6. Demonstrate ability to train torpedo tube out, prepare it for firing, and fire by percussion.

7. Make any preliminary or final adjustment on a torpedo (officers, GM, TM, and GM and TM strikers only).

B. *Written examinations.--*

1. Thorough knowledge of below listed weapons, particularly in regard to accurate firing and safety precautions:

a. 20-mm. machine gun.

b. 50-cal. machine gun.

c. Thompson submachine gun.

d. Springfield rifle.

e. 45-cal. pistol.

2. Motor Torpedo Boat Tactics and torpedo control, including flag signals (officers, advanced knowledge; enlisted personnel, elementary knowledge).

3. Thorough knowledge of torpedoes and depth charges (officers, GM, TM, and GM and TM strikers only).

4. Thorough knowledge of routine maintenance of torpedoes, guns, and explosives (officers, GM, TM, and TM strikers only).

II. Seamanship and Navigation

A. *Practical factors.--*

1. Get under way from the dock and make a landing.

2. Plot, satisfactorily, a 100-mile cruise on a chart in coastal waters, noting compass courses to be steered.

3. Take a star sight, identify star, and work out for line of position (sun sight if no opportunity exists for taking star sights)--officers only.

4. Demonstrate how to tow another PT boat.

5. Anchor a PT boat.

6. Handle a boat in a rough sea.

7. Demonstrate how to fuel underway from a tender.

8. Demonstrate ability to handle fenders, lines, and make necessary knots.

9. Use hand lead.

B. *Written examination.--*

1. Piloting (officers, QM and QM strikers, advanced; all others elementary).

2. Celestial navigation (officers only).

3. Rules of the Road (including thorough understanding of wake damage)-- officers, QM, and QM strikers, advanced; all others, elementary.

4. Deck logs, particularly in regard to navigational records (officers, QM, and QM strikers, advanced; all others, elementary).

5. Safety precautions, handling emergencies and watches.

III. Communications

A. *Practical factors.--*

1. Set up and operate radio on a PT, including changing frequency.

2. Operate radio direction finder; actually get accurate bearings.

3. Send and receive, at below speeds, by semaphore, blinker, and radio telegraphy:

Rank or rating	Semaphore	Blinker	Radio telegraphy
Officers	8	8	10.

Quartermasters	10	10	10.
Radiomen	8	10	20.
All others	6	Alphabet	Alphabet.

4. Demonstrate working knowledge of electrical installations in PT's (officers, RM, and RM strikers, advanced; all others elementary).

5. Demonstrate ability to operate Very's and pyrotechnic pistols.

B. *Written examinations.--*

1. Phonetic equivalents of the alphabet.

2. Voice radio and semaphore procedure (officers, QM, and QM strikers, advanced semaphore procedure; all others, elementary semaphore procedure).

3. Radio telegraphy procedure (officers, RM, and RM strikers only).

4. Electrical installations in PTs (officers, RM, and RM strikers, advanced; all others, elementary).

5. Thorough knowledge of international flags.

6. Recognition and emergency identification signals.

7. Security.

IV. Engineering

A. *Practical factors.--*

1. Start, operate, and secure engines and auxiliary machinery. Demonstrate knowledge of proper instrument readings, proper engine room temperature control when starting.

2. Start and secure auxiliary generator. Demonstrate knowledge of proper instrument readings.

3. Demonstrate knowledge of procedure and safety precautions to be followed in fueling.

4. Demonstrate detailed knowledge of maintenance upkeep, and handling of casualties (officers and engineering ratings only).

5. Demonstrate thorough understanding of dry docking of a PT boat.

B. *Written examination.--*

    1. Thorough knowledge of the hull.

V. Miscellaneous

A. *Practical factors.--*

    1. Demonstrate thorough knowledge of first aid.

    2. Pass "Class A" swimming test.

B. *Written examination.--*

    1. First aid.

    2. Motor torpedo boat squadrons doctrine.

| Name or rating | General quarters | | | Getting underway--station and reports | Anchoring | Mooring | Cleaning |
	Attack	Defense	Fire				
Capt	Conn; torpedo control.	Conn	Conn				
Exec	Wheel and throttles.	Wheel and throttles.	In charge at scene.				
GM	Port tubes or D. C.	20-mm	Remove ammunition from scene of fire.	Lines forward; ammunition on board. Guns OK.	Stand by anchor	Lines forward,	Topside guns and ammunition.
TM	Starboard tubes or D. C. smoke generator.	Smoke generator; 20-mm	Set D. C.'s on safe and jettison on order.	Lines forward; impulse charges on board. Torp. and tubes OK.	do	do	Tubes, D. C.'s and topside.

QM	Navigation (stand by to relieve wheel).	Navigation	Hand CO_2 bottles.	Fenders forward; shift colors; steering gear, lights tested; charts on hand. At night: Blackouts boat.			Bridge and deck house.
RM	Radio	Radio	Cut load switch	Radio; radio operative, batteries chg., recog. sig. and codes on hand. Captain of yard or D. O. notified of departure.		Fenders.	Radio shack and tank compartment.
MM	Engineroom	Engine room	Trip Lux release by hand on order.	Engine room. Fuel, engine OK.			Engine room and lazarette.
MM	Port .50 cal.	Port .50-cal.	CO_2 bottles at fire.	Engine room.			Do.
MM	Starboard .50 cal.	Starboard .50-cal.	Rubber boat; CO_2 if moor.	Lines and fenders aft	Stand by anchor.	Lines aft.	Passageway and forepeak.
SC	20 mm	20-mm	Blankets and mattress.	Food, fresh water. Water tight integrity, OK	do	do	Galley and crews compartment.
Sea	20 mm	Ammunition, .50-cal.	Hand CO_2 bottle			Fenders.	Crews compartment and head.

CONDITION TWO

Station	Port watch	Starboard watch
Bridge	Captain	Executive officer.
Helm	Radioman	Quartermaster.
Port lookout and M. G.	Ship's cook	Torpedoman.
Starboard lookout and M. G.	Gunner's mate	Engineer.
Engine room	Engineer	Do.
20-mm	Seaman	Man from base if one is available.

Condition Two will be used for war cruising when it is not necessary to keep all hands at their General Quarters stations. When cruising in the combat zone, either Condition Two or General Quarters should be maintained at all times.

FIRST-AID EQUIPMENT (FOR TORPEDO BOATS)

[Stock No. S2-1365 (modified)]

Stock No.	Item title	Unit	Quantity	Remarks
1-410	Jelly of tannic acid	4-ounce tube	4	Apply over burned or scalded areas of body; apply gauze dressing.
1-495	Morphine tartrate 0.032 gms., 1 1/2cc. tube with sterile needle.	5 in package	1	Clean site, inject under skin of arm or leg to relieve pain in severe injury or burn.
1-885	Spirits of ammonia, tube and paper cup.	4 in package	1	Stimulant--give contents of tube in cup of water for fainting, inhalations for collapse.
1-975	Acid, acetylsalicylic 0.324	100 bottles	1	ASPIRIN--for headache, sore throat, fever; 1-2 tablets.
1-1015	Extract of cascara sagrada, 0.259 gms.	100 bottles	1	DO NOT USE IF COMPLAINING OF ABDOMINAL PAIN. Mild laxative; 1-2 tablets.
1-1185	Tincture of iodine, mild; 10 cc. applicator vial.	3 in	1	POISON! Antidote: Starch or flour in water. Apply to wounds with vial applicator.
2-060	Bandage compress, 2-inch	4 in package	2	For wounds--do not touch inside of pack.
2-065	Bandage compress, 4-inch	1 in	4	Do.

		package		
2-130	Bandage, triangular, compressed	1	2	For use as arm sling, tourniquet, or to retain dressings in place.
2-135	Bath, eye	1	1	To use with boric acid solution as eyewash.
2-350	Cotton, absorbent, compressed	1 ounce package	2	Use as padding for splints.
2-390	Dressing, battle, large	1	2	For large wounds--do not touch inside of dressing.
2-395	Dressing, battle, small	1	4	Do.
2-420	Gauze, plain	5-yard package	1	For dressing wounds after applying antiseptic.
2-835	Plaster, adhesive, 2 inches by 5 yards	Spool	1	For securing dressings.
2-1310	Tourniquet, web	Package	10	For immediate temporary control of bleeding. Loosen every 15 minutes; then reapply if still bleeding.
2-970	Splint, wire mesh for, 5 by 36 inches	Piece	1	To splint fractures.
4-970	Shears, 6-inch	1	1	For cutting bandages.
S1-2290	Brandy, U. S. P. 2 ounces in bottle	10 in carton	1	To be used as medication after exposure to cold and wet.
S1-3813	Sulfanilamide, powdered (for tropical application), 5-gm. pack.	25 in package	1	Apply contents of pack directly to wound as directed on package.
S2-920	Dressing, gauze and adhesive plaster 1 by 3.	100 box	1/4	For small cuts.
	Basque wood splints 18 by 3 1/2 inches		6	Supporting broken bone.
	Wood splints 54 by 4 by 1/2 inch		4	Do.
1-745	Sodium bicarbonate	1 pound carton	1	For upset condition of stomach.

You Know Captain, I'm Beginning to Doubt My Noon Position, Too

---

Table of Contents
Next Part (2)

Transcribed and formatted for HTML by Larry Jewell & Patrick Clancey, Hyperwar Foundation

Motor Torpedo Boat Manual
February 1943

⚓

U.S. Navy

PART II. GUNNERY INSTRUCTIONS

Chapter 1

Notes on torpedoes, routine upkeep, preliminary and final adjustments, preparation of warheads and exercise heads, treatment of torpedoes after run, maintenance of other equipment.

OERLIKON 20-MM. A.A. GUN

SECTION A. GENERAL DESCRIPTION

1. The Oerlikon is primarily a close-range high-angle A. A. gun. It can be used against surface vessels, but a . 50-caliber machine gun can be used with better success against landing forces, etc. Against dive bombers the 20-mm. is an excellent gun.

2. The major difference between this gun and others is that the force of the explosion is absorbed in checking and reversing the forward motion of a relatively heavy bolt, or breechblock, that is never locked. In most guns the force of the explosion is taken by the locked breechblock and by the recoil cylinders and mechanism.

3. **Firing**.--This gun fires in automatic only, which means that the gun will fire as long as the trigger is pressed and there is ammunition in the magazine. When the last round of each magazine is loaded into the gun the trigger mechanism is returned automatically to the cocked position regardless of the position of the trigger. This feature prevents the breechblock mass from counterrecoiling on an empty gun after the last round is fired and, because there is no explosion to reverse the breechblock, a recocking by hand would be necessary before firing could be continued. A safe fire lever is fitted close to the right handgrip. The rate of fire is approximately 450 rounds per minute.

The magazine is easily and quickly changed. It is retained by lugs on its fore end and a magazine catch at the rear.

The gun and mount consists of three major assemblies:

1. Gun.
2. Magazine.
3. Mount.

4. **Gun**.--The gun consists of all that part of the weapon (except the magazine and cradle) that rotates about the trunnion bearing axis.

The gun may be considered in three sections.

1. Barrel, mounted in the breech casing. The breech casing is mounted in the cradle. The cradle is considered to be part of mount.

2. The various stops and locking gear together with the trigger group, all mounted in the breech casing.

Note.--The above two groups do not recoil.

3. Parts that do recoil. The breech block and bolt with the striker pin, the breech bars and springs, and the barrel spring with its casing.

5. **Magazine**.--The ammunition is supplied from a magazine that holds 60 rounds. The magazine is detachably mounted on the gun. It is filled and also serviced while removed from gun.

6. **Mount**.--The mount extends from the cradle, in which the gun is fixed, to the pedestal

bolted to the deck. The cradle rotates about the trunnion axis. The mount permits the height of the gun trunnion above the deck to be altered easily and rapidly for any sight angle to suit the convenience of the gunlayer. This is done by the column-raising handwheel mounted on the pedestal head.

SECTION B

1. **Barrel**.--The barrel is a forged steel piece 4 feet inches in length, bored out to a caliber of 20 mm. or approximately 0. 8 inch. There are nine grooves in the barrel. The outside of the center section has fins that support the barrel springs, holding these springs away from the barrel and permitting air circulation for cooling. The first 2 inches of the muzzle bore flares outwards as a flash shield.

The barrel can be removed easily and quickly and another barrel substituted, without disassembly of other parts. Interrupted thrust collars machined on the barrel secure it to the

breech, casing. The barrel is assembled from the front with its interrupted thrust collars in the unlocked position. The barrel is then locked by rotating it 60° clockwise (looking from

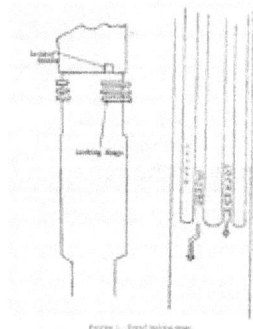

Figure 1. Barrel locking rings.

the muzzle toward the breech). Assembly marks are provided. (See fig. 1). The barrel is prevented from accidental unlocking by the barrel locking gear described later.

The barrel is removed by rotating the barrel-locking handle into the position marked "Unlock." Rotate the barrel approximately

60° counterclockwise (looking from the muzzle to the breech) and pull out to the front (asbestos gloves are provided with the tools and spare parts to remove a hot barrel).

Note.--The clearances between the barrel and its housing in the breech casing have to be very small; therefore, a barrel may feel tight. A special tool is provided for rotating the

barrel.

2. **Barrel locking gear**.--The barrel locking gear consists of three parts:

1. Barrel locking handle pinned to--

2. An axis bolt (upon which the double loading stop is free to rotate).

3. Barrel locking lever, attached to the axis bolt.

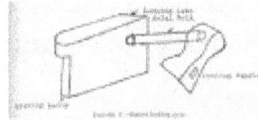

Figure 2. Barrel locking gear.

The purpose of the barrel-locking gear is to prevent the barrel from rotating and thereby freeing itself from the interrupted thrust collars during the firing of the gun.

The barrel-locking handle carries a catch lever that moves a pin, holding the barrel-locking handle in either of two positions, "Locked" or "Unlocked. " When the catch lever is pressed in toward the breech casing, and the handle is moved from "Unlocked" to "Locked," the axis is turned, thereby rotating the barrel-locking lever into a slot in the barrel. This locks the barrel so that it cannot rotate about its own axis. (See fig. 2.)

A stop pin is mounted in the left side of the breech casing and engages a slot in the rear end of the barrel.

--73--

When inserting a barrel and rotating it into place, the stop pin positions the barrel so that the locking lever can be engaged in its barrel slot; by turning the locking handle. (See fig. 3.)

The stop pin also serves to stop the rotation of the barrel in the opposite direction, so that the interrupted collars are in position to permit withdrawal of the barrel from the breech casing.

The double loading stop prevents loading a round of ammunition

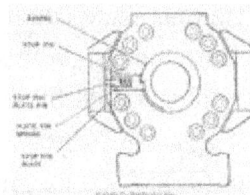

Figure 3. Barrel stop pin.

into the barrel unless the chamber is already clear at the double loading; stop. A hole is drilled through the top wall of the Chamber of the barrel, and in this hole the double loading stop plunger operates. The operation of the double loading stop is described later on.

3. **Breech casing**.--The breech casing is a steel forging, bored but longitudinally, and, its chief functions are to:

1. Carry the barrel at its front end.

2. Carry the trigger group at its rear end.

3. Act as a guideway for the breech block which recoils, and returns to the firing position, with a reciprocating motion.

4. Carry the magazine on its top.

5. Attach to the mount.

The gun is secured to the cradle of the mount by:

1. Two shoes that are a part of the breech casing (located at the front and rear) and fit into keyways in the cradle.

2. A gun securing bolt in the cradle which enters into a corresponding recess in the front shoe of the casing and takes the main fore and aft thrust on firing.

When gun is being mounted in the cradle, the inside of the securing bolt hole in the breech casing and the securing bolt itself should be thoroughly greased for protection against corrosion.

4. **Magazine catch gear and ejector**.--Magazine catch gear and ejector is mounted in the breech casing and consists of three sections.

1. Catch gear to retain the magazine in position.

2. Ejector.

3. Front portion of the magazine interlock gear.

The magazine catch gear is operated by a magazine catch lever (a) (see fig. 4) rotating on an axis bolt (1) mounted oh the casing. A front toe (n) on this lever engages with a face on the ejector (e). A rear toe (m) on this lever engages with the upper rear end of the ejector. The ejector (e) is free to move slightly in a longitudinal direction and therefore can be moved to the fear by rotating the magazine catch lever (a) toward the muzzle,

The ejector normally tends to move to the front because of the pressure of the magazine catch spring. However, the ejector can be held cocked to the rear, by the magazine catch (p). The magazine catch is pivoted at the rear and is able to rise in front, tends to force the catch into engagement with the front end of the ejector.

On the front end at the top of the ejector is a lug (b) that engages a corresponding lug (o) on the magazine and holds the magazine to the gun. If the ejector is held cocked to the rear by the catch, the lug is clear of the magazine so that the latter

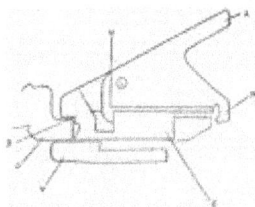

Figure 4.--Magazine catch gear and ejector.

can be shipped or unshipped. The ejector can be moved rearward to the cocked position by rotating the magazine catch lever toward the muzzle.

When the magazine is shipped, the ejector is moved forward automatically, into position for locking the magazine. A projection on the magazine pushes down the front ends of the catch, disengaging it and allowing the ejector to move forward under the influence of the catch spring, into position to lock the magazine.

The catch may be disengaged without the necessity of shipping a magazine by pressing down the forward ends of the catch, using any suitable tool.

CAUTION.--**When shipping a magazine the catch gear must be in the cocked position. The magazine securing lug on the ejector is back of the front end of the catch. No attempt should be made to cock the gear by forcing a magazine past the lug.**

5. **Double loading stop operation**. (See figs. 5-8).--The purpose of the double-loading stop gear is to make it impossible for the breech block to counterrecoil and load a round into the firing chamber unless the chamber is already empty. This avoids the jam that would occur if the rear end of a cartridge case had been torn away, leaving a portion of the case jammed in the firing chamber.

The double loading stop (d) with its operating lever (c), upper plunger (b) and lower plunger (a) are shown in the position they occupy when the gun is cocked. The double loading stop plunger (a) is projecting into the chamber and is the end actuated by the cartridge case. This lower plunger (a) lifts the upper plunger (b) against the rear toe of the double-loading stop operating lever (c) lowering its front end, this permits the double-loading stop to rotate about its axis under the pressure of its springs (f). The double-loading stop (a) acts as a catch to hold the bolt mass to the rear.

The front end of the double-loading stop (d) is raised by spring (f) and the rear end has fallen until it is in the path of the stop plates mounted one on each breech bar.

The left breech bar recoils to the rear carrying with it the stop plate marked "l" (on the right breech bar the stop plate is marked "r"). The rear end of the stop plates is sloped to lift the double-loading stop against the pressure of its springs. The springs assert themselves after the hardened stop plates have passed the double-loading stop. Faces on the rear end of the double-loading stop (r) then intercept the hardened stop plates on the breech bars as the breech bars counterrecoil and thereby hold the whole recoiling mass to the rear.

When the gun is operating normally the fired cartridge case is ejected before the breech bars have recoiled far enough to reach the double-loading stop (d). When ejection of the fired cartridge case occurs, the double-loading stop lower-plunger (a) is no longer held outward by the cartridge case and the whole system is then returned to its inward position by the spring under the double-loading stop lever (c).

Interception of the breech bars by the stop plates on breech bars intercepting the double-loading stop (d) occurs only if a

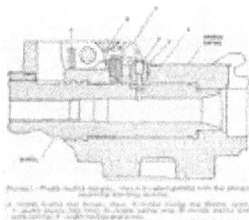

Figure 5. Double loading stop gear.
A--Double loading stop plunger, lower; B--double loading stop plunger, upper; C--double lkoading stop lever; D--double loading stop; E--double loading sdtop guide busing; F--double loading stop spring.

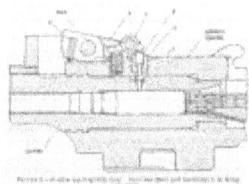

Figure 6. Double loading stop gear. Gun has fired and cartridge is in firing chamber.

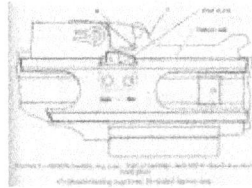

Figure 7. Double loading stop gear. Part of cartridge shell left in chamber as recoil takes place.
C--Double loading stop lever; D--double loading stop.

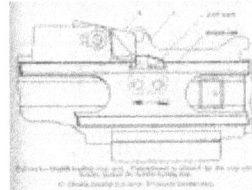

Figure 8. Double loading stop gear. Counterrecoil is arrested by the stop plate bearing against the double loading stop.
C--Double loading stop lever; D--double loading stop.

portion of the fired cartridge case remains in the chamber in line with plunger (a).

The double-loading stop plunger (a) is shaped to lie flush with the curve of the firing chamber wall. This lower plunger (a) has a shoulder on its outer end that prevents it from turning and also limits the travel of the lower plunger. The upper plunger (b) is limited on its inward travel by a shoulder on the guide bushing (e) and on its outward travel by the rear end of operating lever (c).

Note.--The double-loading stop operates in the event of a torn cartridge case being left in the chamber and in contact with the lower plunger. If the portion of the torn cartridge case left in the chamber is forward of the stop, the double-loading stop will not operate and a jam will occur.

SECTION C. TRIGGER FUNCTION

The chief function of the trigger group is that a trigger hook (a, fig. 9) mounted on the breech casing (b) (a nonrecoiling part) can hook onto the recoiling sear (d) that is on the end of the breech bolt (e) and thereby hold the recoiling mass in the cocked position (fig. 9).

Further features are:

(a) The trigger hook (a) can be kept in the released position by keeping the trigger pressed in order to allow fire.

(b) The trigger hook automatically intercepts the recoil sear and holds the recoiling mass in the cocked position, when the trigger is released or when the last round in the magazine has been fired (fig. 11). It is therefore unnecessary to recock by hand to resume firing or after changing magazines.

The recoiling mass is shown in figure 9 held in the cocked position. The barrel springs are compressed and are tending to pull the breechblock toward the muzzle (looking at fig. 9 this would be to the left). The recoil sear (d, fig. 9) is attached to the rear end of the breech bolt by an axis bolt (f).

The trigger hook (a) is hooked on the recoil sear (d), thereby preventing the breechblock and its bolt (e) from moving forward. This trigger hook (a) is pivoted on an axis bolt (g) in the trigger hook holder (h). The trigger holder (h) rests in the trigger casing (c).

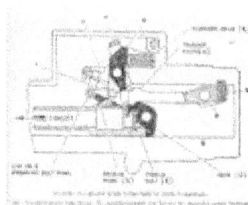

Figure 9. Recoil mass being held in cocked position.
M--Parallelogram rear lever; N--parallelogram top lever; Q--parallelogram bottom lever; V--parallelogram front lever.

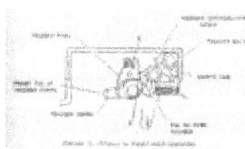

Figure 10. Trigger to trigger crank operation.

The trigger hook is always endeavoring to disengage from the recoil sear. This attempt to disengage is due to the action of two forces:

a. The spring (w) at the end of the trigger hook (a, fig. 9) is exerting pressure on the end of the trigger hook (a) to lift the opposite end from the recoil sear (d).

b. There is an upward thrust on the trigger hook that is caused by the forward pull of the barrel spring acting on the inclined faces of the sear and trigger hook. This is illustrated in figure 9.

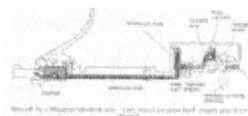

Figure 11. Magazine interlock gear. Last round has been fired, trigger gear is now tripped.

NOTE.--These faces, it will be noted, do not constitute an interlocking hook, but are at such an angle that the barrel spring pull on the recoil sear tends to force the trigger hook upward and out of the engagement; simultaneously, the trigger hook spring is exerting its pressure on the trigger hook trying to disengage it from the recoil sear.

2. In the cocked position (fig. 9) upward movement of the trigger hook is blocked by the lever (m). This lever forms the rear member of a parallelogram consisting of the following:

1. Parallelogram top lever (n), figure 9.

2. Parallelogram front lever (v).

3. Parallelogram bottom levers (q) (left and right).

4. Parallelogram rear lever (m).

The four corners of the parallelogram are formed by axis pins thus allowing the four levers to pivot on each other. The pin

connecting the top and rear levers (n and m) is also mounted in the trigger casing (fig. 10).

As previously stated there is an upward thrust on the trigger hook that is caused by the forward pull of the barrel spring acting on the inclined faces of the sear and trigger. This upward thrust combined with the pressure of the spring loaded parallelogram lever plunger--rear (k, fig. 9) tends to rotate parallelogram rear lever (m) counterclockwise and thus pull the bottom levers (q)

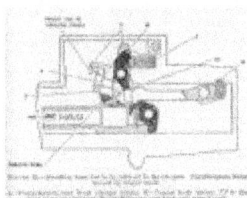

Figure 12. Recoiling mass as to be released to fire the gun.Parallelogram being moved by trigger crank.
A--Parallelogram rear lever plunger spring; B--Trigger hook spring; FF is the poinot of contact between the parallelogram rear lever and trigger hook.

to the right. These bottom levers (q), however, cannot go to the right because they are held to the left by the breech bolt pawls (x) bearing against the lugs on the bottom levers (q). There are two levers (q) and they form the bottom levers of the parallelogram against which the right and left breech pawls (x, fig. 9) bear. These two breech pawls (x) are pivoted on the breech bolt (e). The full weight of compressed barrel springs on the breech bolt makes possible for the two levers (q) to be pulled to the right and, therefore, prevents the trigger hook from disengaging.

3. Pressing the trigger will so move the parallelogram levers (fig. 12) that the trigger hook will be released from the recoil sear and the trigger hook will be kept clear of the path of the recoiling sear as long as the trigger is pressed or until the magazine is empty. The firing is entirely automatic.

When firing, the pressing of the trigger (s, fig. 10) turns the trigger retaining bolt (z) in a counterclockwise direction. The trigger intermediate lever (aa, fig. 10) engages a pin on the trigger pawl holder and, as illustrated, this trigger pawl holder is made to turn on its axis in a clockwise rotation.

The trigger pawl holder (fig. 12) has an axis pin, and on it is placed the trigger pawl. In between the pawl holder and the pawl is a spring (ee) that is under compression in order to keep a toe on the pawl in engagement at point (y) with a notch on the trigger crank. As stated above, pressing the trigger turns the trigger bolt (z, fig. 12) counterclockwise; the trigger intermediate lever being on the same bolt is also turned counterclockwise and carries the trigger pawl with it as a unit. As stated above, the toe of the trigger is in engagement with the notch on the trigger crank, and, therefore, when the trigger pawl is rotated clockwise the trigger crank also is rotated clockwise.

At the front end of the trigger crank is another toe that lies under a lip at point (p) of the parallelogram top lever (n). Movement of the trigger crank pushes up the front end of parallelogram top lever (n) causing it to rotate about its axis pin and forcing the parallelogram to slew into the position shown in figure 12. Parallelogram bottom left and right levers (q, fig. 12) are rotated about their axis on the parallelogram rear lever (m). The front end lugs (q) of parallelogram bottom levers that were bearing against the breech pawls (fig. 12) are now disengaged. The attempt of the trigger hook to disengage itself from the recoil sear, is now about to be realized, because the levers (q) cannot restrain it, inasmuch as they are freed of the breech pawls and barrel spring. Levers (q) can now go to the right, thus forcing lever (m) counterclockwise. Springs also assist in this action as follows:

Parallelogram: rear lever plunger spring (a, fig. 14); trigger hook spring (b).--The movement of the parallelogram rear lever (m) brings it into line with a recess in the trigger hook allowing the trigger hook to rotate upward about its axis and into the

position shown in figure 13, where it is clear of the recoil sear. This disengagement from the recoil sear releases the entire breech block mass so that it counterrecoils under the push of the barrel spring, and fires the gun.

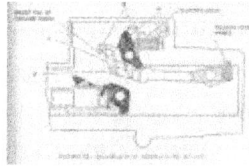

Figure13. Recoiling mass released to fire the gun.

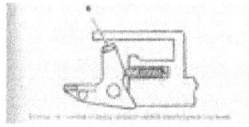

Figure 14. Action of spring plungers against parallelogram top lever.

The trigger pawl is on an axis pin in a trigger pawl holder. In between the pawl holder and the pawl is a spring that is under, compression in order to keep a toe on the pawl in engagement at point (y) with a notch on the trigger crank. During the firing travel of the trigger pawl it remains in engagement with the trigger crank.

This action retains the trigger gear in the position shown in figure 13 as long as the trigger is kept pressed to the rear and there are cartridges in the magazine. In the position illustrated in figure 13, the lugs on the parallelogram bottom levers (q) are clear of the recoil and counterrecoil path of the breech pawls. The trigger hook is kept clear of the recoil sear by the trigger hook spring.

Releasing the trigger allows the trigger intermediate lever (aa, figure 10) trigger pawl holder, trigger pawl, and trigger

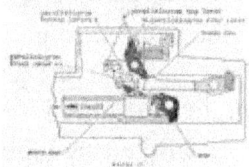

Figure 15.

crank to return to the position shown in figure 10. The parallelogram top lever (n) is lowered by its plunger spring (fig. 14). This drops parallelogram front lever (v, fig. 13) and parallelogram bottom right and left levers (q) into such a position that the lugs on bottom levers (q) lie in the recoil and counterrecoil path of the breech pawls.

On the breech block mass recoil, the breech pawls ride under the bottom levers (q, fig. 15) and, during the subsequent counterrecoil, engage them again. The parallelogram lever (m) is still in the recess in the trigger hook as shown in fig. 15, and it is being kept in the recess by its spring. When the lugs on bottom levers (q) are engaged by the breech pawls the effect is to pull the bottom levers (q) forward. This movement rotates the parallelogram rear lever (m) clockwise causing a face on it to press on the toe (ff, fig. 14) of the trigger hook forcing it down into engagement with the recoiling sear. The breech block mass is thus intercepted and held in the cocked position. See figure 9, "Recoiling mass in cocked position. "

Safe fire gear.--A safe fire lever is fitted close to the right handgrip. When put to the "Safe" position it turns as axis bolt and rotates the safety cam.

The toe of the safety cam contacts the rear toe of the trigger intermediate lever thus locking it and preventing any movement. When put to the "Tire" position (see fig. 10) the safety cam is rotated clear of the trigger intermediate lever.

SECTION D. MAGAZINE INTERLOCK GEAR

1. The purpose of the magazine interlock gear is to stop the gun in the cocked position after the last round of each magazine is loaded into the gun, regardless of the position of the trigger. Otherwise, the breech block mass would counterrecoil on an empty gun, making it necessary to recock by hand before firing could be continued with a fresh magazine.

2. The positions of the various parts of this gear, while the gun is firing, are shown in figure 16. The front portion of the magazine interlock gear is shown in figure 16. It should be noted that the interlock lever (d) is fastened by its axis bolt (g) to the interlock carrier (f) and the interlock rod (k) is also fastened to the interlock carrier (f) by pin (J). The interlock carrier spring (c) acts rearward on the carrier (f) when lever (d) is out of its catch recess (I). The interlock lever spring (h) acts on the lever (d) tending to keep the lever in its catch recess (i) and the front end upward.

The loading power of the magazine is by a clock spring behind the cartridge feeder in the magazine. This feeder operates against the last round in the magazine.

When the last round is fed into the gun, the cartridge feeder emerges at the mouth of the magazine (fig. 16). A bolt on the rear end of the cartridge feeder then bears down against the front end of the magazine interlock lever that is pivoted within the magazine interlock carrier and disengages it from the catch recess In the ejector. This leaves the magazine interlock carrier together

with the magazine interlock lever free to move rearward within the ejector under the influence of the interlock carrier spring. As the carrier moves to the rear, it takes with it the magazine interlock rod. The rear end of the rod pushes against the magazine interlock fork, figure 16, thus rotating the fork on its axis bolt. As the fork rotates, a part of the fork presses against a bolt that bears in turn against the claw of the trigger pawl. The movement of this bolt then trips the trigger pawl disengaging

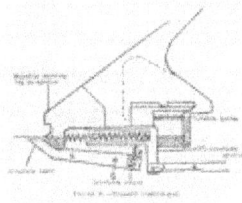

Figure 16. Magazine interlock gear.

it from the trigger crank permitting the trigger crank to drop. This lowers the front end of the parallelogram into the position shown in figure 15. This brings the lug on the parallelogram bottom levers (q) in line with the path of travel of the breech pawls on recoil and counterrecoil. As the breech block recoils, the breech pawls slide under and past the lugs on parallelogram bottom levers (q) and on the counterrecoil engage these lugs and lock the trigger hook as shown in figure 15.

3. The action of moving the magazine catch lever toward the muzzle to free the empty magazine for unshipping (fig. 17) forces

the ejector to the rear so that it overtakes the magazine interlock carrier. This allows the magazine interlock lever, pivoted with the magazine interlock carrier, to be forced by its spring into engagement again with the recess in the ejector, thus locking the interlock carrier to the ejector once more. This movement of the ejector compresses the catch spring (fig. 17) moving the magazine catch about its pivot causing its front ends to contact the front end of the ejector thus holding the ejector in its rear position.

When shipping a new magazine a projection at the mouth presses down the forward ends of the catch (fig. 17) leaving the

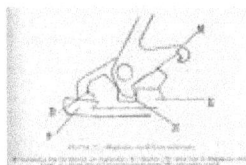

Figure 17. Magazine catch lever assembly.

ejector free to move forward because of the pressure of magazine interlock catch spring (fig. 17) and lock the magazine to the gun as previously described under heading "Magazine Catch Gear and Ejector. " In the course of this action of locking the magazine when the ejector moves forward, the magazine interlock carrier is carried with it (because it is engaged in the catch recess in the ejector (fig. 17)), and the magazine interlock rod is also moved forward (because it is fastened to the carrier). This forward movement of the magazine interlock rod freezes it from the magazine interlock fork.

The magazine interlock fork and the trigger pawl tripping bolt then return to their original position (fig. 1) because of the pressure of the trigger pawl tripping bolt spring. The trigger pawl is thus left free to reengage itself with the trigger crank because of the pressure of the compressed spring between the trigger pawl holder and trigger pawl.

Note.--The magazine is held locked to the gun during the period of ejection of the cartridge. When the breech bolt mass is recoiling, the impact of the fired cartridge case against the ejector slides the ejector rearward into engagement with the recess (M) (fig. 17) of the magazine catch lever thereby preventing it from rising. Thus the magazine is held locked to the gun during the period of the ejection of the cartridge.

SECTION E. RECOILING PARTS AND BUFFERS

The chief components of the recoiling group are:

1. Breech block, carrying the hammer, striker pin and breech face piece.

2. Breech bolt, carrying the sear.

3. Breech bars, left and right, connecting the breech block to the barrel spring case.

4. Breech bolt cotter and securing bolts holding recoil parts together, as follows:

   a. Breech bolt cotter, holds breech block to breech bolt.

   b. Securing bolts and spring pins, secure barrel spring case to breech bars.

   c. Securing bolts and spring pins, secure breech bars to breech bolt cotter.

5. Barrel spring case, mounted on the forward portion of the barrel.

6. Barrel springs, mounted on the center portion of barrel, between the barrel spring case and the breech casing.

   NOTE.--All the above six components move in recoil and counterrecoil.

In addition to the barrel springs, there are 2 other sets of buffer springs. A set of 12 are mounted in the front end of the gun casing, to cushion the last inch or so of recoil. A set of 15 in the

trigger casing, cushions the shock on the trigger mechanism when the trigger hook stops the gun in the cocked position.

2. The action of the striker gear is shown in figure 18 showing the striker pin being held to rear

when the breech bolt is traveling forward; the hammer imparting a blow to the striker pin and the striker pin being withdrawn by the hammer.

Note.--The striker pin reaches its full firing travel by momentum and not by a direct thrust all the way by the hammer.

In order to understand the action of the hammer it should be noted in figure 18 that the front toe and rear toe are positioned out of line with each other. There are two front toes, one on each side of the hammer. The rear toe is an extension of the enter part of the hammer. The upper part of the hammer rests

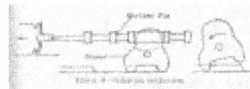

Figure 18. Striker pin and hammer.

in, and operates the striker pin. The hammer plate is secured to the breech casing and has a center cam surface to operate the rear toe of the hammer and impart a thrust on the striker pin. Momentum carries the striker forward, thus firing the cartridge. (See fig. 18.)

The hammer plate has two other cam surfaces, one on each side, to operate the hammer front toes and thus withdraw the striker pin from the fired cartridge. The hammer plate cam surfaces are arranged so that the front toes are clear when the rear toe is operating, and the reverse is also true.

The three conditions of the operation of the striker gear are: (a) Breech block is traveling forward; it has picked up a cartridge, but has not quite reached the firing chamber. All three hammer toes are riding against the side of the breech casing thereby holding the striker pin to the rear. The rear toe is about to strike the rear end of the center cam surface of the hammer plate.

(b)The breech block has reached the end of its travel. The cartridge is being fired. The rear toe of the hammer is riding on the center cam surface of the hammer plate, causing the hammer to rotate forward. The hammer has driven the striker pin fully forward penetrating the primer of the, cartridge. The front toes have entered a cutaway recess in the breech casing.

Note.--The striker pin should protrude 0. 045 inch to 0. 070 inch from the breech bolt face piece when the striker pin is fully forward.

(c)The breech block has started, on recoil carrying with it the fired cartridge. The front toes have ridden up the front slope of the hammer plate causing the hammer to rotate rearward. The hammer has retracted the striker pin from the fired cartridge.

3. The breech block is connected to the breech bolt by the same cotter that connects the breech

bolt to the breech bars. The purpose of breech bolt is to extend the breech block to the rear, in order to contact the trigger group. The breech bolt carries the recoil sear at the rear on an axis bolt. The right and left breech pawls are near the rear of the breech bolt. The recoil sear and breech pawls work with the trigger group as described and illustrated.

The breech block face piece is mounted in the front end of the breech block. It is retained by a shoulder that fits into a recess machined in the breech block, and is locked in place by a leaf spring. A hole is drilled in the center of the breech block face piece, to carry the rear end of the cartridge case.

4. The breech bars are connected at the rear by the breech bolt cotter that passes through the breech block and its extension, the breech bolt. The breech bars are connected at the front to trunnions forced on the barrel spring casing, The trunnions fit in holes in the breech bars. Tubular securing bolts that are secured by two-legged spring pins fasten the breech bars to the barrel spring casing trunnions at the front, and to the breech bolt cotter at the rear.

The right breech bar has a catch plate or lug for a hand cocking cable.

The right and left breech bars have hardened stop plates that contact the double-loading stop whenever a portion of a torn

cartridge case remains in the firing chamber under the double loading stop pin.

5. There are two barrel springs; a long front one in the barrel spring case and a short rear one, with a center sleeve between them. These springs are wound in opposite directions so as to prevent twist on the spring casing and on the breech bars that might be caused by twisting of a single spring. The purpose of these springs is to absorb the rearward momentum of the recoiling parts, and to return these parts to their forward position.

> NOTE.--The compression on the barrel springs is 66 pounds when the recoiling parts are in their fully forward position. The compression amounts to 534 pounds when the buffer strikes the breech casing.

The casing for the barrel springs carries the recoiling end of these springs. A barrel spring front sleeve fits into the front end of the casing and is the front seat for the springs. A barrel spring center sleeve is the intermediate support for the barrel springs and is located between the two springs. It is a loose fit on the barrel. A barrel spring seating ring that is locked in the front end of the breech casing is the rear seat for the barrel springs. The recoil buffer springs, described below, assist the barrel springs.

6. A set of 12 buffer springs are mounted in the forward end of the breech casing.

These recoil buffer springs assist the barrel springs to absorb the recoil and also assist the breech block mass in counter-recoiling. They operate only during the last inch of recoil and during the first inch of counterrecoil. The total compression of the 12 buffer springs, plus the barrel springs at full metal recoil, is 3,143 lbs.

NOTE.--The gun will continue firing with recoil buffer springs broken, but it is inadvisable to allow this, except in action, as the recoil tends to become metal to metal. Parts are then liable to be damaged and the gun becomes less steady for laying and the rate of fire drops.

A recoil buffer retains the buffer springs in the breech casing, and the rear end of the barrel spring casing contacts this buffer during the last inch of recoil, compressing the springs. The

buffer is held in the breech casing by the barrel spring seating ring.

7. One of the duties of the trigger group is to intercept the recoiling mechanism, in order to keep the gun cocked whenever the trigger is released during firing, and, as the recoiling mass is moving forward at high speed, there is a severe shock at the moment of interception. The trigger buffer springs cushion this shock, thereby protecting the sear and trigger hook.

There are 15 trigger buffer springs mounted in the trigger casing.

This trigger casing also carries the trigger hook and the trigger parallelogram levers, and is locked in the breech casing by the hand grip mounting piece. The trigger casing is free to move forward a short distance by compressing the trigger buffer springs against the breech casing. This cushions the interception of the recoiling mass.

SECTION F. MAGAZINE

1. The magazine consists of a cylindrical drum containing 60 rounds of ammunition that are driven around spirals, inside the drum, by a clock spring that is hand wound from outside the magazine. The tension of the spring can be adjusted.

The feed system maintains a pressure on the innermost round, by means of a wound clock spring that is always endeavoring to push the rounds around the spirals and out of the magazine mouthpiece. The lips of the magazine mouthpiece are partly closed so that a round can pass through it only by being pushed out longitudinally at a right angle to the direction of the feed drive, a gap being cut in the front, or muzzle end, of the mouthpiece to allow the rounds to slide in or out.

2. The pressure on the innermost round is from a clock spring that is housed in the magazine casing. The outer end of the spring is held to a spring case by a securing pin. The spring case is bolted to the magazine casing by screws, thus fixing the outer end of the magazine clock spring. The inner end of the spring is hooked on the spring axis, and any tension on the spring tends to turn this spring axis. This spring axis can either rotate freely on the mainshaft, or can

be coupled to it by a spring coupling sleeve having ratchet teeth. When this coupling sleeve is in

engagement the tension of the clock spring is transmitted to the mainshaft tending to rotate it.

The feed block driven by the main shaft carries the feed arm which can slide through the feed block to the radius of any point in the spiral path. The cartridge feeder link is pinned to the feed arm and to the feed head by two articulating bolts. These two articulating bolts have rollers that guide the feed system around the spiral. The cartridge feeder swivels on the feed head, pushing the cartridge around the spiral.

3. The spring axis has a spiral groove cut on its flange, and this spiral groove actuates an indicator block that slides in a radial direction. This block is an indicator of the amount of tension in the spring, and it also stops the winding or unwinding of the spring when the end of the spring axis spiral groove is reached.

NOTE.--This block does NOT indicate how many rounds of ammunition are in the magazine, but shows the amount of tension in the magazine clock spring. **The zero position of the indicator block shows that it has reached the end of the spring axis groove and is holding whatever tension remains in the clock spring. In this position the ratchet teeth of the coupling sleeve can be disengaged from the main shaft thus freeing it from all spring drive.**

The last round of ammunition should be fed into the magazine mouthpiece just before the indicator block reaches the end of the spring axis groove.

> NOTE.--The amount of residual tension in the magazine spring is of importance as it indicates how much drive will be imparted to feeding, the last round.

4. **Loading the magazine.**--

NOTE.--The last two rounds loaded in each magazine should have blind loaded projectiles. This practice is generally adopted to obviate the danger of firing of an H. E. projectile through the muzzle cover.

1. Place the magazine in the loading frame.

   NOTE.--See if the indicator block is at zero, and if it is not, the spring tension must be relieved as instructed.

2. Pull out the coupling sleeve as far as possible, and while holding it out, turn it to a point where, when released,

it is on the lugs of the main shaft and will not snap down and engage the ratchet teeth again. Turning the coupling sleeve about an eighth turn should hold it disengaged.

3. Place the loading lever on the end of the main shaft. This will permit the feed axis to be revolved and thereby rotate the cartridge feeder.

4. Revolve the loading lever clockwise, until the cartridge feeder is in the magazine mouth.

5. Remove loading lever from coupling sleeve, leaving the coupling sleeve in its pulled out position.

6. Push, by hand, through the magazine opening against the cartridge feeder, and move it back just far enough to leave space for the insertion of one or two cartridges. *Never leave space for more than two cartridges.*

7. After a cartridge is inserted, press by hand against it, moving it back far enough to insert one or two cartridges. Continue inserting cartridges until magazine is full. Capacity of magazine is 60 cartridges.

   Note.--It is essential that all cartridges be pushed all the way down to the bottom of the magazine so that their bases are in alignment and firmly seated on the magazine rear plate. This is important because the breech block moves very rapidly and the magazine must feed the cartridges to it properly, so that the face piece can readily pick up the cartridge.

CAUTION.--GREAT CARE SHOULD BE TAKEN NOT TO PUSH THE CARTRIDGES AND FEEDER A FURTHER DISTANCE THAN IS NECESSARY FOR THE INSERTION OF TWO CARTRIDGES. IF THE CARTRIDGES WITH THE CARTRIDGE FEEDER ARE PUSHED IN TOO FAR, THEY MIGHT BECOME UPSET, AND JAM. A JAMMED MAGAZINE CAN BE CAUSED BY PUSHING THE FEEDER BACK TOO FAR BY HAND, OR BY USING THE LOADING LEVER ON THE FEED AXIS. IF THIS HAPPENS IT IS NECESSARY TO DISMANTLE THE MAGAZINE TO CLEAR THE JAM.

It is sometimes impossible to push by hand a number of cartridges back into the magazine in order to make room for more, and this is particularly true toward the end of the loading

of the magazine. When this condition occurs, use the loading lever. Rotate the loading lever counter clockwise very slightly for a distance necessary for the insertion of one but NEVER OVER TWO cartridges.

CAUTION.--If the loading lever is rotated farther than this* the cartridges would have

room to fall into an oblique position, thereby preventing further loading, and making it necessary to dismantle the magazine and clear the jam.

(8) When the magazine has been correctly filled to capacity (60 rounds), the coupling sleeve must be revolved by hand until it drops into engagement with the ratchet teeth.

Note.--The magazine clock spring must then be either completely, or slightly, tensioned as instructed in the following:

Completely tensioning a magazine spring.

(9) When the loaded magazine is to be used immediately, the spring is tensioned completely in the loading frame. Place the loading lever on the spring axis. Revolve the loading lever counterclockwise. Continue revolving the loading lever until a stop becomes distinctly noticeable. This indicates that the clock spring is completly tensioned. Remove the loading lever. Remove the loading magazine from the loading frame and install on a gun. DO NOT STORE A FULLY TENSIONED MAGAZINE, BECAUSE OF THE UNNECESSARY STRAIN ON THE WOUND CLOCK SPRING.

5. The indicator scale on the front cover of the magazine shows "0", "15", "30", "45", and "60" and these figures are a measure of the magazine spring tension Magazines are given either a partial spring tensioning when being stored for future use, or a complete tensioning when being used immediately. The amount of spring tensioning will depend upon how many cartridges there are in the magazine, as for example, a load of 30 or 45 cartridges requires a different spring tension than a full load of 60 rounds.

Partial tensioning of a magazine for storage purposes requires only a slight spring pressure, and the number of cartridges in the magazine makes no difference

In the case of a magazine completely filled to its capacity of 60 rounds, and fully tensioned, the indicator will read "60".

In case the magazine has a partial load of cartridges, then the spring is tensioned according to the load in the following manner: There are openings in the hack plate of the magazine through which the rear ends of the cartridges are visible. Tension the spring for 10 more cartridges than there are in the magazine

Note.--Hold the coupling sleeve with the fingers to prevent its turning when tensioning the spring on a partly loaded magazine. If it is permitted to turn, the cartridge feeder will be backed away from the cartridges and a jam may result.

(a) When a fully or partly filled magazine is to be stored, the spring is given a slight initial tensioning that is just sufficient to hold the cartridge upright.

Note.--A short tensioning with the loading lever in the position is sufficient. If the magazine is fully loaded or only partly filled, this slight initial tensioning is necessary to prevent a jam in the magazine.

(b) If no initial tensioning is given the magazine spring, the cartridges are liable to fall out, become disarranged, or Be tipped over when the magazine is lifted from the loading frame.

It may become necessary to relieve the spring tension on the magazine feed block to unload, to store, or to strip the magazine.

6. (a) Place the magazine in the loading frame in the same manner as when loading. Place loading lever in the spring tensioning axis.

NOTE.--The loading lever will not clear the magazine handle, so place it in such a position that it has room to move clockwise from one side of the handle to the other.

(b) The tension of the spring causes pressure on the ratchet teeth of coupling sleeve. Therefore, press counterclockwise on the loading lever to relieve this pressure and at the same time disengage the coupling sleeve with the other hand by pulling outward and turning about one-eighth turn, so that the sleeve stays disengaged.

(c) Allow the loading lever to move clockwise, as far as it can (until it contacts the magazine handle). Turn the coupling

sleeve slightly and allow it to snap down and mesh the ratchet teeth.

(d) Press on the loading lever ratchet pawl and revolve the loading lever back to position from which it started in step 1. Then release the pawl.

(e) Repeat step c. until the spring tension is completely relieved and no pressure can be felt against the lever.

Note.--If the cartridges are to be left in the magazine, the spring must be given a slight initial tension before taking the magazine out of the loading frame in order to prevent their falling out or being tipped over.

7. If a magazine is loaded with cartridges and has been fully spring tensioned, and it is desired to unload the cartridges and relieve the tension of the magazine clock spring, this can be done by pushing the cartridges out, one hj one. This action removes the cartridges and relieves the spring tension at the same time. It is not necessary to use the loading lever or disconnect the coupling sleeve.

8. It is advisable to relieve the initial spring tension completely and this is done by using Steps a, b, c, and d, these being the same as for "Relieving Magazine Spring Tension". In this case of initial tensioning, the loading lever will relieve the slight initial tensioning in the first four steps, and the fifth step will be unnecessary. Place the loading lever so that it is all the way down and revolve it clockwise with one hand, so that a cartridge is constantly being pressed against the magazine mouthpiece. Use the other hand, and push out the cartridges as they appear at the mouthpiece.

NOTE.--The loading lever must be made to revolve continuously as the cartridges are being removed, or the cartridges will upset and jam. IF THIS HAPPENS IT IS NECESSARY TO DISMANTLE THE MAGAZINE TO CLEAR THE JAM.

9. It is advisable to relieve the spring tension by using steps (a), (b), (c), (d), and (e), paragraph 6 above, and then unload the cartridges as instructed above.

NOTE.--The magazine should be stripped by an artificer.

1. Place the magazine in loading frame.

2. Empty the magazine of cartridges unless the stripping is being done to eliminate a jam, in which case it will be

necessary to proceed with cartridges still in the magazine.

3. There are eight screws that hold the cover plate on the magazine. Remove six of these, leaving in place any two that are directly opposite each other.

4. Install the loading lever on the spring axis and relieve spring tension pressure as instructed.

5. With coupling sleeve disengaged, place the loading lever on the feed axis, and revolve it counterclockwise, until the cartridge feeder is at the inner end of its travel.

6. Turn the coupling sleeve so that it snaps down and engages the ratchet teeth.

7. Install the loading lever on the magazine spring axis and turn the loading lever counterclockwise just far enough to take the slight remaining spring tension.

8. Hold the loading lever in the position described in step 7, and remove the two remaining screws from the cover plate. Keep the loading lever in the position given in Step 7, and loosen the cover plate from the magazine with a screw driver or suitable tool, being very careful not to pry up the spring casing flange.

Note. ---The loosening of the cover plate with a screw driver frees it from the spring casing, and now the remaining spring tension may be allowed to rotate the loading lever clockwise.

9. All spring tension is now eased off and the loading lever can be unshipped.

10. Rotate the spring housing assembly until one of the holes in the coupling sleeve is in line with the head of ratchet cross pin.

11. Lift the spring case until its flange clears the dowel screw in the front plate, and turn it until the letters "D" in the front plate and cover plate are in line. Remove the spring case completely with the spring axis. The spring can be removed from the casing by pushing the spring up on the bolt and holding it to the casing. This will permit the enlarged part of the hole to be lifted over the bolt. The spring can then be removed from the spring axis by twisting the axis so as to disengage the lugs from the holes in the inner end of the spring.

12. Remove the snap ring from the rear end of the main shaft, using pliers.

13. Remove the complete main shaft, feed block, feeder link and cartridge feeder from the front.

14. The feeder link, feed block, and cartridge feeder can be separated by removing the bolt cotter pins and tapping out the two articulating bolts, and feeder swivel bolt, using punch.

15. The magazine casing should not normally be stripped into its component parts.

10. **Thoroughly lubricate all parts**.--See Magazine Maintenance.

1. Assemble the main shaft, feed block, feeder arm, feeder link, two articulating bolts with their rollers, feed head, bolt washers, bolt cotter pins and cartridge feeder.

2. Lubricate, and insert this feed group assembly into the magazine from the front. Engage the rollers in the spiral guideway. Insert the rear end of the main shaft into its bearing in the rear plate.

3. Assemble the snap ring at the rear end of the main shaft. To check the action, turn the feed system so that the cartridge feeder is outward at the limit of its travel in the empty position.

4. Place the enlarged part of the hole in the magazine spring over the bolt in the spring casing, and pull the spring down onto the bolt shoulder and out of the enlarged part of the hole. Pack the magazine spring with Gulf Plastic AS Special grease. Insert the magazine spring in its case over the spring axis, and turn the axis so as to engage the

axis lugs. Insert this assembly into the magazine with the letters "D" in line. Rotate the spring case until the dowel hole marked "O" in its flange engages the dowel screw in the front plate of the magazine.

Note.--Examine the spring case holes that are counterclockwise from the hole marked "O. " In a few cases they may be marked "1," "2," "3," and up. If these markings are found, then turn the spring case so that the hole with the highest number, instead of the hole marked "O," is

engaged with the dowel screw on the front plate of the magazine.

5. Place the cover plate on the magazine, and do not install any screws in it. Move the indicator block with a knife blade, or any similar tool, so that it engages in the spiral groove on the spring axis.

    NOTE.--Up to this point it is permissible to have the cover plate in any position; also the indicator block can be engaged in the spiral groove of the spring axis in any position.

6. Turn the cover plate counterclockwise until the indicator shows zero and the indicator block can be felt coming up against the clock spring.

7. Assemble the coupling sleeve with its spring, the retaining ring and the cross pin.

8. Ship the loading lever on the spring axis and turn the loading lever counterclockwise about seven-eighths of a revolution or until the letter "A," stamped on the cover, is in alignment with letter "A" stamped on the magazine casing.

9. Maintain this position by holding the loading lever, and install eight cover screws.

    CAUTION.--The counterclockwise rotation of the cover from the zero position in Step 6 to "A" alignment in Step 8, has to be done against the clockwise pull of the clock spring. Approximately seven-eighths' revolution of the cover by loading lever should bring the alignment marks "A" opposite each other. BE VERY CAREFUL NOT TO TURN MORE THAN THIS AMOUNT. ALSO, DO NOT ALINE MARKS "A" BY TURNING THE LOADING LEVER CLOCKWISE.

11. If a magazine becomes dry or corroded internally, it must be disassembled, cleaned, and lubricated with Gulf Plastic AX special grease. See instructions for disassembling and reassembling magazine.

12. The magazine clock spring was packed with grease, when the magazine was issued. However, this grease tends to squeeze out in service. Watch this spring for evidences of corrosion,

and if corrosion is found, disassemble, clean and repack with Gulf Plastic AX special grease.

13. The spring that is behind the magazine interlock bolt may become corroded, or operate slowly, due to the use of too thick an oil, or because the oil thickened in cold weather. This magazine interlock bolt is the part on the magazine cartridge feeder that causes the gun to be held in a cocked position when the magazine has fed its last round to the gun. Therefore, any corrosion or slow operation due to thick or thickened oil will cause the gun to fail to remain in a cocked position after firing the last round of each magazine. Use Gulf Plastic AX special grease, or ice machine oil, and apply sparingly and often.

14. All moving parts should be lightly coated with Gulf Plastic AX special grease. A light coat of the same grease should be applied to the spiral guideways in the magazine.

SECTION G. GUN MAINTENANCE

1. The cleaning and oiling of the gun should be carried out as required and not at any fixed intervals.

It should be realized that in this type of gun the force of explosion is absorbed in checking and reversing the forward movement of a relatively heavy bolt that is never locked. The proper functioning of the gun depends on the free movement of the recoiling parts and on the free operation of the various springs used.

Any dirt, corrosion, or lack of lubrication that is present to a degree that will impede free movement and free operation will cause stoppages during firing.

2. **Clean and Oil--**

    a. As soon as possible after firing.

    b. If the gun gets wet.

    c. If the gun gets dirty.

    d. If there is any reason to expect corrosion to start.

In order to clean and oil the gun properly it is necessary to first partly disassemble it.

3. Use mineral oil or any good quality lubricating oil of medium viscosity. **CAUTION.--Do not add white lead, black lead, red lead, or make any addition of any similar substance to the oil.**

4. The double loading stop plunger, upper, and the double loading stop plunger, lower, in the barrel tend to become stuck with oil that is gummed by the heat of the gun. These parts should be cleaned periodically and lubricated with a light viscosity oil, applied sparingly and often.

To remove the double loading stop plunger, lower, from the barrel, take out the retaining pin using the special screw driver. The plunger can then be taken out for cleaning and lubrication.

CAUTION.--If the parts of the double loading stop gear become gummed or corroded, the stop plunger, lower, might not be operated, resulting in stoppage.

5. The parts of the double loading stop gear and also the buffer are exposed to salt-water corrosion and, therefore, require particular care in maintenance. See "Caution" note above.

6. When the gun is being mounted in the cradle, the inside of the securing bolt hole, the breech casing, and the securing bolt itself, should be thoroughly greased for protection against corrosion.

7. If the gun stops of its own accord, for any reason other than an empty magazine, the following immediate action should be carried out:

(a) Put the safety catch to "Safe" and note whether the recoiling parts are in the forward position. If the recoiling parts are in the forward position, a misfire, a broken striker, a broken hammer, or failure to feed from the magazine, is indicated. Safety precautions for a misfire should be observed.

If there is a live round in a hot gun and the stoppage cannot be cleared then douse the barrel with water, to prevent the round from heating up.

If the magazine is empty and the gun stops in the forward position, it may be due to sticking, or sluggish action of the magazine cartridge feeder bolt which trips the interlock lever. If examination shows that this bolt does not work freely, the magazine should not be used again until the condition has been corrected.

(b) Examine the double loading stop. If the horns are in the down or operating position, there is a round or part of a broken case in the chamber.

(c) Remove the magazine and recock the gun. If the magazine is difficult to remove, it will come off as the breech block

is withdrawn when cocking the gun. In the event of it being impossible to remove the magazine without recocking, care should be taken to cock the gun in one continuous movement, and on no account must the breech block be allowed to go forward.

(d) Examine chamber and breech face piece. If the lip of the breech face piece is broken off, a new one must be installed.

(e) Examine the bore from the muzzle, making sure it is clear. This is necessary to avoid a premature or bulged barrel. An ejector tool is provided in the tool roll, to remove any HE shell or practice shell left in the bore. This ejector should be used gently, and, if excessive resistance is felt when removing an HE shell, then change the barrel.

(f) Stoppages of the gun have occurred which appeared to have been caused by the presence of hair from ammunition packing material getting into the mechanism. Steps have been taken to eliminate this type of packing, but a large amount of ammunition has already been issued. At the first opportunity, and in any event before loading it into the magazine drums, ammunition should be examined to see that it is free of hair; and if hair or dirt is found, it should be removed. If grease is removed in this process, it must be replaced.

8. The outside of the barrel, and the outer and inner surfaces of the barrel springs, should be smeared with dry graphite or grate polish.

NOTE.--Oil should not be used on the outside of the barrel nor on the barrel springs as it smokes when the barrel gets hot, and the smoke will interfere with the sighting of the gun.

9. The bore and firing chamber should be lightly cleaned out IMMEDIATELY AFTER FIRING using the cleaning rod equipment in the tool roll.

Place a light coat of a good quality lubricating oil, medium viscosity, in the bore and firing chamber.

CAUTION.--Do not fire with a heavily greased bore or firing chamber.

The proper functioning of the gun requires easy and regular extraction of the empty cartridge case, when it is blown backward by the firing chamber gases. Care must be taken, therefore, to maintain the firing-chamber walls in good condition, thereby avoiding any unnecessary friction with the walls of the

cartridge case. The firing-chamber walls have a high lapped polish when the barrel is issued. FIRING-CHAMBER WALLS MUST NEVER BE CLEANED WITH EMERY PAPER.

10. The amount of life that a barrel will give, depends on how hot the barrel becomes during firing.

Five magazines, containing 60 rounds each or a total of 300 rounds, can be fired continuously without harm to the barrel.

Nine magazines of 60 rounds each, or a total of 540 rounds, will cause serious wear if fired continuously.

If short pauses occur between the firing of each magazine, the wear will remain small, even after several thousand rounds.

During any prolonged firing, keep the barrel as cool as possible, either by frequent changes with the spare barrel, or by dousing the barrel with water.

11. The barrel is removed by rotating the barrel locking handle into the position marked "unlock. " Rotate the barrel approximately 60° counterclockwise looking from the muzzle to the breech and pull out to the front (asbestos gloves are provided with the tools and spare parts to remove a hot barrel) .

Note.--The clearances between the barrel and its housing in the breech casing are very small. Therefore, a barrel may fit very tightly and a special tool is provided for rotating the barrel.

12. The barrel can be removed easily and quickly and another barrel substituted without disassembly of any other parts.

Interrupted thrust collars, machined on the barrel, secure it to the casing. The barrel is assembled from the front with its interrupted thrust collars in the unlocked position. The barrel is then locked by rotating it 60° clockwise looking from the muzzle toward the breech. Assembly marks are provided. The barrel is prevented from accidental unlocking by the barrel locking gear as already described.

The barrel, when rotated into its position, is stopped by a pin mounted in the breech casing that fits into a slot in the rear end of the barrel. This locates the barrel in the proper position to engage the barrel locking lever. The double loading stop prevents loading a round of ammunition into the barrel chamber unless the chamber is already clear at the double loading stop. A hole is drilled through the top wall of the chamber of the barrel and in this hole the double loading stop plunger operates. The operation of the double loading stop has already been described.

13. If violent recoils, causing metal to metal contact of the buffer against the breech casing, occur habitually, and more than one lot of ammunition has been used during these metal to metal recoils, then the cause is probably a collapse of the barrel springs and not a result of ammunition loading.

A metal-to-metal contact always occurs between the barrel spring casing and the buffer during the last inch of recoil. However, the buffer should not normally strike the breach casing. Weak barrel springs will cause the buffer springs to be overloaded and result in metal-to-metal contact of the buffer against the breach casing.

The remedy is to change to the spare barrel springs. H spare barrel springs are not available then insert flat washers at the rear end of the barrel spring up to a maximum thickness of three-fourths of an inch.

CAUTION.--Whenever possible keep the gun UNCOCKED in order to relieve the spring tension and prevent the possibility of a permanent set of the springs.

14. If the buffer becomes corroded it may not have the free movement necessary to transmit the last of the recoil shock to the buffer springs, and the free movement necessary to assist the barrel springs on counterrecoil.

15. The ratchet type hand cocking tool supplied with some of the Mark 2 guns is principally for use when the gun is dismounted from its carriage. This hand-cocking tool can also be used on the Mark 4 gun.

16. To use the hand-cocking tool, first remove the shoulder piece from the breech casing and install the hand-cocking tool in its place on the threads of the breech casing. Hook the end of the chain on the cocking catch plate on the rear end of the right breech bar.

17. Pull the breech block mass back by using the hand-cocking tool handle. The breech pawls can be heard to, click over the parallelogram bottom levers when the breech block mass has been pulled far enough to the rear. The hand-cocking tool handle can then be eased back until the sear engages the trigger hook by following the instructions under "Uncocking with the ratchet type hand-cocking tool."

18. Three other types of hand-cocking devices will be found in use with various guns.

(1) **Double lanyard**.--A stirrup which slips over the barrel and comes up against the barrel spring casing has a lanyard attached to each side. These lanyards are knotted to provide hand holds. The gun can be cocked by having two or three men pull on each lanyard.

(2) **Single lanyard**.--Another device is a single lanyard with a ring on one end and several knots to provide hand holds. The ring is slipped over the left end of the cotter and the gun is cocked by the pull of four or five men on the lanyard.

(3) **Block and tackle**.--A block and tackle type cocking device is used by hooking the front end in one of the holes in the left breech bar. The rear end is shipped over the hand grip and the gun cocked by the use of the block and tackle.

NOTE.--Normal cocking is done most quickly with the single or double lanyard device. To clear a jammed cartridge from the chamber may require considerable force. For this purpose use the ratchet type tool, the block and tackle, or the mount cocking rope.

19. The hand cocking tool supplied with some Mark 2 guns can be used to uncock the gun by removing the shoulder piece from the breech casing and installing the hand cocking tool in its place on the threads of the breech casing. Hook the end of the chain on the cocking catch plate

on the rear end of the right breech bar.

DO NOT SLAM THE BREECH MASS ON AN EMPTY GUN. Ratchet the hand cocking tool lever so as to make the chain taut enough to hold the breech mass from slamming. Remove the magazine by pressing the magazine catch lever forward while lifting the rear end of the magazine clear of its catch and the ejector. Press down with any suitable tool on the end of the magazine interlock lever, in order to release the interlock. Press the trigger and the breech mass will be held from running forward by the hand cocking tool.

Pull on the handle to relieve pressure on the holding pawl. Release holding pawl by pressing forward on the holding pawl lever. While holding lever allow handle to rotate forward a convenient distance. Remove finger pressure from holding pawl lever. Apply finger pressure to handle pawl and revolve the

handle back to its starting position. Then release the pawl. Continue to repeat the above procedure until the breech mass has been eased forward.

The other types of cocking devices described previously can be used to prevent the breech mass from slamming on an empty gun.

20. The normal method used during firing or drill for cocking a gun that is assembled on the mount is to use the mount cocking rope.

Rotate the handwheel so as to lower the gun and its carriage to their lowest position. Elevate and lock the gun at 87°.

Attach one end of the wire cocking rope on the breech cotter. Attach the other end of the cocking rope to the mount cocking bracket.

Turn the gun and its carriage so that the cocking rope is in a direct line to the left side of the gun.

Rotate the handwheel so as to raise the gun and carriage. The downward pull of the cocking rope on the breech block mass will cock the gun.

The breech pawls can be heard to click over the parallelogram bottom levers when the breech block mass has been pulled sufficiently to the rear. The breech block mass can be eased forward by lowering the gun and carriage with the handwheel until the sear is engaged by the trigger hook.

21. Do not slam the breech mass on an empty gun. Rotate the handwheel so that the gun and carriage are at their lowest position. Elevate and lock the gun at 87°. Attach one end of the cocking wire rope to the breech block cotter, and the other end to the mount cocking bracket. Turn the gun on its carriage pivot so that the cocking rope is in a direct lead to the left side of

the gun. Rotate the handwheel to raise the gun upward from the mount so that the cocking wire rope is taut enough to hold the breech mass from slamming. Remove the magazine clear of its catch and the ejector. Press down with any suitable tool on the end of the magazine interlock lever in order to release the interlock. Press the trigger, thereby releasing the recoiling mass. The cocking rope will then hold it from running forward. Ease the recoiling mass forward by lowering the carriage by turning the handwheel.

SECTION H. PARTIAL STRIPPING

1. DO NOT SLAM THE BREECH MASS ON AN EMPTY GUN. Rotate the handwheel so that the gun and carriage are at their lowest position. Elevate and lock the gun at 87°. Attach one end of the cocking wire rope to the breechblock cotter, and the other end to the mount cocking bracket. Turn the gun on its carriage pivot so that the cocking rope is in a direct line to the left side of the gun. Rotate the handwheel to raise the gun upward from the mount so that the cocking wire rope is taut enough to hold the breech mass from slamming. Remove the magazine by pressing the catch lever forward while lifting the rear end of the magazine clear of its catch and the ejector. Press down with any suitable tool on the end of the magazine interlock lever in order to release the interlock. Press the trigger, thereby releasing the recoiling mass. The cocking rope will hold it from running forward. Turning the handwheel in the direction to lower the carriage will ease the breech mass forward.

2. Remove the four breech bar securing spring pins. Remove the four securing bolts securing the breech bars to the cotter and to the barrel spring casing. Take the pull of the barrel springs off the breech bolt cotter by having a second man push the barrel spring casing slightly toward the rear. Slide the cotter out to the left. Instruct the second man to release the barrel spring casing. Remove the breech bars by disengaging them sideways and slide the barrel spring casing clear over the muzzle. Also slide the barrel springs and the guide sleeves clear over the muzzle.

3. Press the catch that retains the handgrips and remove the handgrips by unscrewing counterclockwise.

4. Slide the trigger cover plate off to the rear. Pull out the trigger casing to the rear, complete with the trigger gear and trigger buffer springs. Remove the trigger buffer springs. Remove the trigger snap ring using the special pliers in tool roll. Pull the assembled trigger hook holder out to the rear. The trigger hook on its axis bolt and its spring will be pulled out with the trigger hook holder.

NOTE.--A strong pull is required. Drive out the trigger hook axis bolt and lift out the trigger hook and its spring.

5. Slide the breechblock and the breech bolt out the rear of the breech casing. Remove the recoil sear axis bolt snap ring with the special pliers in the tool roll. Drive out the recoil sear axis bolt and lift out the sear and its spring.

6. Insert a punch (from tool roll) in the recess under the lip of facepiece securing spring and bend the spring clear of the face-piece. Turn the facepiece 90°, either way, with facepiece spanner tool and pull the facepiece out.

7. Remove the hammer axis bolt by turning it 180° and pushing it out. The hammer is free and can be lifted out. The striker pin will then drop to the rear, out of the breech block.

8. Rotate the barrel locking handle into the position marked "Unlock. " Rotate the barrel counterclockwise, looking from the muzzle to the breech, until stopped by the stop pin (approximately 60°) and pull out to the front.

NOTE.--The clearances between the barrel and its housing in the breech casing have to be very small and consequently the barrel may feel tight. A special tool is provided for rotating the barrel. Asbestos gloves are provided for the handling of hot barrels.

9. Remove the retaining pin, using the special screw driver from the tool roll. The double loading stop plunger can then be taken out.

10. Drive out the barrel locking handle pin, using tool. Drive out the barrel locking lever axis bolt from the left to the right, using special punch in tool roll. This will free the barrel locking handle for removal. Lift out the double loading stop, together with its two plungers and two springs. Lift out the barrel locking lever. Lift out the barrel locking lever plunger and its spring. Remove the double loading stop axis bolt securing spring with special pliers in the tool roll. Tap out double loading stop lever and its plunger and its spring. Bend down the upturned lug on the double loading stop guide bushing locking washer. Unscrew the double loading stop guide bushing with spanner in tool roll. This will carry the double loading stop plunger (upper) along with it. Lift out the locking washer.

11. Press in on the barrel spring seating ring retaining catch. Unscrew and remove the barrel spring seating ring, using spanner in tool roll.

--111--

NOTE.--The barrel spring seating ring has a right-hand thread. Pull the buffer out to the front. Remove the 12 buffer springs.

12. Rotate the magazine catch lever toward the muzzle so as to engage the catch. Press in the axis bolt securing spring and drive out the axis bolt. Remove the magazine catch lever. Release the magazine interlock catch by pressing down with a suitable tool on the front ends of the catch. This releases the ejector. Slide out to the front the ejector complete with the magazine interlock rod, interlock lever, interlock carrier, interlock lever spring, interlock carrier pin, and

interlock carrier axis.

Inspection and Adjustment After Partial Stripping

This completes partial stripping and next steps are:

1. Clean and oil the gun as instructed.

2. Inspect and adjust as follows:

The gun should be carefully examined, after partial stripping, for cracks in:

    a. Buffer springs.
    b. Lip of the breechblock facepiece.
    c. Striker pin.
    d. Hammer.
    e. Sear.
    f. Trigger hook.

There is a tendency for the striker pin to "set up" after long use.

See that the striker pin works freely in the breechblock.

Examine all springs. Spares are supplied in the spare parts box for every spring.

The limits for protrusion, in service, are between 0. 045 inch and 0. 070 inch. This measurement is to be made with the striker pin pushed fully forward in the bolt.

NOTE.--If the protrusion is too high, the point of the striker should be dressed back. If the protrusion is too low, there in no adjustment, and a spare striker pin should be shipped.

CAUTION.--Make certain that the striker pinhole in the breechblock is free of burrs, dirt and corrosion.

As previously stated, the striker pin reaches its full firing travel by momentum and not by a direct thrust all the way by

---

the hammer; therefore, wear of the hammer and hammer plate is not important.

Reassembling

1. Assemble the interlock rod and the interlock lever together with its spring to the carrier. Insert one of the springs into the interlock carrier. Slide the interlock carrier, complete with the interlock rod (as assembled above) into the ejector from the rear and push forward against the

spring until the carrier is held by the lever springing into the catch recess in the ejector. Insert the magazine interlock catch into its recess in the breech casing. Insert the two remaining springs and slide the ejector (as assembled above) into the breech casing from the front, taking care that the rod passes through its guide block. Hook the front toe of the magazine catch lever into its recess in the ejector. Pull the lever and the ejector bodily backwards against the springs until the rear toe of the lever can be hooked behind the catch and thereby hold the ejector temporarily in position. Then insert the magazine catch lever axis assembly through the lever.

2. Install double loading stop guide bushing locking washer. Install double loading stop guide bushing using spanner in the tool roll. Install double loading stop plunger upper. Install double loading stop spring case and its spring for the double loading stop lever. Install barrel locking lever plunger and its spring. Install double loading stop lever, install its axis bolt, tapping it from right to left; install its securing spring using special pliers in the toll roll. Install barrel locking lever. Install double loading stop together with its two plungers and two springs.

NOTE.--To accomplish this, first insert the two sets of springs and plungers into the stop. Face toward the muzzle and hold these in place with the first fingers of each hand. Then insert the stop without letting the plungers come out. Install the barrel locking handle. Install the barrel locking handle pin.

3. Install the 12 buffer springs in the breech casing. Install the buffer from the front. Screw in the barrel spring seating ring using spanner from tool roll.

NOTE.--The barrel spring seating ring has a right-hand thread.

CAUTION.--Hold the barrel spring seating ring retaining catch inward while tightening this seating ring.

4. Insert the double loading stop plunger lower in its hole in the barrel. Lock this in place inserting the retaining pin and, tightening securely with the special screw driver. Check to be certain the double loading stop plunger operates freely in the barrel. Place the barrel locking handle into the position marked "Unlock. "

Insert the barrel with the "Insert" arrow in line with the arrow on the breech casing.

When inserting the barrel, press down the horns of the double loading stop. This will prevent the double loading stop plunger in the breech casing from scoring the surface of the barrel.

Note.--Push completely in.

Rotate the barrel clockwise, looking from the muzzle, until it is stopped by the barrel stop pin (approximately 60°) . Place the barrel locking handle in the "Locked" position; then make certain that the barrel is locked against rotation by trying to turn it counterclockwise, looking from the muzzle.

5. Insert the striker pin. Push it into the forward position and see that its slot is in line to receive the top portion of the hammer. Insert the hammer into the slot in the striker pin. Insert the hammer axis bolt in the hole in the hammer nearest the toes. Lock the axis bolt by rotating it 180° so that it lies flush with the surface of the breech block.

6. Place the sear spring and sear in position on the breech bolt and install the sear axis bolt. Install the sear axis bolt snap ring using the pliers in tool roll. Install the breach bolt as assembled above in the breech block. Slide the two together into the breech casing and push into the forward position.

7. Place the trigger hook and trigger hook spring in position in the trigger hook holder. Install trigger hook axis bolt. Install the assembled trigger hook and holder from the rear into the trigger casing.

NOTE.--A strong push is necessary when inserting the trigger hook into the trigger casing.

Install the trigger snap ring using the special pliers in tool roll. Install the trigger buffer springs. Slide the trigger casing assembly

into the breech casing from the rear. Slide the trigger cover plate, on, from the rear.

8. Screw on the handgrips. They should stop with the engraved number UP and with the handgrip catch engaged to prevent rotation.

NOTE.--AT THIS POINT OF REASSEMBLY TEST THE OPERATION. Test the trigger gear, breechblock, and breech bolt for correct action by bringing the breechblock and bolt, with the cotter in place, to the rear and then pushing them forward again until they are held by the trigger gear. Trip the magazine interlock gear, press the trigger and see that the block and bolt are thereby fully released.

9. Install the short barrel spring to the rear. The smaller-diameter end of the spring goes to the rear. Install the barrel spring center sleeve. Install the long barrel spring. Install the barrel spring front sleeve. Larger outside diameter end of this sleeve goes toward the front. Slide the barrel spring casing on, with the engraved number UP. Place the breech bar securing bolts. Have a second man take the pull of the barrel springs by pushing on the barrel spring casing toward the rear. While holding the pull of the barrel springs, insert the breech cotter from left to right and pass it through the left-side breech bar, breechblock, breech bolt, and right-side breech bar. Instruct the second man to release the barrel spring casing. Assemble the four breech bar securing bolts and their four spring pins. This connects the breech bars to the barrel spring casing and to the breech cotter.

NOTE.--The flanged ends of the securing bolts should be UP and the two tongues of the spring pins should be left athwart the gun. If left fore and aft, they will have a tendency to become disengaged on firing.

SECTION I. CARE OF THE GUN

1. If the gun is left in the secured position it should be uncocked in order to relieve the stress on the barrel springs.

The magazine catch has to be tripped in order to uncock the gun and should be left in that state in order to ease the springs in the ejector.

2. The muzzle cover should be placed over the end of the barrel.

NOTE.--An HE shell should not be fired through a muzzle cover. The last two rounds loaded in each magazine should have blind loaded projectiles.

3. DO NOT SLAM THE BREECH MASS ON AN EMPTY GUN. Rotate the handwheel so that the gun and carriage are at their lowest position. Elevate and lock the gun at 87°. Attach one end of the cocking wire rope to the breech block cotter and the other end to the mount cocking bracket. Turn the gun on its carriage pivot so that the cocking rope is in a direct line to the left side of the gun. Rotate the handwheel to raise the gun upward from the mount so that the cocking wire rope is taut enough to hold the breech mass from slamming. Remove the magazine by pressing the catch lever forward while lifting the rear end of the magazine clear of its catch and the ejector. Press down with any suitable tool on the end of the magazine interlock catch in order to release the interlock. Press the trigger, thereby releasing the recoiling mass. The cocking rope will then hold it from running forward. Turning the handwheel in the direction to lower the carriage will ease the breech mass forward.

The use of the different hand methods for uncocking are given in section G, par. 18.

4. All 20-mm. antiaircraft ammunition MUST BE COMPLETELY COVERED WITH A LIGHT COAT OP A SUITABLE GREASE BEFORE BEING LOADED INTO THE MAGAZINE.

As previously stated, the ammunition is packed greased; however, this grease tends to dry off and must be regreased before being loaded into the magazine.

Note. -A small amount of a suitable grease applied, shortly before firing, to the cartridge case that is . visible in the magazine mouthpiece will assist in preventing a jam in the gun barrel.

Dry ammunition or ammunition with insufficient grease will jam in the gun chamber when fired and extraction will be very difficult, if not impossible.

NOTE.--Oil must not be used as a substitute for miners 1 grease.

Sufficient grease should be present on all cartridge cases to be easily felt by the fingers but an excess should be avoided, Caution.--Do not grease the rear end of the cartridge cases as the grease has a tendency to percolate inward, past the percussion cap. NEVER USE OIL.

5. If the gun stops of its own accord, for any reason other than an empty magazine, the following immediate action should be carried out:

(a) Put the safety catch to "Safe" and note whether the recoiling parts are in the forward position. If the recoiling parts are in the forward position, a misfire, a broken striker, a broken hammer, or failure to feed from the magazine is indicated. Safety precautions for a misfire should be observed. If there is a live round in a hot gun and the stoppage cannot be cleared, then douse the barrel with water to prevent the round from heating up. If the magazine is empty and the gun stops in the forward position, it may be due to sticking, or sluggish action of the magazine cartridge feeder bolt which trips the interlock lever. If examination shows that this bolt does not work freely, the magazine should not be used again until the condition has been corrected.

(b) Examine the double loading stop. If the horns are in the down or operating position, there is a round or part of a broken case in the chamber.

(c) Remove the magazine and recock the gun. If the magazine is difficult to remove, it will come off as the breech block is withdrawn when cocking the gun. In the event of it being impossible to remove the magazine without recocking, care should be taken to cock the gun in one continuous movement, and on no account must the breech block be allowed to go forward.

(d) Examine chamber and the breech facepiece. If the lip of the breech facepiece is broken off, a new one must be installed. (e) Examine the bore from the muzzle, making sure it is clear. This is necessary to avoid a premature explosion or bulged barrel. An ejector tool is provided in the tool roll, to remove any HE shell or practice shell left in the bore. This ejector should be used gently, and if excessive resistance is felt when removing an HE shell, then change the barrel.

(f) Stoppages of the gun have occurred which appeared to have been caused by the presence of hair from ammunition packing

material getting into the mechanism. Steps have been taken to eliminate this type of packing, but a large amount of ammunition has already been issued. At the first opportunity, and in any event before loading it into the magazine drums, ammunition should be examined to see that it is free of hair; and if hair or dirt is found, it should be removed. If grease is removed in this process, it must be replaced.

SECTION J. 20 MM. GUN COMPLETE STRIPPING AND ASSEMBLY

1. The stripping operations listed under "Partial stripping" are sufficient for normal inspection and cleaning.

In case of damage to, or failure of, the smaller parts, further stripping may be necessary.

A number of these operations are independent of any other and care should be taken not to disassemble further than necessary, as for instance:

Example.--The barrel is not the first operation on the list for partial stripping, yet it may be removed normally without taking off any other part.

The complete stripping instructions given below are a continuation of the partial stripping.

(a) Under partial stripping the following were removed:

      Trigger cover plate.
      Trigger hook and holder.
      Trigger casing complete.
      Trigger buffer spring.

Drive out the parallelogram lever axis bolt-rear top in either direction. Remove the trigger parallelogram complete. Remove the parallelogram spring box by driving out its axis bolt in either direction. A special punch is in tool roll.

(b) Remove the two retaining pins from the parallelogram lever axis bolt-bottom, front.

Remove the spacing sleeve pin, and lever axis bolt, top front sleeve. Drive out the parallelogram lever axis bolt-top front. Drive out the parallelogram lever axis bolt-bottom front.

NOTE.--Special punches are in the tool roll.

(c) Drive out the two vertical pins that are used to secure the two outer plungers.

Remove the horizontal pin that is used to secure the central plunger.

NOTE.--There are two parallelogram lever plungers, front, and there is one parallelogram lever plunger, rear, that can be pulled out with their two springs and one spring.

(d) Drive out the trigger pin in the hub of the trigger using special punch in tool roll. Tap out the trigger retaining bolt inward using special punch in tool roll. Lift out the trigger. Tap out the trigger crank inward using special punch in tool roll. Lift out the trigger pawl and the pawl holder together. Note.--The pawl can be separated from the pawl holder by-driving out the pawl axis pin from left to right. Lift out the trigger intermediate lever.

(e) Drive out, from left to right, the safety gear axis bolt pin. This pin secures the safe/fire lever to the axis bolt. Drive out the safety gear axis bolt.

NOTE.--This frees the safe/fire lever and the safety cam. (f) Follow operation 5, of "Partial stripping," necessary for examination of the sear for fractures. Remove the "magazine interlock lever from the carrier by driving out its axis bolt. Note.--This also releases the magazine interlock lever spring. I Lift out the interlock catch. Remove the magazine interlock fork by driving out its axis bolt in either direction.

(g) Drive out the trigger pawl tripping bolt spring case retaining pin. This pin secures the spring case to the breech casing. Remove the spring case complete with the trigger pawl tripping bolt and its spring. The trigger pawl tripping bolt and its spring can be removed from the spring case by driving out the trigger pawl tripping bolt retaining pin transversely through the spring case.

(h) Drive out the interlock rod guide block retaining pin and press the block out from the breech casing.

(i) Remove the breech pawls by prying out the right and left axis pins. The breechpawls and their springs will then fall out. (j) Lift the end of the hammer plate securing spring clear of the hammer plate and tap the hammer plate upward to remove, (k) Drive out the retaining catch axis bolt and lift out the retaining catch. Drive out the retaining catch plunger pin and remove its spring and the retaining catch plunger.

--119--

(l) Drive out in either direction the barrel spring seating ring retaining catch retaining pin. Lift out the retaining catch and its spring.

(m) Press in the breech casing barrel stop pin plate using a pointed tool from tool roll. Drive out, in either direction, the barrel stop pin plate. Lift out the barrel stop pin, the barrel stop pin plate pin, and the barrel stop plate spring.

(n) Push the trigger intermediate lever spring case out by pushing on its rear end at the rear face of the breech casing. Remove the trigger intermediate lever spring case distance piece. Drive out the trigger intermediate lever plunger retaining pin Lift out the trigger intermediate lever plunger and its spring.

2. The complete reassembly instructions given below are a continuation of the reassembling a partially stripped gun.

(a) Place the trigger intermediate lever plunger and its spring, in the trigger intermediate lever spring case. Install the trigger intermediate lever plunger retaining pin. Install the trigger intermediate lever spring case distance piece. Push the real end of the trigger intermediate lever spring case into the rear face of the breech casing.

(b) Install the barrel stop pin plate spring, the barrel stop pin plate pin, and the barrel stop pin. Drive in, from either direction, the barrel stop pin plate.

(c) Install in the breech casing the retaining catch and its spring. Drive in from either direction the barrel spring seating ring retaining catch retaining pin.

(d) Install in the retaining catch the retaining catch plunger its spring and drive in the retaining catch plunger pin. Install the retaining catch in the breech casing and drive in the retaining catch axis bolt.

(e) Tap the hammer plate downward into its recess in the breech casing. Make certain the hammer plate securing spring is in place.

(f) Install the breech pawl springs in the breech casing. Install the right breech pawl and left breech pawl on their spring, installed above. Install the breech pawl axis pins.

(g) Note.--Follow operation 1 of "Reassembling a partially stripped gun" in section H under Reassembling.

--120--

(h) Install the trigger pawl tripping bolt spring and the bolt in place in the trigger pawl tripping bolt spring case. Drive the trigger pawl tripping bolt retaining pin transversely through the spring case. Place the spring case (as just assembled) and the trigger pawl tripping bolt spring and tripping bolt in the breech easing. Drive in the trigger pawl tripping bolt spring case retaining pin. This pin secures the spring case to the breech casing.

(i) Install the magazine interlock fork to the breech casing by inserting the fork in its position and drive in its axis bolt from either direction.

(j) Install the safe/fire lever and the safety cam and drive in the axis bolt. Install the safe/fire lever on its axis bolt and drive the axis bolt pin in from right to left. This pin secures the safe/fire lever to the axis bolt.

(k) Assemble the trigger pawl and its spring to the pawl holder by inserting the pawl axis pin from right to left. Drop this trigger pawl and holder assembly into its position in the breech casing. Insert the trigger crank from inside of the breech casing.

NOTE.--The pawl, pawlholder, and trigger crank are all stamped with the letter "I" and when correctly assembled all three letters must be visible from above. IF NOT VISIBLE, THE ASSEMBLING HAS BEEN INCORRECTLY DONE.

(l) Insert the trigger intermediate lever so as to engage the pin on the pawlholder.

(m) Reassemble the trigger, trigger retaining bolt from inside the breech casing. Install the trigger pin. Reassemble the trigger hook and its spring in the trigger holder and drive in the trigger hook axis bolt.

(n) Place the two outer plungers (parallelogram lever plunger-top) and place the central plunger (parallelogram lever plunger-rear; and their three springs in the parallalogram spring box. Install the horizontal pin that is used to secure the central plunger. Install the two vertical pins that are used to secure the two outer plungers. Reassemble the parallelogram. Install the parallelogram lever axis bolt, top front. Install the parallelo-gram lever axis bolt, bottom front. Install the parallelogram.

lever axis bolt, top front sleeve and the sleeve pin. Install the two retaining pins on the lever axis bolt, bottom front.

NOTE.--The parallelogram levers are all marked "L" and "R". A correctly assembled parallelogram will have all the letters "L" visible and on the left side, and all of the letters "R" visible and on the right side. The parallelogram top lever is marked with the word "Up" and this must be visible from above.

Install the parallelogram spring box assembled above and drive in its axis bolt. Drive from either direction. Place the parallelogram assembled above in the trigger casing, pushing it rearward against the spring plungers in the spring box in order to get the holes in line for the lever axis bolt rear top. A strong push is required. Drive this lever axis bolt in from either direction.

(o) Install the trigger hook holder assembled in Operation 13 into the rear of trigger casing. A strong push is required. Replace the trigger snap ring that secures the trigger hook holder in the trigger casing, using the special pliers in the tool roll. Replace the trigger buffer springs.

(p) Complete the reassembly by following the instructions for reassembly, operations 2 through 9 inclusive, given in detail in section H under Reassembly.

SECTION K. MOUNT

1. The mount permits the height of the gun trunnion above the deck to be easily and rapidly altered for any sight angle, thus enabling the gunlayer to assume the easiest position. This is done by the column-raising handwheel mounted on the pedestal head. A tubular column supports the trunnion bracket and carries an internal thread that mates with a screw, driven by the handwheel. The rotatable pedestal head may be locked in any position by the clamping lever. On the base of the pedestal in also located the bracket for the cocking wire rope.

The gun can be trained through 360° and continued around by means of the rotatable combined trunnion bracket and pivot. There is no stop; therefore, the training can be continued on any target without stopping.

The gun can be elevated from minus 5° to plus 87° by means of the rotatable cradle.

The pedestal of the Mark 4 has two brackets for the cocking wire rope. The wire rope is hooked in the lower bracket for use when cocking the gun. When the gun has been cocked, the upper end of the cocking wire rope is unhooked from the breech bar, wrapped around the pedestal, and hooked over the upper bracket.

The Mark 2 mount has the cocking wire rope attached to a spring-controlled reel that winds up the cocking rope inside the pedestal when it is not in use.

2. There are five principal parts in the mount as follows:

(a) Fixed pedestal supports the mount and is bolted to the deck. A cocking wire rope bracket is bolted to the outside and is used to hook the wire rope on when cocking the gun. A bottom cover plate is bolted underneath the pedestal and is the main support for the equalizing springs, the column-raising spindle and the vertical shaft of the gear train. This bottom cover plate has a shim pack which provides the means of adjustment for free movement of the column. A guide tube is fixed within the pedestal and is provided with a vertical keyway in which slides the key on the tubular column.

(b) Tubular column is constructed with internal threads at its lower end. These internal threads engaged external threads on the column-raising spindle. The handwheel operates the column-raising spindle. The helical springs are inside the column-raising spindle and the pivot and they are placed in series in compression, being separated by a spacing ring. Guide tubes hold these springs, the lower external guide tube being supported by a thrust bearing in a bushing on the bottom cover plate.

CAUTION.--These compressed helical springs must not be disassembled unless a special fixture is used. The heavy compression these springs are under will cause serious injury unless the compression is eased off.

(c) Pedestal head, through which the column rises, is able to rotate around the top of the fixed pedestal but can be held in any desired position by a spring steel clamping band that is operntod by a lever. The pedestal head contains the handwheel drive, a double gear consisting of a bevel apd spur for the purpose of transmitting the drive, and the clamping band with its lever.

(d) Combined trunnion bracket and pivot is free to rotate around the top of the column on thrust bearings, which take upward and downward thrust, and in roller bearings located between the column and the trunnion bracket and pivot. It carries the trunnion arms that have plain bearings for the trunnion pins of the cradle.

NOTE.--Two holes, each being 1 $^1/2$ inches in diameter, are provided in the trunnion arms. These holes are directly above the center of gravity of the mount and a cable through these holes will support the mounting in a vertical position.

(e) Cradle rotates freely about the right trunnion pin. The left trunnion pin is keyed to the cradle in order to form an abutment for the counterbalance torsion spring. This torsion spring is used to compensate the weight of the gun when the gun is in elevation. The gun is carried in two machined and grooved slides in the cradle. The breech casing of the gun is positioned in a fore and aft direction by the gun securing bolt operated from underneath.

3. When gun is being mounted in the cradle, the inside of the securing holt hold in the breech casing and the securing bolt itself should be thoroughly greased for protection against corrosion. Two cavities at the rear of the cradle are filled with lead to act as balance weights. A canvas bag is attached to the cradle to catch the fired cartridge cases.

4. The pedestal head can be turned by hand to any position desired when the clamping lever is raised. The pedestal head can be locked in any position by depressing the clamping lever.

NOTE.--The column raising handwheel tends to turn idly during the rotation of the pedestal head, and the rotation of the head can be assisted by turning the handwheel.

5. When the pedestal head is locked so that it cannot rotate, the action of turning the handwheel drives the gear train. The column has threads that are engaged in the threads of the column raising spindle and is prevented from turning by a key that is in a verticle keyway in the guide tube. The column, therefore, rises with the gun and the weight of the rising parts is taken

by the compressed internal helical springs which aid in raising the gun. The rise of the gun is limited by the upper stop ring secured to the top of the spindle. A. lug on the spindle spur gear acts as the lower stop.

NOTE.--A locking catch is provided to lock the handwheel and thus fix the column at any height. A housing catch is also fitted to lock the combined trunnion bracket and pivot, when It is in its lowest position to the pedestal. A locking bolt enables the cradle to be locked to the trunnion bracket at elevations of plus 5° and plus 87°.

6. There are two ring-shaped internal oil wells. One of these is at the top of the pedestal head and the other is in the head of the pivot of the trunnion bracket.

NOTE.--The oil wells are fitted with spring type dust proof oilers and the wells should be kept filled with ice machine oil.

The trunnion bearings are lubricated by spring ball pressure fittings that are screwed into the upper part of the trunnion bearings.

The following lubrication is necessary during reassembly.

(a) Coat the column raising spindle with grease before assembling it in the pedestal.

(b) Pack grease all around the bevel and spur wheel gear before the pedestal head is installed. Spread grease over all of the teeth of this gear completely covering all the teeth.

(c) Pack grease on the teeth of the handwheel spindle and bevel pinion piling the grease on the face of the gear opposite its spindle before assembling it to the pedestal. d) Pack grease on the teeth of the column raising spindle " spur wheel and vertical shaft spur wheel lower.

(e) Fill the bottom cover with grease before assembling it to the pedestal.

(f) After assembling the bottom cover to the pedestal, complete the filling of the cover with grease by screwing a pressure grease fitting into the pipe tap hole that is in the cover and fill with; grease by using pressure gun.

--125--

SECTION L. AMMUNITION FOR 20-MM. ANTIAIRCRAFT GUN MARK 4 OR MARK 2

There are six types of ammunition and they are listed as follows:

(a) High explosive, with tracer; projectile type "HL" loaded with pentolite, an explosive formed by combining equal parts of TNT and PETN. Color of projectile, BLUE.

(b) Same as (a) except projectile is loaded with tetryl. Color of projectile, LIGHT GREY.

(c) High explosive without tracer; projectile type "HB" loaded with pentolite. Color of projectile, YELLOW.

(d) Same as (c) except projectile loaded with tetryl. Color of projectile, WHITE.

(e) Blind loaded with tracer. Color of projectile, DARK GREEN GREY with $1/8$-inch wide YELLOW BAND.

(f) Blind loaded and plugged. Color of projectile, DARK GREEN GREY.

NOTE.--The above colorings apply to 20-mm. antiaircraft ammunition only for Mark 4 and

Mark 2. Do not confuse with colors used in other ammunition.

(a and b) This projectile has about one-half of the cavity loaded with pyrotechnic tracer mixture designed to burn about 3 3/4 seconds. The forward part of the projectile cavity space is loaded with pressed tetryl or pentolite. These explosives are approximately equivalent in destructive value. The fuze used is a simple air-column type with no moving parts. Its action is initiated by impact, an air-column is instantaneously formed by impact, either head-on or glancing, The closing disk being displaced into the fuze body by impact, an air-column is instantaneously compressed and wire drawn through an inner disk. The rate of temperature-pressure rise is sufficient to ignite lead azide, which in turn ignites pressed tetryl in the detonator, and ignition of the burster charge is affected. The fuze is designed definitely not to function on the equivalent of 0. 012 inch duraluminum plate (or lighter), but definitely to function on the equivalent of 1/8-inch mild steel plate or heavier. The fuze is not equipped with any bore-safe feature, and will act whenever the closing disc is displaced into the fuze with sufficient force. This projectile is not equipped with a self-destruction feature.

--126--

(c and d) This projectile is similar to the "Leaded and fuzed projectile with tracer" described above, but has a burster charge that is approximately twice as great.

(e) This projectile has the burster charge cavity inert loaded to weight, except for the tracer, and is plugged at the nose with a fuze body, assembled with no detonator.

(f) This projectile has the burster charge cavity inert loaded to weight, and is plugged at the nose with a fuze body assembled with no detonator.

The powder is an FNH type of nitrocellulose powder. It is a single-perforated grain with weight of charge to give 2,725 foot-seconds at 90° F. with standard projectiles. Surveillance and break-down of 20-mm. antiaircraft cartridges are covered in separate correspondence. Instructions regarding this ammunition are similar to those currently effective regarding 1. 10-inch, 75-caliber ammunition.

The cartridge case is of the usual type with a conventional percussion cap.

SECTION M. GENERAL INFORMATION ON 20 MM.

An HE shell must never be fired through a muzzle cover. To prevent such an occurrence the last two rounds loaded in each magazine should have blind loaded projectiles.

The first shipments of ammunition are being made in wooden boxes. Later shipments will be in metal boxes containing 180 rounds in each box. The completely filled metal box weighs 1.25 pounds. Rounds are packed in separate cardboard tubes and each tube is lined with greaseproof paper so that the grease on the cartridges will not be absorbed. The cardboard tube is open at both ends but is fitted with an inner ferrule, to prevent the cartridges from clearing the tube fuze first. The cartridge is a light friction fit in the tube.

Use care in withdrawing greased cartridges from their packing tubes. The most efficient way of getting them free of the tube is to push on the nose of the fuze with a finger of the hand, while firmly holding the packing tube. As previously stated, there is an inner ferrule in the tube to prevent the cartridge from clearing the tube fuze first. Pushing on the nose of the fuze starts the cartridge out of the tube, when it immediately

becomes a loose fit and care must be taken not to permit the greased cartridge to come adrift and fall.

Stoppages of the gun have occurred which appeared to have been caused by the presence of hair from ammunition packing material getting into the mechanism. Steps have been taken to eliminate this type of packing, but a large amount of ammunition has already been issued. At the first opportunity, and in any event before loading it into the magazine drums, ammunition should be examined to see that it is free of hair; and if hair or dirt is found it should be removed. If grease is removed in this process, it must be replaced.

NOTE.--Pay attention to the need of a complete covering of mineral grease on all cartridge cases.

All 20-mm. antiaircraft Mark 2 and Mark 4 ammunition MUST BE COMPLETELY COVERED WITH A LIGHT COAT OF MINERAL GREASE BEFORE BEING LOADED INTO THE MAGAZINE.

The ammunition is usually packed greased. However, this grease tends to dry off. Whether cartridges are packed greased or not, they should be regreased before loading the magazine.

Note. ---A small amount of mineral grease, applied shortly before firing, to the cartridge case that is visible in the magazine mouthpiece, will assist in preventing a jam in the gun barrel.

Dry ammunition or ammunition with insufficient grease will jam in the gun chamber when fired, and extraction will be very difficult, if not impossible.

NOTE.--Oil must not be used as a substitute for mineral grease.

Sufficient grease should be present on all cartridge cases to be easily felt by the fingers. An excess should be avoided.

CAUTION.--Do not grease the rear end of the cartridge cases as the grease has a tendency to percolate inward past the percussion cap. NEVER USE OIL.

Care must be used in handling the greased cartridges. They must not be dropped or struck a heavy blow on either the nose or the cartridge base. Any cartridge that has been dropped over

5 feet is to be set aside and turned in to any naval ammunition depot at the first opportunity.

NOTE.--Rounds that have been possibly damaged as described above, are not to be considered unsafe, except for firing. If used

for firing, they might result in dud action and, therefore, should be refuzed before firing.

If prolonged firing is necessary, then the cartridge bag should be emptied frequently. A cartridge bag that gets too full, gets in the way of the gun layer at high gun elevations.

Secure, and turn in to a naval ammunition depot, all ammunition boxes, internal containers, fired cartridge cases, packing tubes, dropped or damaged cartridges. The tear strip of the top of the internal container may be discarded.

Chapter 2. BROWNING MACHINE GUN (.50 CAL., AIR COOLED, M2, BASIC)

SECTION A. GENERAL DISCUSSION

1. The fundamental operating principle of the Browning machine gun, cal. . 50, M2 pattern, is the same as that of cal. . 50 Browning machine guns of previous manufacture. The force of recoil is used to perform the various mechanical operations of the gun. The mechanism consists of a barrel attached to a barrel extension, and a bolt, which are positively locked together when the mechanism is in the forward position. Upon the discharge of a cartridge the energy set up in the barrel starts the action of recoil which is transmitted to the bolt and resisted by the barrel extension. When the mechanism has recoiled 3/4 of an inch, the positive lock between the bolt and barrel extension starts to release and the separation occurs in an additional 3/8-inch travel. The 2 1/8 inch distance of recoil may be considered as the power stroke. Following this separation of the bolt, a portion of the recoil forces in the barrel extension is transmitted to the bolt by an accelerator and the remaining energy to a back plate through a hydraulic buffer mechanism. The energy of recoil of the gun if finally delivered to the mount.

2. The functions of the accelerator are as follows:

(*a*) To act between the rear surface of the barrel extension and the bottom projection on the bolt as a lever of increasing length to relay recoil energy to the bolt. This utilization of energy serves to slow up the barrel and barrel extension recoil, and to speed up the recoil of the bolt.

(*b*) To boost the recoil energy of the bolt at the period when extraction occurs.

(*c*) To hold the barrel and barrel extension in the recoil position, with the oil buffer spring compressed to prevent the barrel returning to its forward position before the bolt has completed its recoil.

(d) To relay energy from the bolt on its forward movement to the barrel extension in order to insure that the barrel extension and the barrel move forward ahead of the bolt so that when the breech lock in the barrel extension rises it will be properly timed with the bolt to insure hooking without binding or interference. That is, the accelerator serves as both an energy transmitter and as a timing element to insure proper closing and locking as well as unlocking of the breach lock from the bolt.

3. Through relayed energy of the accelerator the bolt continues to recoil, compressing its driving spring, and is brought to rest by the back plate buffer. During the recoil of the bolt several functions have occurred, including extraction of the fired cartridge case, and extraction of a live round from the ammunition belt and placing it in position for chambering.

4. The counterrecoil of the bolt, due to the energy stored in its driving springs, begins immediately after the recoil of the bolt has been arrested by the back plate buffer. At this time the fired cartridge case is ejected and chambering of the live round begins. This counterrecoil continues until the bolt trips the accelerator. This tripping of the accelerator causes the counterrecoil of the barrel extension and attached barrel to occur ahead of the bolt. The energy used to trip the accelerator momentarily delays the movement of the bolt, assuring the proper timing for completing chambering of the live round and the positive locking of the mechanism.

5. In order that the trunnion adapter of the aircraft gun may be quickly disassembled from the receiver, a component called the trunnion block shim is provided so that the mating components will be interchangeable without the threads having to be qualified.

(a) There are 12 different thicknesses of trunnion block shims manufactured. They are marked with numbers running consecutively from 1 to 12. No. 1 shim is 0. 0675 inch thick and the thickness of each higher numbered shim is increased by 0. 0025 inch.

(b) Upon original assembly of the machine guns at place of manufacture the shim of correct thickness is assembled and the number of that particular shim and the next three higher numbers are marked on the side plate and the rear oil cap trunnion

adapter or barrel jacket. The three next higher numbered shims accompany the machine gun as a thicker shim may be required later.

Example.--If number 3 shim is used in the machine gun assembly then shims numbered 4, 5, and 6 will accompany the machine gun and the numbers 3, 4, 5, 6 will be marked on the side plate and the rear oil cap.

6. **General data**.--The following general data applies to all types of Cal. . 50, machine guns. General data pertaining to the individual types of gun are given in this section which covers the particular type.

Caliber	inches	.50
Weight of 1 metallic belt link (approximate)	oz	$^1/_2$
Weight of 100 rounds in metallic link belt	pounds	50.25
Weight of complete round of M2 ball ammunition (approximate)	oz	4
Weight of powder charge (approximate)	do	$^1/_2$
Weight of bullet, M2 ball (approximate)	do	2
Maximum of chamber pressure per square inch	pounds	52,000.00
Muzzle velocity of bullet	feet per second	2,900.00

7. **General data**.--Browning machine gun, cal. .50, M2, aircraft.

Weight of gun (fixed mounting)	pounds	64.51
Weight of gun (flexible mounting)	do	68.51
Weight of barrel assembly (barrel and sleeve)	do	9.85
Over-all length of gun (fixed mounting)	inches	57.09
Over-all length of gun (flexible mounting)	do	56.40
Over-all length of barrel	do	36.00
Rate of automatic fire	shots per minute	500-650

SECTION B. FUNCTIONING

1. **General remarks**.--This section outlines the functioning of the Browning machine gun, cal. .50, M2.

2. **To load**.--Loading may be considered to include two distinct operations, namely, entering the loaded belt properly into the belt opening and thereafter operating the mechanism of the gun until it is closed, with the cartridge in the chamber and

a cartridge in the feedway gripped by the extractor for extraction on the next recoil stroke.

(a) The first of these operations may be performed with the cover either open or closed. In either case, enter the double-loop end of the belt through the feed opening until the first cartridge is beyond the belt holding pawl. Close the cover, if open. Pull the belt completely to the rear by means of retracting slide (operating slide or bolt handle) and release it.

(b) The second operation consists of pulling the bolt once completely to the rear and then allowing it to spring forward. This operation must start with the action fully closed and the extractor gripping the cartridge in the feedway.

3. **To unload**.--(a) Lift cover, remove belt, retract bolt, and make visual inspection of feedway, T-slot, and chamber, to make Certain that the gun is unloaded.

(b) Release belt and lower cover.

(c) Press the trigger or sear mechanism to relieve tension on the firing pin spring.

4. **Backward movement of recoiling parts**.--(a) The explosion of the cartridge forces the barrel to the rear, carrying with it the barrel extension and the belt which is locked to the barrel extension by the breech lock.

(b) When the barrel has recoiled about % inch, the breech lock pin strikes the cam surfaces of the breech lock-depressors. This unlocks the belt from the barrel extension and permits the belt to continue to the rear.

(c) As the barrel extension moves to the rear it strikes the accelerator and turns it backward.

5. **Backward action of the accelerator**.--(a) As the accelerator turns backward it strikes the bottom projection on the bolt and accelerates it to the rear.

(b) The shoulders on the barrel extension shank engage behind the claws of the accelerator, locking the barrel and barrel extension in a rearmost position, to the oil buffer body.

6. **Backward movement of the bolt**.--(a) As the bolt moves backward the driving springs are compressed.

(b) The bolt brings with it a cartridge from the belt gripped by the extractor and an empty case from the chamber gripped in the T-slot.

(c) The cam lug on the extractor rides along on top of the switch until near the end of the backward movement of the bolt, then the extractor by action of the cover extractor cam is forced downward until its cam lug is below the switch.

7. **Action of the oil buffer**.--As the barrel and barrel extension move backward together, and since the oil buffer piston rod is linked directly with the barrel extension by means of the hook

on the shank projecting from the rear of the barrel extension and the hook on the forward end of the oil buffer piston rod, the oil buffer spring is compressed, the oil buffer piston rod head and the oil buffer piston valve are driven rearward in the oil buffer tube forcing the oil through the restricted openings in both the piston rod head and valve, uncovering the openings and permitting the oil to pass readily from the forward to the rear side of the piston rod head and valve, thus permitting the rapid return of the parts to the firing position.

8. **First action of feeding**.--(a) As the bolt moves backward, the stud on the belt feed lever, riding in its cam groove in the top of the bolt, moves the belt feed pawl laterally into position behind the next cartridge.

(b) The ammunition belt is prevented from falling out of the gun by the belt holding pawl.

9. (a). As the bolt moves backward, the upper end of the cocking lever is forced forward by the top plate bracket attached to the top plate, which brings the lower end to the rear.

(b) When the lower end of the cocking lever moves to the rear it brings with it the firing pin extension, withdrawing the firing pin from the face of the bolt and compressing the firing pin spring against the sear stop pin.

(c) The shoulder of the firing pin extension, engages in the notch in the sear under pressure of the sear spring.

10. Action of the driving springs.--When the rear end of the bolt strikes the buffer plate, its remaining force is absorbed in the fiber buffer discs. The driving springs, which have been compressed by the backward action of the bolt, then force the bolt forward. On guns manufactured after June 1940 two driving springs, one inside the other and wound in opposite

directions, are used. By use of two springs, greater initial Spring load is provided which is an advantage in feeding ammunition during high angles of fire. The new assembly will be available for replacement of old type assemblies now in service.

11. **Forward movement of the bolt**.--(a) When the bolt starts forward the cam lug on the extractor riding under the switch rotates the extractor downward. This causes the extractor to force the cartridge down the T-slot in line with the chamber. If there is an empty case in the T-slot, the live round, held by the extractor and ejector, or the ejector if there is no live round, strikes the empty case at this point and forces it out of the T-slot.

(b) The upper end of the cocking lever is forced backward and the lower end moves forward away from the rear of the firing pin extension.

12. **Release of recoiling parts**.--(a) The bottom projection on the bolt strikes the accelerator and rotates it forward. This unlocks the barrel extension from the oil buffer body. The barrel extension remains linked with the oil buffer piston rod.

(b) When the accelerator has been tripped the barrel extension and the barrel move forward, assisted by the oil buffer spring.

(c) Part of the forward force of the bolt acts through the accelerator to push the barrel extension forward.

13. **Loading and locking action**.--(a) The extractor rises as its cam lug moves along the top of the extractor cam and the ejector moves outward, leaving the cartridge in the chamber engaged by the T-slot. The extractor grips the first round in the belt and is held down firmly, ready to extract it, by the cover extractor spring.

(b) The breech lock is forced upward by the breech lock cam and locks the breech just before the recoiling parts reach the firing position. (The breech lock engages in a recess cut in the bottom of the bolt and thus locks it firmly to the barrel extension and against the rear end of the barrel.)

14. **Second action of feeding**.--(a) As the bolt goes forward the stud of the end of the belt feed lever, riding in its cam groove in the top of the bolt, moves the belt feed slide and belt feed pawl in a lateral direction.

(b) The belt feed pawl carries the first cartridge against the cartridge stops, ready to be gripped by the extractor.

NOTE.--The aircraft guns use the cartridge alining pawl when feeding from the left side. The cartridge alining pawl is not reversible and when aircraft guns are fed from the right the old design rear cartridge stop, not having the cartridge aline pawl, is used.

(c) The next cartridge is carried over the belt holding pawl, which rises behind it and holds it in position to be engaged by the belt feed pawl on its return movement.

15. **Trigger action in automatic fire**.--If the side plate trigger is held to the rear, the sear is disengaged just before the bolt has reached its forward position, thereby releasing the firing pin extension. The gun thus fires automatically, repeating the operating of functions already described. (The release of the firing pin extension actually takes place when the recoiling parts are still about 1/8 inch from the forward position but after the breech is locked.)

16. **Adjustment of oil buffer**.--(a) The oil buffer is so arranged that it is possible to adjust the speed of the firing of the machine gun. This is accomplished by turning the oil buffer tube the required number of clicks, depending on whether a high rate of fire is desired or a slower rate.

(b) Turning the buffer tube to the right tends to cut off or close the oil buffer which allows it to absorb more recoil and reduce the rate of fire.

(c) Turning the buffer tube to the left allows the oil buffer to open and allows the oil to pass through larger throttling parts which results in an increased rate of fire.

(d) Guns of early manufacture were equipped with a regulator having an index finger. The index finger has a key which fits into a slot in the rear of the buffer tube. The letter "O" on the left side of the back plate indicates the "open position" for the oil buffer and the letters "CL" on the right side indicates the "closed position. " Turning the index finger to the right or left opens or closes the oil buffer as desired.

(e) Guns of new manufacture have a hole in the back plate through which the oil buffer may be adjusted with a screwdriver blade.

SECTION C. DISASSEMBLING, HEADSPACE ADJUSTMENT, REPLACING GROUPS IN GUN, AND METHOD OF CHANGING AIRCRAFT GUN FROM LEFT-HAND FEED TO RIGHT-HAND FEED

1. **General information on disassembling**.--(a) Disassembling will be considered under two general headings: Removal of groups to the extent required for ordinary cleaning and for minor repairs, and detail disassembling, involving removal of all components from each group.

(b) A group is a number of components which either function together in the gun or are intimately related to each other and should, therefore, be considered together.

(c) The removal of groups is outlined in this section as the procedure is similar for the water-cooled antiaircraft guns.

(d) Detail disassembling is outlined in subsequent sections which cover the particular type of gun.

2. **Removal of groups from gun**.--(a) Release the cover latch and open the cover. The cover need not be removed as the other parts of the gun may be taken out without removing it.

NOTE.--Removal of the cover group is not recommended unless necessary for repair as it is difficult to reassemble due to the force required to compress the detent pawl spring.

(b) Release back plate latch lock and back plate latch and lift out the back plate.

(c) Press forward and away from the side plate on the end of the driving spring rod to release retaining pin in head of rod from hole in side plate. Draw bolt to the rear until the bolt stud is in line with hole in center of slot in side plate. Remove bolt stud from bolt.

(d) Remove the bolt, complete, out of the rear end of the gun casing. The assembled driving spring unit need not be removed from the bolt.

(e) Compress oil buffer body spring lock, using a cartridge point or a drift through hole in right-hand side plate and remove oil buffer, barrel extension, and barrel assembly by pulling out to the rear.

NOTE.--When the guns are mounted in a close or remote position the release tool is used to compress the oil buffer body spring lock.

(f) Detach the oil buffer assembly from the barrel extension by pressing the accelerator forward.

3. **Headspace**.--The headspace of a military weapon with a cartridge fully seated in the chamber is the distance between the base of the cartridge and the face of the bolt. In Browning machine guns, the headspace is adjusted by obtaining the proper distance between the forward part of the bolt and the rear end of the barrel. The headspace adjustment must be checked before firing.

4. **Head-space adjustment**.--(a) In the past the head space has been adjusted with the barrel, barrel extension, and bolt out of the gun. However, the best adjustment is obtained with the gun fully assembled. This method has the additional advantage of avoiding the loss of the cooling liquid.

(b) To adjust the head space.--Unscrew the barrel from the barrel extension until the action works freely. Then using the point of a cartridge screw the barrel into the barrel extension until the action will just close without being forced. Then unscrew the barrel TWO ADDITIONAL notches.

CAUTION.--Care must be exercised to avoid roughening the barrel surface during adjustment. Care must also be exercised on water-cooled guns to eliminate binding of the barrel by the packing, or a false adjustment may otherwise be obtained.

5. **Effect of head-space adjustment**.--Probably the most important adjustment of the machine gun is the head-space adjustment. Tests show that shot patterns are not adversely affected by the head space when the guns are adjusted as outlined above. In fact, better uniformity of shot patterns will be obtained when the guns are operated with the above adjustment which is based on the fundamental design of the weapon. Tests have also proved that guns may be damaged and in some cases put out of action by using unapproved methods of adjusting the head space. Many reports show that difficulties with improperly guided belts and with firing mechanisms have been attributed to undue concern over head-space adjustment.

(a) **Insufficient headspace**.--When the head-space adjustment is too tight, poor functioning will result as the breech lock will not fully enter its recess in the bolt. This condition may damage the barrel extension, bolt, or breech lock. Extraction trouble may also occur due to improper timing of locking and unlocking.

Furthermore, with a tight head-space adjustment the gun operates sluggishly because of the binding of the moving parts.

(b) **Excessive head space**.--If the head space is too great, a separation of the cartridge may occur. Should there be any weakness in the base of the cartridge case, such as a split case, the possibility of a rupture is increased by excessive head space.

NOTE.--When assembled correctly for right-handfeed, the enlarged portion of the bolt switch is toward the rear of the bolt.

(c) **Assemble extractor assembly to bolt**.

6. **Belt feed mechanisms**.--(a) Open cover and remove belt feed lever. Transfer the belt feed lever plunger and spring from upper hole in belt feed lever to lower hole.

(b) Remove belt feed slide assembly from cover.

(c) Drive out belt feed pawl pin and remove belt feed pawl and arm from the belt feed slide.

(d) Hold the belt feed pawl with the arm pointing toward the body (spring seat in pawl up and arm down) and change the belt feed pawl arm from left side of pawl to the right side of pawl.

(e) Reassemble belt feed pawl and arm to belt feed slide.

(f) Reassemble belt feed slide assembly to cover, with belt feed pawl arm pointing toward left side of gun. (g) Reassemble belt feed lever to cover.

7. **Gun casing**.--(a) Remove belt holding pawl pins from right and left sides.

(b) Transfer the front rear cartridge stops and the link stripper from the right to the left side of the gun.

NOTE.--Guns of new manufacture when fed from the left side have a rear cartridge stop assembly which cannot be used when the gun is fed from the right side. In changing from left-to right-hand feed it is necessary to substitute a rear cartridge 1stop and stripper of old design. The rear cartridge stop assembly referred to above has a cartridge alining pawl which prevents "short round" stoppages.

(c) Transfer the belt holding pawl and belt holding pawl spring from left side of gun to right-hand side.

(d) Assemble the belt holding pawl pins to the gun.

(e) Assemble the bolt assembly in the gun and complete the assembly of the gun in the usual manner.

8. **Inspection before firing gun**.--After changing the gun from left-hand feed to right-hand feed, or vice versa, and also before firing, the gun should be inspected in order to determine that it has been properly assembled. Note should be made of the following when the gun is arranged for right hand feed:

(a) When the cover is open the upper end of the belt feed lever should position itself toward the right-hand side of the cover.

(b) The belt feed pawl arm should point toward the left with the arm assembled to the upper side of the pawl (cover raised).

(c) The front and rear cartridge stops and the link stripper should be assembled on the left side of the feedway.

(d) The belt holding pawl should be in position on the right side of the feedway.

(e) Looking down on top of the bolt as it is assembled in the gun, the enlarged portion of the bolt switch should be toward the rear.

9. **Cooling**.--Aircraft machine guns are air-cooled and as mounted at present there is very little difference in the cooling whether the gun is fired on the ground or in the air.

(a) With the standard 36-inch cal. .50, M2 barrel weighing 9. 85 pounds, a maximum burst of 75 rounds may be fired from a flexible gun. Approximately one minute after firing a 75-round burst, firing may be resumed and 20 rounds fired and repeated each minute thereafter.

(b) The long burst will heat the barrel to the maximum permissible temperature, and repeated firing after one minute delay with a reduced number of rounds per minute will maintain the barrel at the high temperature. Thus the initial burst of 50 to 75 rounds or a 50- to 75-round burst followed by firing 20 rounds for each succeeding minute, requires a cooling time or cessation of fire for approximately 15 minutes before the long burst can be repeated.

(c) If long bursts are not fired, approximately 25 rounds may be fired each minute over long periods.

SECTION D. CARE AND CLEANING

1. **General care**.--The importance of a thorough knowledge of how to care for and clean the machine gun can not be over-

emphasized. The kind of attention given to a weapon of this type determines largely whether or not it will shoot accurately and function properly when needed. The bore and chamber must be kept in perfect condition for accurate shooting. Also, it is just as important that the receiver and moving parts be kept clean, lubricated, and in perfect condition for efficient functioning. Care and cleaning will not be confined to the gun alone but will include all accessories. Belt links and ammunition must be kept clean and dry.

2. **Cleaning, cleaning materials, and lubrication.**--

(a) **Cleaning bore.**--Disassemble groups from gun.

(1) Place barrel, muzzle down, in a vessel containing hot water and issue soap, a sal soda solution, or lacking these, hot water alone.

(2) Insert cleaning rod, with a flannel patch assembled, in the breech. Move rod forward and back for about one minute, pumping water in and out of bore.

(3) Use a brass or bronze wire brush while the bore is wet, running it forward and back through the barrel three or four times.

(4) Pump water through bore again to clean.

(5) Dry the cleaning rod and remove barrel from water. Using dry, clean flannel patches, thoroughly swab bore until it is perfectly dry and clean. Thoroughly dry and clean the chamber using a flannel patch on a stick if necessary.

(6) Saturate a patch with sperm oil and swab bore and chamber with the patch. Allow a thin coat of the oil to remain in the bore.

(7) Guns should be cleaned not later than the evening of the day on which the gun is fired.

(8) Inspect and clean the guns for 3 days following cessation of firing.

(b) **Cleaning parts other than gun.**--(1) Wipe receiver clean, care being taken to remove dirt from belt holding pawl. Thoroughly clean cover, bolt, barrel extension, oil buffer, and back. plate, using a small stick covered with a flannel patch to remove dirt from all recesses.

(2) Wipe all parts with an oily rag.

(c) **Preparation for storage.**--(1) Clean and prepare the guns with particular care. All parts of the gun should be cleaned

and wiped thoroughly dry with rags. In damp climates particular care must be taken to see that the rags are dry. After drying, the bare hands should not touch the parts; handle with an oily rag.

(2) Apply rust-preventive compound to all metal parts of the gun. Rust-preventive compound, medium (U. S. A. Spec. 2-84A) , is a sluggish liquid which pours at a temperature of 81° F. It is used for short-time protection and should not be used on, guns put in permanent storage. It may be applied with a brush or by dipping. In applying, heating is not necessary except in very cold temperatures. Application of the rust-preventive compound to the bore of the machine-gun barrel is done best by dipping the cleaning brush in rust-preventive compound and running it through the bore two or three times. Prior to placing the weapon in storage the bolt should be in the forward position with the firing pin released. In fact it is good practice to relieve the firing-pin tension whenever the weapon is not in use.

(3) The wooden supports in the packing box must be painted with rust-preventive compound before storing the gun. Place the gun in the wooden packing box, handling the gun with oiled rags.

(d) **Guns received from storage**.--Machine guns received from storage are completely coated with rust-preventive compound. Use dry-cleaning solvent to remove all traces of this grease, particular care being taken that all recesses in which springs or plungers operate are cleaned thoroughly. After using the dry-cleaning solvent make sure it is completely removed from all parts by washing with soap and water, and drying thoroughly. The bore and chamber of the barrel must be thoroughly cleaned. All surfaces having been thoroughly cleaned they should then be protected with a thin film of lubrication oil applied with a rag.

NOTE.--Failure to clean the firing pin and driving spring and the recesses in the bolt in which they operate may result in gun failure at normal temperatures, and will most certainly result in series malfunctions if the guns are operated in low temperature areas as rust-preventive compound and other foreign matter will cause the lubrication oil to congeal or frost on the mechanism.

(e) **Lubricant to be used on gun**.--(1) Proper oiling is second in importance only to intelligent cleaning. It is a vital necessity for the working parts but should be used sparingly. Oil all bearing surfaces of gun before firing, taking particular care to see that exterior of barrel is oiled at breech end, also that cover extractor spring, cover extractor cam, and cover detent pawl are oiled. Oil cocking lever, groove in the bolt for belt feed lever, grooves in barrel extension to take bolt ribs, breech lock cam, switch, extractor cam, sear mechanism, and the Ways of belt feed slide.

CAUTION.--In oiling aircraft guns, special care should be taken not to use an excess of oil, as low temperatures that may be encountered will thicken the oil and may cause the gun to malfunction. The parts are best oiled by wiping with a well-oiled rag. (2) If the gun is to be fired in areas where the temperature is 45° or above, sperm oil should be used, when available. When not available, motor oil, weight 20, or any light grade machine oil, may be used in an emergency.

(3) On all types of machine guns when operated in areas where the temperature is below 45° F., and all aircraft machine guns when operated in the air, regardless of ground temperature, aircraft-instrument and machine-gun lubricating oil should be used.

(f) **Preserving machine guns after rust-preventive compound has been removed**.--Sperm oil is the most suitable oil for preserving the mechanism when in regular or intermittent use. This oil is efficient for preserving the polished surfaces, the bore and the chamber for a period of from two to six weeks, dependent on the climatic and storage conditions. Aircraft instrument and machine gun lubricating oil should not be considered as a suitable preservative; however, for aircraft guns and other guns operated regularly in cool areas it should be used, and application made more often, as it is a material disadvantage to use sperm oil or other heavy bodied oils, as it is absolutely essential that such oils be removed with cleaning fluid, and aircraft instrument and machine gun lubricating oil applied before an attempt is made to fire the gun in such areas. Sperm oil should invariably be used for preserving the chamber and bore, however, as the light oil cleaning compound is used to remove fouling from the barrel and other parts of the gun.

(g) **Rust-preventive compound**.--This is a heavy dark-colored sticky grease provided to protect metal surfaces of the gun from corrosion while in storage. It is not a lubricant and should not be used as a lubricant. The compound is of two grades, i.e., heavy and medium.

(1) Rust-preventive compound, heavy (Spec. U. S. A. 2-82B) , must be made fluid prior to use. A practical method to obtain fluidity is to place container in a vessel of water, heating it to a temperature of not over 180° F., the exact temperature being determined by the thickness of the film desired. In no case should it be heated above 180° F. ; at this temperature deterioration of the compound sets in. The higher the temperature of the compound, the thinner is the film applied to the metal. The compound should be heated to the temperature at which used for about half an hour before using. Best results will be obtained if the compound is heated to 180° F., and then allowed to cool to the desired consistency before using. The best method of applying the compound is by dipping as there is much less danger of the inclusion of air bubbles in the grease film by this method.

(2) Rust-preventive compound, medium (Spec. U. S. A. 2-84A) , is a sluggish liquid which pours at a temperature of 81° F. It is used for short time protection and should not be used on guns put in permanent storage. It may be applied with a brush or by dipping. In applying, heating is not necessary, except, in very cold temperatures. Application of the rust-preventive compound to the bore of the machine gun barrel is best done by dipping the cleaning brush in rust-preventive compound and running it through the bore two or three times.

NOTE.--Navy slushing compounds of similar grades may be used.

(h) **Metal fouling solution**.--This is a perishable mixture; to be prepared as needed, and used for dissolving primer residue and metal fouling from the bores of machine gun barrels.

Prepare the solution as follows:

(1) Ingredients.--Ammonium persulphate, 1 ounce or 2' medium heaping tablespoonfuls, ammonium carbonate, 200> grains or 1 heaping tablespoonful; ammonia (28 percent) , 6 ounces or 3/8 pint or 12 tablespoonfuls; water, 4 ounces or 1/4 pint. or 8 tablespoonfuls.

NOTE.--The foregoing amount is sufficient for cleaning about six machine gun barrels.

(2) Powder the ammonium persulphate and ammonium carbonate together (place them inside a clean cloth and grind with a tool handle) ; dissolve in the water and add the ammonia: mix thoroughly until about 90 percent of the powder is dissolved and allow to stand for one hour before using. The solution should be kept in a strong bottle, tightly rubber corked, and in a cool place. The solution shall be used within 30 days after mixing and should not be used more than twice. Used solution should not be mixed with unused solution but should be bottled separately.

(i) **Ammonia swabbing solution**.--This is a dilute metal fouling solution used for swabbing out the bores of machine gun barrels. Prepare the solution as follows:

(1) *Ingredients*.--Ammonium persulphate, 60 grains or $^1/2$ tablespoonful, smooth off. Ammonia (28 percent) , 6 ounces or 3/8 pint or 12 tablespoonfuls. Water, 4 ounces or 1/4 pint or 8 tablespoonfuls.

(2) First dissolve the ammonium persulphate in the water, then add the ammonia. Keep the solution in a strong bottle, tightly rubber corked, and in a cool place. Pour out that which is necessary at the time only, and keep the bottle corked.

3. **Points to be observed, before, during, and after firing**.-- When the machine gun is to be fired, it must be cleaned, properly assembled, and lubricated. While in use it must be kept as nearly as possible in the same condition. After firing it must again be put in readiness for later use, Certain rules, the observance of which will aid fulfillment of these conditions, are called points to be observed before, during, and after firing.

a. **Points to be observed before firing**.--The gunner must be thoroughly impressed with the value of observing these points and testing his gun by their observance each time it is to be fired, doing it, furthermore, before the moment for firing has actually arrived. They are not intended as a guide for a detailed inspection of the gun, nor should points to be observed before firing be so considered. They are intended to constitute a procedure that can be carried out quickly as a preliminary to going into action with the gun or firing a score at target practice with it.

(1) See that the bore is clear and clean.

(2) See that the working parts of the gun are oiled.

(3) See that oil buffer tube is filled with oil.

(4) See that the adjusting screw is screwed in tight against buffer disks in back plate.

(5) Try gun action several times by hand to see that the mechanism works freely and smoothly.

(6) Test headspace adjustment.

(7) Examine the gun for leakage or excessive friction of the barrel packing. Adjust the packing adjusting ring and muzzle gland, if necessary. Test adjustment of packing by operating the gun by hand. A wide adjustment of the formed packing is provided, and the gun will rarely need repacking.

(8) Verify cleanliness of the sights and tightness of their adjusting screws.

(9) See that water jacket is filled and that the hose connections are tight.

(10) See that ammunition belts are clean and correctly loaded. Secure sufficient supply of ammunition.

(11) Verify presence of tools and spare parts.

b. **Points to be observed during firing**.--It is to be understood that these points are observed as occasion arises or opportunity during cessation of fire permits. Firing is not interrupted merely for the purpose of observing them.

(1) Clean bore and chamber.

(2) In case of misfire (with bolt fully forward and firing pin released) wait ten (10) seconds before pulling bolt to the rear, for to extract a cartridge having a hangfire is hazardous to personnel and might cause irreparable damage to the gun.

c. **Points to be observed after firing**.--(1) Unload the gun.

(2) Clean bore and chamber. Inspect bore each day for several succeeding days and clean until all signs of fouling have been eliminated.

(3) Disassemble and clean gun thoroughly. Inspect all parts. Make needed repairs and replacements.

(4) On assembling, check the Operation with dummy cartridges and release the firing pin spring, after insuring that functioning and adjustments are correct.

4. **Precautions to be observed in cold weather.**--

a. Test the gun frequently to see that it functions properly. b. During cold weather when the gun is silent, the movable parts in the receiver of the gun must be kept absolutely dry and free from oil but before firing the gun the moving parts should be oiled.

5. **Precautions to be observed during a gas attack.**--

a. Cover guns with waterproof sheet if available.

b. Work recoiling parts if the gun is not being fired.

c. Guns should be cleaned as soon as possible after a gas attack.

d. Oiling will prevent corrosion for about 12 hours.

e. Clean all metal parts in boiling water containing a little soda.

f. All traces of gas must be removed from ammunition with a slightly oiled rag, then thoroughly dry ammunition.

g. Rust-preventive compound resists gas corrosion more than lighter oil.

6. **Method of filling oil buffer.**--Remove the two oil buffer tube filling screws from the base of the buffer tube. Use the oil buffer filling oiler filled with machine gun recoil oil (Spec. U. S. A. 2-77). In an emergency any light recoil oil may be used, adding glycerin in freezing temperatures if necessary. Start the flow of oil by pressing on the base of the oiler. While the oil continues to pour from the oiler, insert nozzle into either filling hole and with a continued pressure, on the base of the oiler allow oil to flow into the buffer tube. DO NOT RELEASE PRESSURE ON OILER UNTIL NOZZLE HAS BEEN REMOVED PROM PILLING HOLE, THUS AVOIDING GETTING AIR BUBBLES INTO THE BUFFER TUBE. Repeat the operation until the buffer is overflowing. Replace the filling screws. Any excess oil in the buffer will be relieved by the relief valve in the forward end of the buffer body. The reason that two filling holes are provided is to show visually by overflow when the buffer tube is completely full.

SECTION E. MALFUNCTIONS

1. **Explanation.**--(a) A malfunction is an improper action of some part of the gun resulting in a stoppage; for example, a failure to extract the empty cartridge case.

(b) Any accidental cessation of fire is a stoppage. It may bo a faulty cartridge or a malfunction of some part of the gun. The fact that all the ammunition in the belt being fed into the gun has been exhausted should not be called a malfunction since it is a cessation of fire from natural results.

(c) **Immediate action** is the term applied to that operation required to clear a temporary stoppage.

2. **Prevention of stoppages**.--Proper care of the gun and attention to the points before, during, and after firing as outlined before will greatly reduce liability to stoppages, particularly if the gunner has an intelligent understanding of the reasons why stoppages generally occur. Prevention is the best remedy for all stoppages. Nevertheless, stoppages will occur in spite of all that can be done to prevent them.

3. **Classes of stoppages**.--Stoppages may be classed under two main headings:

(a) *Temporary,* which are due to--

1. Failure of some part of the gun of which a duplicate is carried.

2. Faulty ammunition.

3. Neglect of points before or during firing.

4. Lack of knowledge of the operation and functioning of the gun.

(b) *Prolonged,* which are due to a failure of some part that cannot, as a rule, be remedied by the gun squad under fire or without skilled assistance.

4. **Classified table of stoppages**.--(a) Stoppages are classified according to the position in which the bolt stud is found when the gun stops firing.

1. *Firing position*.--Bolt stud all the way forward.

2. *Second position*.--Bolt stud just in rear of all the way forward to half way back.

3. *Third position*.--Bolt stud just in rear of half way back to all the way back.

(b) A table of stoppages classified according to the position of the bolt stud follows:

Classified table of stoppages

Position of bolt stud:

First-position stoppage:

1. Misfire due to defective primer.

2. Short or broken firing pin.

3. Weak or broken firing pin spring.

4. Faulty engagement of firing pin and sear notch.

5. Sear spring weak, broken, or out.

6. Belt improperly loaded. (May cause a second position stoppage.)

7. Short round.

8. Bent or worn belt feed lever. (May cause a second position stoppage.)

9. Belt feed pawl spring weak or out.

10. Belt feed pawl pin out or partially out.

11. Cover extractor spring weak or out.

12. Belt feed lever bent or bolt switch defective. (Stud on end of lever jumps out of cam groove in bolt.)

13. Damaged extractor. (May cause a second stoppage.)

14. Belt holding pawl out or spring weak.

15. Belt holding pawl fails to depress. (May cause a third position stoppage.)

Second-position stoppage:

1. Separated case which stays in the chamber when bolt is pulled to the rear.

2. Separated case which is removed from the chamber by the new round when bolt is pulled to the rear.

3. Separated cases due to too much headspace. (May result in either 1 or 2 above.)

4. Headspace adjustment too tight.

5. Broken or missing barrel locking spring. (May result in either 3 or 4 above.)

6. Bulged round.

7. Tight link in belt.

8. Bullet loose in cartridge case.

9. Broken extractor or ejector.

Third-position stoppage:

1. Battered or thick rim of cartridge.

2. Broken cannelure.

3. Enlarged hole in recoil plate. (Setback primer.)

4. Belt feed pawl arm bent or broken.

5. Broken or damaged T-slot in bolt.

6. Thin rim of cartridge permitting nose of bullet, to drop below the chamber.

5. **Immediate action**.--Immediate action is the immediate and automatic application of a proper remedy for a machine-gun stoppage. When a stoppage is experienced, first note the position of the bolt stud. Never push the bolt forward. Proceed as follows:

(a) Gun fails to fire.--With hand, feel rounds entering feed-way. Straighten, if required. See that cover is latched. Wait ten (10) seconds then pull bolt to the rear twice and release it. Relay and fire.

(b) Gun still fails to fire.--(1) Raise cover and note position of bolt. If bolt is not closed, pull back bolt and remove cartridge in T-slot. Examine it. (If cartridge is warm let it cool for about 30 seconds.) Take first round out of belt. Reload. Relay and fire.

(2) If bolt is closed, pull bolt to the rear once. If a cartridge is ejected, examine for broken firing pin. If no cartridge is ejected, examine feed mechanism and extractor and remedy defect. Reload. Relay and fire.

CAUTION.--After any stoppage which appears to be caused by insufficient recoil, make sure that the bore is clear before continuing firing. It is possible that such a stoppage, as for instance, one caused by incomplete ignition of the powder charge, may result in the bullet lodging in the bore, and in case this happens and another round is fired before the bore is cleared the gun will certainly be seriously damaged.

6. **To remove a cartridge from the T-slot**.--(a) Hold back the bolt and raise the extractor. The cartridge will usually fall out unless it has a thick rim or the T-slot is defective.

(b) If the cartridge will not fall out when the extractor is raised, use a screw driver or similar tool. Hold the bolt to the rear with the extractor raised. Place the screw driver through

the top of the receiver into the top of the cannelure of the cartridge and drive the cartridge downward out of the T-slot by-striking the upper end of the screw driver with the palm of the hand.

7. **To remove a case from the chamber**.--If there is an empty case with broken rim stuck in the chamber, hold back the bolt and remove cartridge from the T-slot if there is one. Insert the cleaning rod from the muzzle and knock the empty case from the chamber. If several cases stick in the chamber in close succession put some oil on the chamber and with a cleaning brush, thoroughly scrub the chamber with the brush, then wipe out the chamber with a dry rag.

8. **Replacing damaged parts**.--(a) Damaged parts will be removed and replaced as quickly as possible. If it is imperative that fire be maintained or immediately resumed, a broken minor part should be replaced by substituting the complete spare part which contains it. Thus a broken firing pin would be remedied by changing bolts; a broken ejector by changing extractors. Later, as opportunity permits, the small parts will be repaired or replaced in order to make the larger part again available for use. Where the complete bolt has been changed, a check should be made on headspace.

(b) It is of extreme importance that all pieces of broken parts be removed when remedying a stoppage due to a broken part. Otherwise, serious damage to the "action" may result on resuming fire.

Chapter 3. THOMPSON SUBMACHINE GUN

SECTION A. DESCRIPTION

1. **General**.--The Thompson submachine gun, caliber .45, M1928A1 (fig. 19), is an air-cooled, recoil-operated, magazine-fed weapon weighing about 15% pounds with loaded 50-round magazine. The exterior surface of the rear portion of the barrel contains a series of annular flanges which serve to dissipate heat and cool the barrel during firing. The hand of the gunner is protected on the under side of the barrel by a wooden fore grip. A rear grip is also provided. Sling swivels are attached to the fore grip and stock for attaching the gun sling. The weapon is provided with a "Cutts" recoil compensator to lessen the recoil and the tendency of the muzzle to rise in full automatic fire. By correctly setting the rocker pivot, the weapon may be used for either full-automatic or semiautomatic fire. The weapon is fed from a drum-type magazine having a capacity of 50 rounds or from a box type magazine having a capacity of 20

rounds.

2. **General data**.--a. Dimension:

(1) Barrel:

Diameter of bore	inches	0.45
Number of grooves		6
Twist in rifling, uniform, right, one turn inches		16
Length of barrel	inches	10.50

(2) Gun:

Over-all length of gun including compensator.	inches	33.69
Sight radius	do	22.30

b. Weight:

Gun without magazine	pounds	10.75
Loaded 20-round magazine	do	1.31
Loaded 50-round magazine	do	4.95
Empty 20-round magazine	do	.38
Empty 50-round magazine	do	2.63

3. **Miscellaneous data**.

Initial velocity	feet per second.	802
Pressure in chamber (approx.)	pounds per sq. inch	12,000-16,000
Weight of ball cartridge (approx.)	oz	3/4
Weight of bullet (approx.)	do	1/2
Weight of powder charge (approx.)	grains.	5
Rate of automatic fire (cyclic rate)	shots per minute	600-700

SECTION B. DISASSEMBLING AND ASSEMBLING

1. **General**.--(a) Disassembling is considered under two general headings, removal of groups and disassembling of the groups.

(b) A group is a number of components which either function together in the gun or are intimately related to each other and should therefore be considered together.

2. **Removal of groups from gun**.--(a) Magazine.--With the bolt in the rearward position, raise magazine catch and slide out magazine.

(b) **Stock**.--Press in on butt stock catch button and slide butt stock to the rear.

(c) **Frame from receiver**.--Turn safety to "fire" position and rocker pivot to "automatic" or "full auto" position. Pull trigger and allow bolt to go forward gradually by retarding actuator with left hand. Place gun upside down on knee or table, muzzle to the left. With thumb of right hand depress frame latch and with left hand slide frame toward rear of gun about 1 inch by pushing or tapping on rear grip. Take gun from table or knees, turn it right side up, grasp receiver firmly with left hand near feedway. With right hand grasp grip in normal firing position, index finger on trigger. Pull the trigger as in firing and withdraw frame to rear of gun, pulling down on frame as well as to the rear as it is withdrawn. Failure to pull down as frame is withdrawn causes frame latch to strike against the rear portion of the trigger and trip, damaging these parts.

--153--

--154--

(d) **Recoil spring**.--Support muzzle of barrel on table or knees with open side of receiver facing operator. Grasp receiver with left hand with thumb in position to depress buffer pilot. With thumb of left hand press down on buffer pilot. With thumb and forefinger of right hand engage flange of buffer and pull down until buffer pilot clears back of receiver. If breech oiler follows, push it back. Hold buffer with thumb and forefinger of right hand and withdraw this entire unit from receiver. Care should be taken to obtain a firm hold on the buffer to prevent the recoil spring, which is compressed, from forcing it out of the operator's hand. When the recoil spring, at rest, measures less than $10^1/2$ inches it should be replaced.

(e) **Bolt, lock, and actuator**.--Grasp receiver, bottom up, with left hand. Slide bolt to the rear and lift out. Slide actuator with lock forward and lift out lock. Slide actuator to rear, turn receiver over, and allow actuator to fall out into right hand.

(f) **Breech oiler**.--Hold receiver upside down in left hand, muzzle to front. Hook end of forefinger of right hand under front end of right side of breech oiler. Pull up and to left until right side of breech oiler is out of groove in receiver. Hold the oiler in this position with the right thumb. Without moving thumb, hook forefinger of right hand under front end of left side of oiler, and pull oiler out of groove in left side of receiver. With forefinger of right hand pull entire front end of oiler up and to the rear. Lift the oiler out of the receiver, front end first. It is not necessary to remove oiler for ordinary cleaning purposes.

3. **Disassembling of groups**.--(a) **Magazine, 50-round**.-- Remove winding key and lift off cover. Lift up on end of rotor retainer and slide it out of its engagement in the hub. The rotor assembly may then be removed from body. Further disassembly of magazine is not necessary and is prohibited.

(b) **Magazine, 20-round**.--Slide out floor plate. Hold fingers over bottom of magazine tube to keep magazine spring from flying out. Remove follower.

(c) **Butt stock**.--Complete disassembly of butt stock is not necessary for ordinary cleaning. However, when necessary for replacement of broken or worn parts, butt stock slide and butt

plate may be removed by taking out the screws holding them in place.

(d) **Frame group**.--(1) Hold frame in left hand and, using back end of actuator (not knob) as a tool in right hand, do-press short finger of pivot plate and push out rocker pivot with thumb of left hand; lift out rocker and pivot.

(2) Again using actuator but steadying hand with thumb against frame to prevent excessive movement, depress long finger of pivot plate and withdraw safety.

(3) Hold frame upright with grip in right hand. Press simultaneously with both thumbs on sear and trigger pivots. These pivots project sufficiently so that by a quick pressure thereon, pivot plate will protrude on the other side far enough to permit withdrawal. While withdrawing pivot plate with left hand, press down on trigger and sear with thumb of right hand to release pressure of spring on pivots. Do not cant pivot plate during withdrawal. The remaining components of the firing mechanism are then free to be removed. Disconnector can be removed from trigger by simply withdrawing it.

(4) To remove magazine catch, rotate it in a counterclockwise direction to its lull limit and pull out to the left. Removal should be limited to replacement of broken parts. Removal of magazine catch submits magazine catch spring to unnecessary strain and is apt to damage it.

(e) **Bolt group**.--

(1) Push hammer pin out of bolt from left side; hammer, firing pin, and firing-pin spring will then tend to spring out under the impulse of the firing-pin spring. Caution should be exercised to prevent these parts from springing away and becoming lost. The firing-pin spring must not be stretched.

(2) Extractor should not be removed for ordinary cleaning or disassembling. To do so submits it to unnecessary strain and is apt to cause it to break or become set.

(3) To remove extractor from bolt, insert corner of actuator flange under head of extractor on face of bolt and pull extractor out and up to withdraw it from its groove. When disassembling extractor from or assembling it to bolt, do not lift extractor higher than necessary for lug to clear anchorage hole as otherwise setting or breakage may occur.

(f) **Receiver group**.--For ordinary training receiver and parts assembled thereto need not be assembled.

(1) To remove rear sight leaf, drive out sight base pin and remove leaf. Take care to see that rear sight leaf plunger and spring do not fly out.

(2) The ejector can be removed by lifting leaf sufficiently to* disengage detent and unscrewing same from receiver. Do not try to unscrew ejector with bolt assembled and in forward position. To do so may damage the ejector and bolt.

(3) Fore grip can be removed by unscrewing fore grip screw-

(4) Barrel should be removed only for purpose of replacement and then only by authorized ordnance personnel.

4. **Assembling of groups**.--In general, groups and their components are assembled and replaced in the gun in the reverse order of that in which they were removed or disassembled. Certain precautions in assembling ((a) and (b) below) must be observed in order that the parts will function properly after gun is assembled.

(a) In assembling trigger mechanism, first see that magazine catch is in place. Assemble springs in their proper recesses. Assemble disconnector to trigger by depressing disconnector spring and sliding disconnector into place.

(1) Place trigger, trip, sear, and sear lever in their respective positions in frame, making sure forward end of sear lever rests on tip of disconnector. To aline these parts, hold frame in left hand and press downward with end of thumb on trigger and base of thumb on sear. Insert pivot plate. To avoid binding, apply gentle pressure with ball of right hand over entire pivot plate.

(2) Insert safety as far as it will go, and using actuator as a tool depress long finger of pivot

plate and push safety home. Turn safety to "fire" position.

(3) Place rocker in position in frame with fiat side against sear lever. Insert rocker pivot as far as it will go. Using actuator as a tool, depress short finger of pivot plate and push rocker pivot home. Turn rocker pivot to "full auto" position. If rocker is assembled backward, the gun will fire full automatic but not semiautomatic.

(b) If extractor has been removed, slide it into place, lifting head only enough to clear stud; avoid excessive pressure. In-

sert firing pin and spring in bolt being careful to avoid stretching firing pin spring. Place hammer in position with rounded edge upward and push hammer pin into place.

5. **Replacing groups in gun**.--Before replacing groups in gun, be sure ejector is screwed all the way home and that breech oiler is in place.

(a) Place receiver on table or knees, bottom up, and insert actuator in receiver, knob to front. Slide actuator forward and place lock in guideways of receiver, with the word "up" correctly readable from the rear and the arrow pointing toward the muzzle. Slide actuator to the rear and place bolt in position by lowering it into the receiver front end first, moving it to the rear, and allowing it to drop into place.

(b) Slide bolt forward and start recoil spring assembled to buffer guide, into its recess in bolt. Push recoil spring down into bolt until buffer pilot clears end of receiver. Let buffer pilot find its seat in the receiver and snap into place.

(c) For guns equipped with drilled buffer guides, assemble about two-thirds of recoil spring on buffer guide, place retaining pin (nail or strong wire) through coil of spring and hole of buffer guide to hold compressed spring on buffer guide. Care should be taken to see that retaining pin is entered in the hole in buffer guide from the side opposite to that of the milled off flat portion of the buffer flange. Slide the bolt forward and start the loose end of recoil spring into recess in actuator which rides in the bolt. Feed loose end of spring into its recess until rear end of pilot can be seated in hole in rear end of receiver, care being taken to see that buffer disk is in place before pilot is placed in the hole in receiver. Move bolt rearward until rear end of bolt is brought up against spring retaining pin. Remove retaining pin which permits spring completely to seat itself within the recess. Release bolt.

(d) Before fitting frame to receiver, be sure that safety is set at "fire" position and rocker pivot at "full auto." Slide frame onto receiver. Frame latch will lock frame in position. Holding trigger depressed, operate actuator back and forth several times to test mechanism.

SECTION C. CARE AND CLEANING

1. **General**.--The attention given to a weapon of this type determines largely whether it will shoot accurately and function properly. The bore and chamber must be kept in perfect condition for accurate shooting. Also, it is just as important that the receiver and moving parts be kept clean, lubricated, and in perfect condition for efficient functioning. Care and cleaning; will include the magazines, which must be kept free from rust, grit, gum, etc., in order to function property. When not on the person, the submachine gun should be habitually transported in a suitable boot provided with the necessary brackets for attachment.

2. **Cleaning and lubrication--General**.--(a) Keep the gun well cleaned and oiled. After each day's firing, clean the bore, chamber, and all parts and surfaces of the receiver, bolt ejector, and extractor that have been in contact with powder gases. Remove frame from receiver and take bolt out; thoroughly clean front end of bolt and extractor. With the bolt removed, the bolt well, the head of the receiver, and the ejector head are readily accessible.

(b) **Bore**.--(1) As the barrel of the submachine gun is not removed for cleaning, it must be cleaned from the muzzle if the submachine gun cleaning rod is used. However, by using the rifle cleaning rod the barrel can be cleaned from the breech. Push rifle cleaning rod through buffer pilot in back of receiver and thread a patch through eye of rod.

CAUTION.--In cleaning bore, care must be taken not to foul cleaning patch in slots of recoil compensator.

(2) Run several wet patches through bore. For this purpose water must be used; warm water is good, and warm soapy water is better. Remove patch, attach cleaning brush, and run brush back and forth through bore several times. Care should be used to insure that brush goes all the way through bore before direction is reversed. Remove brush and run several wet patches through bore. Follow this by dry patches until patches

--159--

come out clean and dry, then saturate a patch in sperm oil and push it through bore.

NOTE.--Sperm oil (U. S. A. Spec. 2-45A) should be used when available. When not available, motor oil, weight 20, or any light grade machine oil may be used in an emergency.

(c) **Chamber**.--The chamber should be cleaned with the chamber cleaning brush at reasonable intervals in extended firing to facilitate extraction of cartridge cases and to prevent pitting and rusting. It is not necessary to disassemble gun for this purpose. The brush is introduced through ejection opening in receiver and should be vigorously used. Upon completion of firing, the brush having been used the chamber is further cleaned and oiled in the process of cleaning the bore.

(d) **Exterior surfaces**.--Wipe off exterior surfaces of gun with a dry cloth to remove dampness, dirt, and perspiration, then wipe off all metal surfaces with an oiled (sperm oil) rag. The stock and grips should be wiped with raw linseed oil.

(e) **Magazines**.--It is imperative that magazines be given the best of care and kept in perfect condition. They should be disassembled, wiped clean and dry, and thinly coated with oil. Dirt that gets into them through careless handling during range or other firing must be removed. Care must be exercised in handling magazine to avoid denting or bending, especially the lips of the mouth of the box type magazines.

(f) **Lubricating the gun**.---To function efficiently, the gun must be properly lubricated. For this purpose use aircraft machine gun lubricating oil (U. S. A. Spec. 2-27) or sperm oil (U. S. A. Spec. 2-45A) .

(1) Having removed frame from receiver, oil should be dropped over pivot points of trigger and trip, sear and sear lever, and disconnector and rocker.

(2) Holding receiver in left hand, open side up, bolt should be slightly drawn back and oil dropped on locking lugs of lock, on sides of lock, and on all sliding surfaces of bolt and receiver.

(3) Felt pads in breech oiler should be kept well saturated with oil.

(4) After assembling frame to receiver, bolt should be drawn back and a little oil should be dropped on rounded front end of

bolt. Actuator knob should be worked back and forth several times to insure penetration of oil to all parts of mechanism.

(5) All sliding surfaces should be oiled frequently and freely to insure perfect functioning of the gun.

SECTION D. FUNCTIONING

1. **General**.--The pressure of the gases generated in the barrel by the explosion of the powder in the cartridge is exerted in a forward direction against the bullet, driving it through the bore, and in a rearward direction against the face of the bolt. This force drives the bolt and the actuator together to the rear against the pressure of the recoil spring. During rearward movement, the process of unlocking, extracting, ejecting empty shell, and compressing the recoil spring are affected; during the forward movement, the processes of feeding, locking, and firing the cartridge are accomplished. To simplify explanation of functioning, the cycle has been divided into three phases as set forth below.

2. **Backward movement of recoiling parts (first phase)**.-- The cartridge having been fired,

the pressure from the exploding cartridge is transmitted through the forward and of the bolt to the lock to the locking surfaces of the receiver. The powder used is fast burning, so that the highest pressure obtained is nearly instantaneous. The lock being made of bronze and the bolt and receiver being made of steel, the high chamber pressure causes the lock to adhere to the locking surface on the receiver, thus locking the bolt in its forward position until this pressure subsides. As soon as the high chamber pressure has subsided, the lock moves upward, clears the locking surfaces in the receiver, and the bolt can move to the rear. The angle of the lock is such that the moment the lock is moved to clear the receiver locking surfaces there is only sufficient powder in the chamber to force the cartridge case and bolt to the rear, eject the empty case and compress the recoil spring, which thus stores up energy for the forward movement. The empty case is unseated by the chamber pressure as the bolt is unlocked. As soon as the bolt moves back from the abutment on the under side of the receiver, the firing pin spring forces the firing pin to

the rear away from the face of the bolt. The empty cartridge is held on the face of the bolt by the extractor. After the bolt has traveled to the rear about 2 inches the ejector, which protrudes in a groove on the left side of the bolt, comes in contact with the base of the empty cartridge and throws it to the right through the ejection opening. The bolt still has about 1 $3/4$ inches to go to the rear before the back of the bolt comes in contact with the buffer. The rearward movement of the bolt, carrying the actuator and compressing the recoil spring, expends nearly all the energy imparted by the chamber pressure, so that the bolt does not strike heavily against the buffer. The buffer pad absorbs the remaining shock. On the under side of the bolt there are two sear notches so that, if the bolt strikes the buffer pad, the rear sear notch will pass over the sear and allow the sear to engage in the front notch. If the movement is not strong enough to cause the bolt to strike the buffer pad, the sear will engage in the rear notch. If the bolt moves to the rear far enough to eject the empty cartridge case and to feed the next cartridge from the top of the magazine, the bolt will normally be back far enough to engage the sear with the rear notch.

3. **Forward movement of recoiling parts (second phase).**-- When the trigger is pulled, the bolt moves forward under the action of the recoil spring, carrying the lock and actuator with it. After the bolt moves forward about 1 inch, the forward end of the bolt comes in contact with the back of a cartridge and pushes it forward until the nose of the bullet comes in contact with the bullet ramp in front of the receiver. The lips of the magazine hold the cartridge in a straight line until the cartridge has almost cleared the magazine. The cartridge is guided into the chamber by the bullet ramp and the lips of the magazine. When the cartridge has been seated in the chamber, the extractor snaps around the rim of the cartridge. Just before the bolt reaches its forward position, the lock is cammed down into the locking grooves in the receiver so that the bolt is completely locked as the hammer on the under side of the bolt strikes the receiver. The hammer being of a triangular shape, the lower point strikes the receiver, causing the hammer to pivot around the hammer pin and strike the head of the firing pin with the upper point, thereby firing the cartridge. The rectangular surface of the

bolt, striking the abutment of the receiver, stops the forward movement.

4. **Action of trigger mechanism (third phase).**--(a) (1) *Rocker pivot set at "single."*--When the trigger is pulled, the trigger rotates around the trigger pivot (the forward pin of the pivot plate) and lifts the disconnector up under the sear lever. The sear lever lifts the front end of the sear; this causes the sear to rotate around the sear pivot (the rear pin of the pivot plate), and in so doing depresses the nose of the sear, disengaging it from the sear notch on the under side of the bolt. As the bolt goes forward, the point of the rocker is in the T-groove on the under side of the bolt. When the point of the rocker strikes the rear end of the T-groove, the rocker is forced forward. The rounded part of the rocker comes in contact with the disconnector and forces the disconnector out from under the sear lever. As soon as the disconnector has been disengaged from the sear lever, the sear spring and the sear lever spring force the sear and sear lever up into firing position, so that the sear notch on the bolt will catch on the next rearward movement of the bolt.

(2) *Rocker pivot set at "full auto."*--The rocker pivot is of eccentric design so that when the rocker pivot is set at "full auto" the rocker is lowered enough to allow the bolt to move forward without striking the point of the rocker. Therefore, the sear remains in its lowered position as long as the trigger is depressed. The rocker pivot cannot be turned from "full auto" to "single" unless bolt is retracted.

(b) (1) *Safety set at "fire."*--When the safety is turned toward the front, the flat-milled surface is in such a position that the sear is allowed to rotate around the sear pivot.

(2) *Safety set at "safe."*--When the safety is turned toward the rear, the rounded part of the safety engages in a groove in the rear of the sear and locks the sear in its uppermost position. The safety can be turned only when the bolt is to the rear.

(c) The magazine catch rotates around its pin and is held down in the engaged position by the magazine catch spring. The stud on the magazine catch is to hold the box-type magazine; the drum type is held by the rectangular catch on the left side. The trip functions only when the box-type magazine is used. As the magazine empties, a fin on the back of the magazine

follower rises up under the trip, causing the trip to rotate around the trigger pin, compressing the disconnector spring holding the disconnector forward of the sear lever. Thus the bolt will not go forward on an empty chamber when the box magazine is used.

SECTION E. STOPPAGES AND IMMEDIATE ACTION

1. **Misfire.**--In the event of misfire, retract or cock bolt with a sharp, quick pull on actuator

knob. This should insure ejection of misfired cartridge. Inspect chamber to see that it does not contain an unexpended round.

2. **Other stoppages**.--For any other malfunction, retract bolt as above and clear throat and chamber of gun by turning gun over on its side and letting case or cartridge roll out. If necessary, remove magazine and allow cartridge or case to fall out the bottom. While manipulating the gun under those circumstances, always set the gun at "safe."

SECTION F. SPARE PARTS AND ACCESSORIES

1. **Spare parts**.--The parts of any submachine gun will in time become unservicable through breakage or wear resulting from continuous usage. For this reason spare parts are provided for replacement of the part's most likely to fail, for use in making minor repairs, and in general upkeep of the submachine gun. Sets of spare parts should be maintained as complete as possible at all times and should be kept clean and lightly oiled to prevent rust. Whenever a spare part is used to replace a defective part, the defective part should be repaired or a new one substituted in the spare parts set. Parts that are carried complete should at all times be correctly assembled and ready for immediate insertion in the submachine gun.

Twenty- or fifty-round magazines are also issued as spares; the former for use with submachine guns issued for use by cavalry motorcyclists and the latter for submachine guns issued for use by cavalry combat vehicle troops. The quantity of magazines issued per gun is based on the allowance of ammunition authorized.

The allowances of spare parts and of magazines are prescribed in SNL A-32.

2. (a) **General**.--Accessories include the tools required for disassembling and assembling and for the cleaning and preservation of the gun. They must not be used for any purpose, other than as prescribed. There are a number of accessories, the names or general chacteristics of which indicate their uses or applications. Therefore, detailed description or method of use of such items is not outlined herein. However, accessories-embodying special features or having special uses are described in 6 below.

(b) (1) *Brush, chamber cleaning, M6*.--The brush consists of a steel wire core with bristles, the core being twisted in a spiral to hold the bristles in place. It is used to clean the chamber of the submachine guns.

(2) *Brush, cleaning, caliber .45, MB*.---The brush consists of a brass wire core with bristles and tip. The core is twisted in a spiral and holds the bronze bristles in place. The brass tip which is threaded for attaching the brush to the cleaning rod is soldered to the end of the core.

(3) *Case, accessory and spare parts, M1918*.--This is a leather box-shaped case, approximately 2 $\frac{1}{4}$ inches wide, 3 $\frac{1}{2}$ inches high, and 5 $\frac{1}{2}$ inches long. It is used to carry

spare parts and a number of the smaller accessories.

(4) *Rod, cleaning, submachine gun.*--This consists of a long steel rod having a circular loop at one end and a cleaning patch slot at the other end. Permanently affixed to the cleaning patch end of the rod is a head having a threaded hole to receive the cleaning brush, caliber .45, M5.

(5) *Sling, gun, M1923 (webbing).*--The gun sling is fastened to the swivels provided on the gun. It consists of a long and short strap, either of which may be lengthened or shortened as desired to suit the particular man using it.

(b) *Thong.*--The thong consists of a tip with cleaning patch slot and a weight tied to the ends of a 30-inch length of cord. It is used in cleaning the bore of the submachine gun.

SECTION G. INDIVIDUAL SAFETY PRECAUTIONS

General rules.--

(a) Before firing--

1. Test trigger mechanism as "safe" and "single."

2. See that bore is clear and clean.

3. Work bolt back and forth rapidly several times to see that it is clean, well-oiled, and works freely.

4. Examine magazines and eliminate faulty ones.

5. See that each magazine is free from dirt and that it is properly loaded.

(b) Insert loaded magazine only on order of the commanding officer. Do not attach loaded magazine until ready to fire.

(c) Carry gun with bolt retracted and safety on "safe" until ordered to attach magazine, and keep safety on "safe" until gun is raised to fire.

(d) Keep the trigger finger outside trigger guard until gun is raised to fire.

(e) From time magazine is attached until gun is cleared and clearance checked, keep gun pointed toward target.

(f) For semiautomatic fire make certain that rocker pivot is set on "single" and the safety on "safe" before attaching magazine.

(g) For full automatic fire, make certain that rocker pivot is set on "full auto" and the safety on "safe" before attaching magazine.

(h) Habitually set the safety at "safe" while changing magazines and during lulls in firing.

(l) To clear gun, first remove magazine.

(j) At CEASE FIRING set the safety at "safe," remove magazine, and see that no cartridge remains in the chamber before turning away from the target.

(k) After gun has been cleared and checked for clearance, close the bolt on an empty chamber.

Chapter 4. MAGAZINE, RIFLE CALIBER .30, MODEL 1903

SECTION A. GENERAL

1. The Navy, which requires a small number of rifles compared with Army, uses in general the same type of rifle and ammunition as the Army and obtains this material from the War Department. This is in order to provide for interchangeability of material and to facilitate the supply.

2. Practically all military rifles in use at the present time have the same general features. They are bolt action magazine rifles of approximately .30 caliber fitted with knife bayonet, equipped with open sight for battle use, and weigh approximately 9 pounds. The bolt must be opened by hand, and the trigger must be pulled for each shot. The ammunition is usually furnished in clips and the magazine of the rifle holds one full clip.

The military rifle must be free from complications, ruggedly constructed, and capable of standing rough usage. Such refinements as telescopes sights, etc., cannot be used on rifles which are issued for general service.

3. The United States Army and Navy are equipped with the United States rifle caliber .30, model 1903. This rifle is usually referred to in the service as the Springfield rifle. The following are the essential features of this rifle:

Caliber, .30.
Weight, 9 pounds.
Weight of bayonet, 1 pound.
Weight of bullet, 172 grains.
Muzzle velocity, 2,700 feet per second.
Maximum powder pressure in chamber, 51,000 pounds.

Length of travel of bullet in bore, 21.70 inches.
Number of grooves in rifling, 4.
Twist of rifling, right hand, uniform 1 turn in 10 inches.
Sight radius, 22.12 inches.
Trigger pull, 4.25 to 5.5 pounds.
Maximum range at 45° elevation, about 5,500 yards.

Mechanical Operation of the Rifle

1. **Assembled parts and their operation**.--Most of the operating parts may be included under the bolt mechanism and the magazine mechanism.

2. (a) **The bolt mechanism** consists of the bolt, sleeve, sleeve lock, extractor, extractor collar, safety lock, firing pin, firing-pin sleeve, striker, and mainspring.

(b) The bolt moves backward and forward and rotates in the well of the receiver; it carries a cartridge, either from the magazine or one placed by hand in front of it, into the chamber and supports its head when fired.

(c) The sleeve unites the parts of the bolt mechanism, and its rotation with the bolt is prevented by the lugs on its sides coming in contact with the receiver.

(d) The hook of the extractor engages in the groove of the cartridge case and retains the head of the. latter in the countersink of the bolt until the case is ejected.

(e) The safety lock, when turned to the left, is inoperative; when turned to the right--which can only be done when the piece is cocked---the point of the spindle enters its notch in the bolt and locks the bolt; at the same time its cam forces the cocking piece slightly to the rear, out of contact with the sear, and locks the firing pin.

3. (a) The bolt mechanism operates as follows: To open the bolt, raise the handle until it comes in contact with the left side of the receiver and pull directly to the rear until the top locking lug strikes the cut-off.

(b) Raising the handle rotates the bolt and separates the locking lugs from their locking shoulders in the receiver, with which they have been brought into close contact by the powder pressure. This rotation causes the cocking cam of the bolt to force the firing pin to the rear, drawing the point of the striker into the bolt, rotation of the firing pin being prevented by the lug on the cocking piece projecting through the slot in the sleeve into its groove in the receiver. As the sleeve remains longitudinally stationary with reference to the bolt, this rearward motion of the firing pin, and consequently of the striker, will start the compression of the mainspring, since the rear end of the latter bears against the front end of the barrel of the sleeve and its front end against the rear end of the firing-pin sleeve.

(c) When the bolt handle strikes the receiver, the locking lugs have been disengaged, the firing pin has been forced to the rear until the sear notch of the cocking piece has passed the sear nose, the cocking piece nose has entered the cock notch in the rear end of the bolt, the sleeve lock has engaged its notch in the bolt, and the mainspring has been almost entirely compressed.

(d) During the rotation of the bolt a rear motion has been imparted to it by its extracting cam coming in contact with the extracting cam of the receiver, so that the cartridge case will be started from the chamber.

The bolt is then drawn directly to the rear, the parts being retained in position by the cocking piece nose remaining in the cock notch and locked by the sleeve lock engaging its notch in the bolt.

(e) To close the bolt, push the handle forward until the extracting cam on the bolt bears against the extracting cam on the receiver, thereby unlocking the sleeve from the bolt, and turn the handle down. As the handle is turned down the cams of the locking lugs bear against the locking shoulders in the receiver, and the bolt is forced slightly forward into its closed position. As all movement of the firing pin is prevented by the sear nose engaging the sear notch of the cocking piece, this forward movement of the bolt completes the compression of the mainspring, seats the cartridge in the chamber, and, in single loading, forces the hook of the extractor into the groove of the cartridge case. In loading from the magazine the hook of the extractor, rounded at its lower edge, engages in the groove of the top cartridge as it rises from the magazine under the action of the follower and magazine spring. The piece is then ready to fire.

4. (a) To pull the trigger, the finger piece must be drawn to the rear until contact with the receiver is transferred from its bearing to the heel, which gives a creep to the trigger, and then until the sear nose is withdrawn from in front of the cocking piece.

(b) Just before the bolt is drawn fully to the rear, the top locking lug strikes the heel of the ejector, throwing its point suddenly to the right in the lug slot. As the bolt moves fully to the rear, the rear face of the cartridge case strikes against

the ejector point and the case is ejected, slightly upward and to the right, from the receiver,

(c) Double loading from the magazine is prevented by the extractor engaging the cartridge ease as soon as it rises from the magazine and holding its head against the face of the bolt until ejected.

(d) It will be noted that in this system of bolt mechanism the compression of the mainspring, the seating of the cartridge in, and starting of the empty case from the chamber are done entirely by the action of the cams.

(e) The piece may be cocked either by raising the bolt handle until it strikes the left side of the receiver and then immediately turning it down or by pulling the cocking piece directly to the rear.

(f) In firing, unless the bolt handle is turned fully down, the cam on the cocking piece will strike the cocking cam on the bolt and the energy of the mainspring will be expended in closing the bolt instead of on the primer; this prevents the possibility of a cartridge being fired until the bolt is fully closed. The opening and closing of the bolt should each be done by one continuous motion.

5. **The magazine mechanism** includes the floor plate, follower, magazine spring, and cut-off.

(a) To charge the magazine, see that the cut-off is turned up, showing "On," draw the bolt fully to the rear, insert the cartridges from a clip, or from the hand, and close the bolt. To charge the magazine from a clip, place either end of a loaded clip in its seat in the receiver and with the thumb of the right hand press the cartridges down into the magazine until the top cartridge is caught by the right edge of the receiver. The cartridge ramp guides the bullet and cartridge case into the chamber. The magazine can be filled, if partly filled, by inserting cartridges one by one. Pushing the bolt forward, after charging the magazine, ejects the clip.

(b) When the cut-off is turned down, the magazine is "off". The bolt cannot be drawn fully back, and its front end projecting over the rear end of the upper cartridge holds it down in the magazine below the action of the bolt. The magazine mechanism then remains inoperative, and the arm can be used as a single loader, the cartridges in the magazine being held in

reserve. The arm can readily be used as a single loader with the magazine empty.

(c) When the cut-off is turned up, the magazine is "on." The bolt can be drawn fully to the rear, permitting the top cartridge to rise high enough to be caught by the bolt in its forward movement. As the bolt is closed this cartridge is pushed forward into the chamber, being held up during its passage by the pressure of those below. The last one in the magazine is held up by the follower, the rib on which directs it into the chamber.

(d) In magazine fire, after the last cartridge has been fired and the bolt drawn fully to the rear, the follower rises and holds the bolt open to show that the magazine is empty.

SECTION B. PRECAUTIONS

1. If it is desired to carry the piece cocked, with a cartridge in the chamber, the bolt mechanism should be secured by turning the safety lock to the right. Under no circumstances should the firing pin be let down by hand on a cartridge in the chamber.

2. To obtain positive ejection, and to insure the bolt catching the top cartridge in magazine, when loading from the magazine, the bolt must be drawn fully to the rear in opening it.

3. When the bolt is closed, or slightly forward, the cut-off may be turned up or down as desired. When the bolt is in its rearmost position to pass from loading from the magazine to single loading it is necessary to force the top cartridge or follower below the reach of the bolt, to push the bolt slightly forward, and to turn the cut-off down, showing "Off."

4. In case of a misfire it is unsafe to draw back the bolt immediately, as it may be a case of hangfire. In such cases the piece should be cocked by drawing back the cocking piece.

5. It is essential for the proper working and preservation of all cams that they be kept lubricated.

6. Never fire the rifle with grease or any obstruction in the bore whether near the breech or the muzzle. Practically all cases of burst barrels can be traced to some obstruction left in the bore, such as a cleaning patch, mud, or the like.

SECTION C

(A) Dismounting and Assembling

1. The bolt and magazine mechanism can be dismounted without removing the stock. The latter should never be done, except for making repairs, and then only by some selected and instructed man.

2. (a) To dismount bolt mechanism, place the cut-off at the center notch, cock the arm and turn the safety lock to a vertical position, raise the bolt handle and draw out the bolt.

(b) Hold bolt in left hand, press sleeve lock in with thumb of right hand to unlock sleeve from bolt, and unscrew sleeve by turning to the left.

(c) Hold sleeve between forefinger and thumb of the left hand, draw cocking piece back with middle finger and thumb of right hand, turn safety lock down to the left with the forefinger of the right hand in order to allow the cocking piece to move forward in sleeve and thus partially relieving the tension of mainspring; with the cocking piece against the breast, draw back the firing-pin sleeve with the forefinger and thumb of right hand and hold it in this position while removing the striker with the left hand, remove firing pin sleeve and mainspring, pull firing pin out of sleeve, turn the extractor to the right, forcing its tongue out of its groove in the front of the bolt, and force the extractor forward and off the bolt.

(d) To assemble bolt mechanism, grasp with the left hand the rear of the bolt, handle up, and turn the extractor collar with the thumb and forefinger of the right hand until its lug is on a line with the safety lug on the bolt; take the extractor in the right hand and insert the lug on the collar in the undercuts in the extractor by pushing the extractor to rear until its tongue comes in contact with the rim on the face of the bolt (a slight pressure with the left thumb on the top of the rear part of the extractor assists in this operation) ; turn the extractor to the right until it is over the right lug; take the bolt in the right hand and press the hook of the extractor against the butt plate or some rigid object, until the tongue on the extractor enters its groove in the bolt.

(e) With the safety lock turned down to the left to permit the firing pin to enter the sleeve as far as possible, assemble the sleeve

and firing pin; place the cocking piece against the breast and put on mainspring, firing-pin sleeve, and striker. Hold the cocking piece between the thumb and forefinger of the left hand, and pressing the striker point against some substance, not hard enough to injure it, force the cocking piece back until the safety lock can be turned to the vertical position with the right hand; insert the firing pin in the bolt and screw up the sleeve (by turning it to the right) until the sleeve lock enters its notch on the bolt.

(f) See that the cut-off is at the center notch; hold the piece under floor plate in the fingers of the left hand, the thumb extending over the left side of the receiver; take bolt in right hand with safety lock in a vertical position and safety lug up; press rear end of follower down with left thumb and push bolt into the receiver, lower bolt handle; turn safety lock and cut-off down to the left with right hand.

3. (a) **To dismount magazine mechanism**.--With the bullet end of a cartridge press on the floor plate catch (through the hole in the floor plate), at the same time drawing the bullet to the rear; this releases the floor plate.

(b) Raise the rear end of the first limb of the magazine spring high enough to clear the lug on the floor plate and draw it out of its mortise; proceed in the same manner to remove the follower.

(c) To assemble magazine spring and follower to floor plate, reverse operation of dismounting. Insert the follower and magazine spring in the magazine, place the tenon on the front end of the floor plate in its recess in the magazine, then place the lug on the rear end of the floor plate in its slot in the guard, and press the rear end of the floor plate forward and inward at the same time, forcing the floor plate into its seat in the guard.

4. **Complete dismounting**.--The bolt and magazine mechanism having been dismounted, proceed as follows:

(a) Turn safety lock to dismounting bevel on sleeve and remove it by striking the thumbpiece a light blow.

(b) To dismount the sleeve lock, drive out sleeve lock pin from the top and remove lock and spring, being careful not to lose the spring.

(c) Remove front sight pin and remove front sight.

(d) Press in rear end of lower band spring and drive forward the lower band by a few sharp blows on the lug and then on top with a hardwood block.

(e) Remove upper band screw and drive upper band forward, in the same manner prescribed for the lower band.

(f) Move upper band forward on barrel until stopped by movable stud, and then remove lower band, by slipping it over upper band and movable stud. To remove upper band entirely from barrel requires the removal of the front sight screw and the movable stud.

(g) Draw hand guard forward until free from the fixed base and remove.

(h) Remove guard screws and guard. It may be necessary to tap gently on the front and rear of the guard bow to loosen.

(i) Remove barrel and receiver from stock.

(j) To remove the lower band spring, drive its spindle out of its hole in the stock from the left.

(k) Unscrew the butt swivel, consisting of the plate, swivel, and pin, permanently assembled, which is issued complete.

(l) Unscrew butt-plate screws and remove butt plate from stock.

(m) Unscrew butt-plate spring screw and remove the butt plate; spring; drive out butt-plate pin and remove butt plate cap.

(n) Remove cut-off by loosening the screw in the end of the thumbpiece until it disengages the groove in the cut-off spindle; insert the blade of a screw driver in the notch in the rear end of the spindle and force it out. Remove the spring and tho plunger, being careful not to lose them.

(o) Remove the ejector by driving out the ejector pin from tho upper side.

(p) Remove sear and trigger by driving out the sear pin from the right, being careful not to lose the sear spring.

(q) Remove trigger from sear by driving out the trigger pin from either side.

(r) Remove floor-plate catch and spring by driving out tho pin from either side.

(s) Remove bolt stop by inserting a small punch or end of striker in the hole in the left end and forcing it from its pocket.

The leaf should never be removed from the movable base except for the purpose of making repairs.

The fixed base and the fixed stud should never be removed from the barrel.

(B) Assembling the Rifle

1. Reverse and follow in inverse order the operations of dismounting. In assembling the sleeve lock to the sleeve, be careful to compress the lock and spring while drh ing in the pin from the bottom of the sleeve.

2. To assemble the safety lock and sleeve, insert the safety-lock spindle in its hole in the sleeve as far as it will go; then, with the thumbpiece vertical and pressed against some rigid object, introduce the point of the tool provided for this purpose between the safety-lock spindle and the safety-lock plunger, forcing the latter into the thumbpiece until it slips over the edge of the sleeve. Further pressure on the safety-lock thumbpiece, together with the gradual withdrawal of the tool, will complete the assembling.

3. The floor-plate spring and the cut-off spring are alike, except in length. The latter being the longer, care should be taken not to substitute one for the other.

SECTION D. CARE OF THE RIFLE

(A) Cleaning

1. The proper care of the bore requires conscientious, careful work, but it pays well in reduced labor of cleaning and in prolonged accuracy, life of the barrel, and better results in target practice. Briefly stated, the care of the bore consists of removing the fouling resulting from firing to obtain a chemically clean surface, and coating this surface with a film of oil to prevent rusting. The fouling, which results from firing, is of two kinds-- one, the products of combustion of the powder and primer composition; two, cupro-nickel scraped off (under the abrading action of irregularities or grit in the bore.) The former, because of its acid reaction, is highly corrosive; that is, it will induce rust and must be removed. Metal fouling of itself is inactive, but may cover powder fouling and prevent the action of cleaning agents

until removed, and when accumulated in noticeable quantities it reduces the accuracy of the rifle.

2. **Methods of removing powder fouling**.--The best method to remove powder fouling is by the use of boiling or hot water, if obtainable, and in the absence of hot water, cold water should be used. The barrel should be washed out five or six times by pouring a cupful at each washing through the barrel with a funnel. After washing, a bristle brush should be run through the barrel several times and then the bore should be dried out by running dry flannel patches through it. After it is thoroughly dry, it should be oiled with sperm oil.

Powder fouling may be readily removed by scrubbing with hot sal soda solution, but this solution has no effect on the metal fouling of cupro-nickel. It is therefore necessary to remove all metal fouling before assurance can be had that all powder fouling has been removed and the bore safely oiled. Normally, after firing a barrel in good condition, the metal fouling is so slight as to be hardly perceptible. It is merely a smear of infinitesimal thickness, easily removed by solvents of cupro-nickel. However, due to pitting, the presence of dust, other abrasives, or accumulation, metal fouling may occur in clearly visible flakes or patches of much greater thickness and much more difficult to remove.

In cleaning the bore after firing, it is well to proceed as follows: Swab out the bore with sal soda solution (see below) to remove powder fouling. A convenient method is to insert the muzzle of the rifle into the can containing the sal soda solution and, with the cleaning rod inserted from the breech, pump the barrel full a few times. Remove and dry with a couple of patches. Examine the bore to see that there are in evidence no patches of metal fouling which, if present, can be readily detected by the naked eye, then swab out with the swabbing solution, a. dilute metal-fouling solution. (See below.) The amount of swabbing required with the swabbing solution can be determined only by experience, assisted by the color of the patches. Swabbing should be continued, however, as long as the wiping patch-is discolored by a bluish-green stain. Normally a couple of minutes' work is sufficient. Dry thoroughly and oil.

3. **To oil the barrel**.--The proper method of oiling the barrel is as follows: Wipe the cleaning rod dry; select a clean, patch

and thoroughly saturate it with sperm oil; scrub the bore with the patch, finally drawing the patch smoothly from the muzzle to the breech, allowing the cleaning rod to turn with the rifling. The bore will be found now to be smooth and bright, so that any subsequent rust and sweating can be easily detected by inspection.

4. **Methods of removing metal fouling**.--If the patches of metal fouling are seen upon visual inspection of the bore, the standard metal-fouling solution prepared as hereinafter prescribed

must be used. After scrubbing out with the sal soda solution, plug the bore from the breach with a cork at the front end of the chamber, or where the rifling begins. Slip a 2-inch section of rubber hose over the muzzle down to the sight and fill with the standard solution -to at least one half inch above the muzzle of the barrel. Let it stand for 30 minutes, pour out the solution, remove the hose and breech plug, and swab out thoroughly with sal soda solution to neutralize and remove all trace of ammonia and powder fouling. Wipe the barrel clean and dry; then oil. With few exceptions, one application is sufficient, but if all fouling is not removed as determined by careful visual inspection of the bore and of the wiping patches, repeat as described above.

5. After properly cleaning with one of the solutions, as has just been described, the bore should be clean and safe to oil and put away; but as a measure of safety a patch should always be run through the bore on the next day, and the bore and wiping patch examined to insure that cleaning has been properly accomplished. The bore should then be oiled, as described above.

6. If the solutions are not available, the barrel should be scrubbed, as already described, with the sal soda solution, dried, and oiled with a light oil. At the end of 24 hours it should again be cleaned, when it will usually be found to have "sweated," that is, rust having formed under the smear of metal fouling where powder fouling was present, the surface is puffed up. Usually a second cleaning is sufficient, but to insure safety it should be again examined at the end of a few days before final oiling. The swabbing solution should always be used, if available, for it must be remembered that each puff when the bore "sweats" is an incipient rust pit.

A clean dry surface having been obtained, to prevent rust it is necessary to coat every portion of this surface with a film of neutral oil. If the protection required is but temporary and the arm is to. be cleaned or fired in a few days, a sperm oil may be used. This is easily applied and easily removed, but has not sufficient body to hold its surface for more than a few days. If rifles are to be prepared for storage or shipment, a heavier oil must be used.

(B) Preparing Arms for Storage or Shipment

In preparing arms for storage or shipment they should be cleaned with particular care, using the metal-fouling solution as described above. Care should be taken, insured by careful inspection on succeeding day or days, that the cleaning is properly done and all traces of ammonia solution removed. The bore is then ready to be coated with heavy oil. In order, therefore, to insure that every part of the surface is coated with a film of oil, the heavy oil should be warmed. Apply the heavy oil first with a brush; then, with the breech plugged, fill the barrel to the muzzle, pour out the surplus, remove the plug, and allow to drain. It is believed that more rifles are ruined by improper preparation for storage than from any other cause. If the bore is not clean when oiled; that is, if powder fouling is present or rust has started, a half inch of heavy oil on the outside will not stop its action, and the barrel will be ruined. Remember that the surface must be perfectly cleaned before the heavy oil is applied. If the instructions as given above are carefully followed, arms may be stored for years without harm.

(C) Preparation of Solutions

1. **Sal-soda solution**.--This should be a saturated solution of sal soda (carbonate of soda). A strength of at least 20 percent is necessary. Soda ash may be substituted for sal soda, in which case it should be borne in mind that 6 ounces of soda ash is equivalent to 1 pound of sal soda.

> Sal soda, one-fourth pound, or 4 heaping tablespoonfuls.
> Water, 1 pint.
> The sal soda will dissolve more readily in hot water.

--178--

2. **Swabbing solution**.--Ammonium persulphate, 60 grains, tablespoonful smoothed off.

> Ammonia (28 percent), 6 ounces, or $^3/_8$ of a pint, or 12 tablespoonfuls.
> Water, 4 ounces, or $^1/_4$ pint, or 8 tablespoonfuls.

Dissolve the ammonia persulphate in the water and add the ammonia. Keep in tightly corked bottle, pouring out only what is necessary at the time.

3. **Standard metal-fouling solution**.--Ammonium persulphate 1 ounce or 2 medium-heaping tablespoonfuls.

> Ammonium carbonate, 200 grains or 1 heaping table-spoonful.
> Ammonia (28 percent), 6 ounces, or $^3/_8$ pint, or 12 tablespoonfuls.
> Water, 4 ounces, or $^1/_4$ pint, or 8 tablespoonfuls.

Powder the persulphate and carbonate together, dissolve in the water and add the ammonia; mix thoroughly and allow to stand for 1 hour before using. It should be kept in a strong bottle, tightly corked. The solution should not be used more than twice, and used solution should not be mixed with unused solution, but should be bottled separately. The solution, when mixed, should be used within 30 days. Care should be used in mixing and using this solution to prevent injury to the rifle. The ammonia solution should not be used in a warm barrel. An experienced petty officer should mix the solution and superintend its use.

Neither of these ammonia solutions has any appreciable action on steel when not exposed to the air, but if allowed to evaporate on steel they attack it rapidly. Care should, therefore, be taken that none spills on the mechanism and that the barrel is washed out promptly with soda solution. The first application of soda solution removes the greater portion of the powder fouling and permits a more effective and economical use of the ammonia solution. These ammonia solutions are expensive and should be used economically.

The standard metal-fouling solution is preferred when available.

SECTION E. GENERAL REMARKS

1. It is a fact recognized by all that a highly polished steel surface rusts much less easily than one which is roughened; also that a barrel which is pitted fouls much more rapidly than one which is smooth. Every effort, therefore, should be made to prevent the formation of pits, which are merely enlarged rust spots, and which not only affect the accuracy of the arm but increase the labor of cleaning.

2. The chambers of rifles are frequently neglected because they are not readily inspected. Care should be taken to see that they are cleaned as thoroughly as the bore. A roughened chamber delays greatly the rapidity of fire, and not infrequently causes shells to stick.

3. Rifles should always be cleaned from the breech, thus avoiding possibly injury to the rifling at the muzzle which would affect the shooting adversely. If the bore for a length of 6 inches at the muzzle is perfect, a minor injury near the chamber will have little effect on the accuracy of the rifle. The rifle should be cleaned as soon as conditions permit. The fouling is easier to remove then, and if left longer it will corrode the barrel.

4.If gas escapes at the base of the cartridge, it will probably enter the well of the bolt through the striker hole. In this case the bolt mechanism must be dismounted and the parts and well of the bolt thoroughly cleaned.

5.Before assembling the bolt mechanism, the firing pin, the barrel of the sleeve, the body of striker, the well of the bolt, and all cams should be wiped with an oiled rag.

6.Many of the parts can generally be cleaned with dry rags. All parts after cleaning should be wiped with an oiled rag.

7.The best method of applying oil is to rub with a piece of cotton cloth upon which a few drops of oil have been placed, thereby avoiding the use of an unnecessary amount of oil; this method will, even in the absence of the oiler, serve for .the cams and bearings, which should be kept continually oiled.

8.Any part that may appear to move hard can generally be freed by the use of a little oil.

9.The stock and hand guard may be coated with raw linseed oil and polished by rubbing with the hand.

10.Sperm oil should only be used for lubricating metallic bearing and contact surfaces.

Chapter 5. AUTOMATIC PISTOL, CALIBER .45, MODEL 1911

SECTION A. GENERAL

1. The Navy, which requires a small number of pistols as compared with the Army, uses in general the same type of pistol and ammunition as the Army and obtains this material from that arm of the service. This is in order to provide for interchangeability of material and to facilitate the supply.

2. The United States Army and Navy are equipped with the United States automatic pistol, caliber .45, model 1911. The following are the essential features of this pistol:

Weight, 2 pounds 7 ounces
Trigger pull, 6 to 7 $^{1}/_{2}$pounds
Total length, 8.593 inches
Length of barrel, 5.025 inches
Diameter of bore, 0.445 inch
Number of grooves, 6
Width of grooves, 0.1522 inch
Depth of grooves, 0.003 inch
Width of lands, 0.072 inch
Twist, left-handed, one turn in 16 inches
Front sight above axis of bore, 0.5597 inch
Maximum range, 45° elevation, 1,955 yards.

SECTION B. DETAILED DESCRIPTION

1. The three principal parts of the pistol are the receiver, barrel, and slide.

2. (a) The receiver has suitable guides for the reciprocating slide, and a hollow handle in which the magazine is inserted from below and locked in place by the magazine catch. The magazine may be removed by pressure upon the checkered end of the magazine catch which projects from the left side of the receiver in a convenient position for operation by the thumb.

--181--

Figure 20.--.45 cal. Automatic pistol.

(b) The magazine catch engages with and locks the magazine under the pressure of the magazine catch spring and is held in the receiver by means of the magazine catch lock.

(c) The magazine consists of a magazine tube closed at the bottom by means of the magazine base secured with two magazine pins. The magazine base has riveted to it the magazine loop, to which the magazine tube is contained the magazine spring, exerting a pressure against the magazine follower which serves as a movable platform for the cartridges.

(d) Secured at each end of the handle of receiver on both sides are screw bushings, onto which are fitted the stocks and into which, to secure the latter, are screwed the stock screws.

(e) In front of the handle of receiver, in the trigger guard, is seated the trigger; in rear and above the handle the firing mechanism is arranged, comprising the hammer mounted on the hammer pin, the sear and (automatic) disconnector mounted together on the sear pin, the grip safety, and safety lock; also the mainspring and the sear spring. The mainspring is seated within the mainspring housing and there held by the mainspring-cap pin. The mainspring housing also contains the mainspring cap and the housing-pin retainer. The conical point of the latter protrudes slightly into the hole for the housing pin, engaging with the groove around the middle thereof, thereby holding the housing pin in place. Into the base of the mainspring housing is fitted the lanyard loop secured by the lanyard-loop pin.

(f) The sear spring has a rib on its lower end which fits into a slot in the rear wall of the magazine seat and keeps the spring from moving vertically. The mainspring housing, bearing against the rear of the spring, locks it in position and gives to it the required tension. The hammer strut is attached to the hammer in rear of its pivot by means of the hammer-strut pin. Its lower end rests in the mainspring cap.

(g) Above the handle on the left side are the slide stop plunger and safety-lock plunger, with their ends protruding from the front and rear, respectively, of the plunger tube. The plunger spring is seated between the plungers within the plunger tube and yieldingly holds them in position.

(h) The ejector is seated at the top of the receiver near the rear end, at the left side. It is held in place by the ejector pin.

(i) The top of the receiver forward of the trigger guard has a semitubular extension which forms the seat for the rear portion of the recoil spring.

3. (a) The barrel of the pistol is largest at the breech, and at the top has two transverse locking ribs, the forward edges of which, together with the forward edge of the breech portion, serve

to positively interlock the barrel with the slide when in the firing position. At its rear is an extension which facilitates the entrance of the cartridge from the magazine into the chamber. The rear end of the barrel is attached to the receiver by the link, link pin, and the pin of the slide stop, and, swinging thereon, can move a limited distance lengthwise and also in a vertical plane.

(b) The side walls of the slide overlap the sides of the receiver, and being provided with longitudinal ribs corresponding with similar grooves at the top of the receiver, the slide is free to move longitudinally.

4. (a) The slide has at its front end a strong tubular abutment which is in line with the forward portion of the receiver, and which permits the slide to move to the rear until the rear end of the abutment comes in contact with the flange of the recoil-spring guide against the shoulder in the receiver at its forward end, thereby positively limiting the rearward movement of the slide. Therefore the latter necessarily is assembled to. the receiver from the front, and is prevented from being thrown rearward from the receiver under any circumstances.

(b) In the abutment at the front end of the slide is seated the forward end of the recoil spring fitted into the plug. The rear end of the recoil spring fitted onto the recoil-spring guide, rests against the shoulder in the front end of the receiver.

(c) On the top of slide are mounted the front sight and rear sight.

(d) The barrel bushing fits into the front end of the slide, supports the muzzle end of the barrel, and holds the plug and recoil spring in place.

(e) When the slide and the barrel therein are mounted upon the receiver and the slide stop is in its place, so that the pin part of the slide stop locks the barrel to the receiver through the link, the slide is thereby positively locked in place upon the receiver.

(f) The firing pin, firing-pin spring, and (shell) extractor are carried in the rear end of the slide and locked by the firing-pin

spring. By pressing the firing pin forward so as to clear the firing-pin stop, the latter is released and may be removed downwardly, leaving both firing pin and extractor free for removal.

(g) The slide stop consists of the pin part, which serves as a pivot and passes through the link, and a body, on which is a thumb piece, for releasing the slide from the open position. 5. (a) The safety lock consists of a thin plate, a projecting pin, a thumbpiece, and a projecting stud. The pin part serves as a pivot for the safety lock and is at the same time a pivot for the grip safety. The upper corner of the plate has an angle which will fit into a correspondingly shaped recess in the slide. When the slide is in this forward position and the hammer is cocked, the safety lock may be pushed up manually by means of the thumbpiece, thereby positively locking the hammer and the slide. While the safety lock is being pushed up into the locking position the stud on the safety lock is being carried upward, and it finally stands in rear of the lower arm of the sear blocking the sear and causing the locking of the hammer. If the safety lock is pressed down so as to release the slide, the projecting stud of the safety lock clears the sear, permitting the sear to be operated by the trigger thereby causing the release of the hammer if the grip safety is pressed inward, as by the hand grasping the handle of the pistol, and the trigger is pulled.

(b) The grip safety is pivoted in the upper part of the receiver. Its lower part projects from the rear face of the handle under pressure of the short leaf of the sear spring, thereby locking the trigger whenever the handle of the pistol is released. But when the handle is grasped, as in the firing position, the grip safety releases the trigger without requiring the attention or thought of the firer.

(c) The (automatic) disconnector is mounted in the receiver at the rear of the magazine seat. In the under side of the slide and near its rear and a recess is provided which stands above the top of the disconnector when the slide is in the forward firing position. With the slide in this position the disconnector is raised to its operative position by the center leaf of the sear spring, and it then will transmit the movement of the trigger to the sear. The forward surfaces of the recess of the slide and of the projecting end of the disconnector are inclining, so that the rearward movement of the slide depresses the connector until the slide again

returns to its forward position. In this depressed position of the •disconnector the trigger is disconnected from the sear, allowing the sear to reengage the hammer. This arrangement automatically and positively prevents firing of the pistol except when all its parts are in the fully closed and locked firing position, and it also prevents more than one shot from following each pull of the trigger.

SECTION C. TO DISMOUNT AND ASSEMBLE THE PISTOL

1. Remove the magazine by pressing the magazine catch.

2. Press the plug inward and turn the barrel bushing to the right until the plug and the end of the recoil spring protrude from their seat, releasing the tension of the spring. As the plug is allowed to protrude from its seat, the finger or thumb should be kept over it, so that it will not jump away and be lost or strike the operator. Draw the slide rearward until the smaller rear recess in its lower left edge stands above the projection on the thumbpiece of the slide stop; press gently against the end of the pin of the slide stop which protrudes from the right side of the receiver above the trigger guard and remove the slide stop. This releases the link, allowing the barrel, with the link and the slide, to be drawn forward together from the receiver, carrying with them the barrel bushing, recoil spring, plug, and recoil-spring guide.

3. Remove these parts from the slide by withdrawing the recoil-spring guide from the rear of the recoil spring, then draw the plug and the recoil spring forward from the slide. Turn plug to right to remove from recoil spring. Turn the barrel bushing to the left until it may be drawn forward from the slide. This releases the barrel, which, with the link, may be drawn forward from the slide, and by pushing out the link pin the link is released from the barrel.

4. Press the rear end of the firing pin forward until it clears the firing pin stop, which is then drawn downward from its seat in the slide; the firing pin, firing pin spring, and tractor are then removed from the rear of the slide.

5. The safety lock is readily withdrawn from the receiver by cocking the hammer and pushing from the right on the pin part

or pulling outward on the thumbpiece of the safety lock when it is midway between its upper and lower positions. The cocked hammer is then lowered and removed after removing the hammer pin from the left side, of the receiver. The housing pin is then pushed out from the right side of the receiver, which allows the mainspring housing to be withdrawn downward and the grip safety rearward from the handle. The sear spring may then be removed. By pushing out the sear pin from the right to the left side of the receiver the sear and the disconnector are released.

6. To remove the mainspring, mainspring cap, and housing-pin retainer from the mainspring housing, compress the main spring and push out the small mainspring cap pin.

7. To remove the magazine catch from the receiver, its checkered left end must be pressed inward, when the right end of the magazine catch will project so far from the right side of the receiver that it may be rotated one-half turn. This movement will release the magazine-catch lock from its seat in the receiver, when the magazine catch, the magazine-catch lock, and the magazine-catch spring may be removed.

8. With the improved design of magazine-catch lock, the operation of dismounting the magazine catch is simplified, in that when the magazine catch has been pressed inward the magazine-catch lock is turned by means of a screw driver or the short leaf of the sear spring a quarter turn to the left, when the magazine catch with its contents can be removed. The improved design will be recognized from the fact that the head of the magazine-catch lock is slotted.

9. The trigger can then be removed rearwardly from the receiver.

10. The hammer strut or the long arm of a screw driver can be used to push out all the pins except the mainspring-cap pin, lanyard loop pin, and ejector pin.

11. **To assemble the pistol**, proceed in the reverse order.

12. It should be noted that the disconnector and sear are assembled as follows: Place the cylindrical part of the disconnector in its hole in the receiver, with the flat face of the lower part of the disconnector resting against the yoke of the trigger. Then place the sear, lugs downward, so that it straddles the

disconnector. The sear pin is then inserted in place, so that it passes through both the disconnector and the sear.

13. The sear, disconnector, and hammer being in place and the hammer down, to replace the sear spring locate its lower end in the cut in the receiver, with the end of the long leaf resting on the sear; then insert the mainspring housing until its lower end projects below the frame about one-eighth of an inch, replace the grip safety, cock the hammer, and replace the safety lock; then lower the cocked hammer, push the mainspring housing home, and insert the housing pin.

14. In assembling the safety lock to the receiver, use the tip of the magazine follower or a screw driver to press the safety-lock plunger home, thus allowing the seating of the safety lock. It should be remembered that when assembling the safety lock the hammer must be. cocked.

15. When replacing the slide and barrel in the receiver, care must be taken that the link is tilted forward as far as possible and that the link pin is in place.

SECTION D

(A) Method of Operation

1. A loaded magazine is placed in the handle and the slide drawn fully back and released, thus bringing the first cartridge into the chamber (if the slide is open, push down the slide stop to let the slide go forward.) The hammer is thus cocked and the pistol is ready for firing.

2. If it is desired to make the pistol ready for instant use, and for firing with the least possible delay the maximum number of shots, draw back the slide, insert a cartridge by hand into the chamber of the barrel, allow the slide to close, then lock the slide and the cocked hammer by pressing the safety lock upward, and insert a loaded magazine. The slide and hammer being thus positively locked, the pistol may be carried safely at full cock, and it is only necessary to press down the safety lock (which is located within easy reach of the thumb) when raising the pistol to the firing position.

3. The grip safety is provided with an extending horn, which not only serves as a guard to prevent the hand of the shooter

from slipping upward and being struck or injured by the hammer, but also aids in accurate shooting by keeping the hand in the same position for each shot, and, furthermore, permits the lowering of the cocked hammer with one hand by automatically pressing in the grip safety when the hammer is drawn slightly beyond the cocked position. In order to release the hammer, the grip safety must be pressed in before the trigger is pulled.

(B) Safety Devices

1. It is impossible for the firing pin to discharge or even-touch the primer, except on receiving the full blow of the hammer.

2. The pistol is provided with two automatic safety devices.

3. The automatic disconnector, which positively prevents the release of the hammer unless the slide and barrel are in the forward position and safely interlocked; this device also controls the fining and prevents more than one shot from following each pull of the trigger.

4. The automatic grip safety at all times locks the trigger unless the handle is firmly grasped and the grip safety pressed in.

5. The pistol is in addition provided with a safety lock by which the closed slide and the cocked hammer can be at will positively locked in position.

(C) Operation in Detail

1. The magazine may be charged with any number of cartridges from one to seven.

2. The charged magazine is inserted in the handle and the slide drawn once to the rear. This movement cocks the hammer, compresses the recoil spring, and, when the slide reaches the rear position, the magazine follower raises the upper cartridge into the path of the slide. The slide is then released and, being forced forward by the recoil spring, carries the first cartridge into the chamber of the barrel. As the slide approaches its forward position it encounters the rear extension of the barrel and forces the barrel forward; the rear end of the barrel swings upward on the link, turning on the muzzle end as on a fulcrum. When the slide and barrel reach their forward position they are

positively locked together by the locking ribs on the barrel, and their joint forward movement is arrested by the barrel lug encountering the pin on the slide stop.

3. The pistol is then ready for firing.

4. When the hammer is cocked, the hammer strut moves downward, compressing the

mainspring, and the sear, under action of the long leaf of the sear spring, engages its nose in the notch on the hammer.

5. In order that the pistol may be fired, the following conditions must exist: The grip safety must be pressed in, leaving the trigger free to move; the slide must be in its forward position, properly interlocked with the barrel, so that the disconnector is held in the recess on the under side of the slide under the action of the sear spring, transmitting in this position any motion of the trigger to the sear; the safety lock must be down, in the unlocked position, so that the sear will be unlocked and free to release the hammer, and the slide will be free to move back.

6. On pulling the trigger the sear is moved and the released hammer strikes the firing pin, which transmits the blow to the primer of the cartridge. The pressure of the gases generated in the barrel, by the explosion of the powder in the cartridge, is exerted in a forward direction against the bullet, driving it through the bore, and in rearward direction against the face of the slide, driving the latter and the barrel to the rear together. The downward swinging movement of the barrel unlocks it from the slide, and the barrel is then stopped in its lowest position. The slide continues to move to the rear, opening the breech, cocking the hammer, extracting and ejecting the empty shell, and compressing the recoil spring, until it--the slide-- reaches its rearmost position, when another cartridge is raised in front of it and forced into the chamber of the barrel by the return movement of the slide under pressure of the recoil spring.

7. The weight and consequently the inertia of the slide, augmented by that of the barrel, is so many times greater than that of the bullet that the latter has been given its maximum velocity and has been driven from the muzzle of the barrel before the slide and barrel have recoiled to the point where the barrel commences its unlocking movement. This construction, therefore, delays the opening of the breech of the barrel until after the bullet has left the muzzle and therefore practically prevents

--190--

the escape of any of the powder gases to the rear after the breech has been opened.

8. This factor of safety is further increased by the tension of the recoil spring and mainspring, both of which oppose the rearward movement of the slide.

9. While the comparatively great weight of the slide of this pistol insures safety against premature opening of the breech, it also insures operation of the pistol, because at the point of the rearward opening movement, where the barrel is unlocked and stopped, the heavy slide has attained a momentum which is sufficient to carry it through its complete opening movement and makes the pistol ready for another shot.

10. When the magazine has been emptied, the pawl-shaped slide stop will be raised by the magazine follower under action of the magazine spring into the front recess on the lower left side of the slide, thereby locking the slide in the open position, and serving as an indicator to remind the shooter that the empty magazine must be replaced by a charged one before the

firing can be continued.

11. Pressure upon the magazine catch quickly releases the empty magazine from the handle and permits the insertion of a loaded magazine.

12. To release the slide from the open position, it is only necessary to press upon the thumbpiece of the slide stop, then the slide will go forward to its closed position, carrying a cartridge from the previously inserted magazine into the barrel and making the pistol ready for firing again.

SECTION E. IMPORTANT POINTS

1. Never place the trigger finger within the trigger guard until it is intended to fire and the pistol is pointed toward the target!

2. Do not carry the pistol in the holster with the hammer cocked and safety lock on, except in an emergency. If the pistol is so carried in the holster, cocked and safety lock on, the butt of the pistol should be rotated away from the body when withdrawing the pistol from the holster, in order to avoid displacing the safety lock.

3. The trigger should be pulled with the forefinger. If the trigger is pulled with the second finger, the forefinger extending

--191--

along the side of the receiver is apt to press against the projecting pin of the slide stop and cause a jam when the slide recoils.

4. Care must be exercised in inserting the magazine to insure its engaging with the magazine catch.

5. Pressure must be entirely relieved from the trigger after each shot, in order that the trigger may reengage with the sear.

6. To remove cartridges not fired, disengage the magazine slightly and then extract the cartridge in the barrel by drawing back the slide.

7. The pistol must be kept clean, free from rust, and properly oiled. Excessive oil left in the mechanism will cause the parts to gum and work stiffly.

8. Care must be exercised to insure that the disconnector is properly assembled to the sear.

9. The hammer should not be snapped when the pistol is partially disassembled.

10. The grips need never be removed, as the pistol can be dismounted and assembled without removing them.

11. Use no hammer either in assembling or dismounting the pistol.

12. Magazine: Reasonable care should be taken to see that the magazine is not dented or otherwise damaged.

13. Never insert the magazine and strike it smartly with the hand to force it home, as this may spring the base or the inturning lips at the top. It should be inserted by a quick continuous movement.

14. Cleaning solutions and methods are the same as those followed for cleaning the magazine rifle.

Chapter 6. MK. 18 MOD. 1 21-INCH LIGHTWEIGHT DECK-TYPE TORPEDO TUBE AND AUXILIARY EQUIPMENT

Operating Instructions--General

1. The torpedo boat is designed to carry four torpedoes in tubes and to discharge them by expansion of ignited gun powder. There are two tubes on each side. Tubes train inboard for cruising and loading, and train outboard for expected action and firing. The forward tubes train outward to an angle of 8° 30' with the ship's centerline, the after tubes to an angle of 12° 30'. All torpedoes are fired forward and at the stated angles with the centerline.

2. Before loading the torpedoes into the tubes, it is intended that the gyro in each torpedo be set to the respective angle of the tube into which it is to be loaded. The direction of setting must be such that after leaving the boat the gyro will correct the course of the torpedo to that of the boat at the instant of firing, plus the spread angle.

3. The boat is designed to release its torpedoes at any speed under any ordinary condition.

4. The following brief description will aid the crew to understand the functions of the various gear:

Torpedo.

5. The tube is designed to use the Mark XIV torpedo, diameter, fully charged, 21.060 inches; length, 240 inches; weight in service condition, 3,017 pounds; permissible pressure on afterbody, 100 pounds per square inch.

6. The same torpedo (Mark XIV) with elongated warhead can also be fitted. In this case the length is increased by 6

inches and the weight by 200 pounds. The head is the only part affected by these increases.

7. An alternative torpedo is the Mark VIII-3D, diameter fully charged, 21.060 inches; length with warhead, 250.88 inches; weight in service condition, 3,050 pounds; permissible pressure on afterbody, 75 pounds per square inch (instantaneous only).

8. Before use, the guide stud should be removed, the tapped holes being left open.

Impulse case.

9. It is intended that 3" cartridge cases Mark VI be supplied for use with these tubes. The Mark VI case is identical in external outline with the 3" case Mark II, which was designed for 3"/23 caliber guns, except that it had been cut down in length to 6.60 inches. The Mark VI case carries the Mark XX combination primer, which screws into the case. If needed, satisfactory cases may be improvised from Mark II cases, by cutting off to 6.60 inches. The Mark II case, however, carries a primer Mark X or mod., which is arranged for percussion firing only. **No attempt should be made to use any other cases than those referred to in the foregoing**.

Tube.

10. The tube proper is made of steel, fabricated by welding. It is pivoted on an aluminum alloy turntable and turntable base. The forward end is mounted on an aluminum alloy support which travels on corrosion-resistant steel plates and is guided by brass Z-bars, cadmium plated. The turntable and the forward support are joined with steel tubing rails. The tube does not recoil.

11. The breech ring and door are of aluminum alloy and are sealed with neoprene gasket inserted in the door.

Combustion chamber.

12. The combustion chamber is a steel casting, tested to 3,000 pounds per square inch for strength and tightness. It is fitted with an interrupted thread piece onto which the firing mechanism locks. With firing mechanism removed, the cartridge should slide into the chamber, when fitted with sealing rings under a moderate hand pressure. The firing mechanism locks it in place. Blow-by around the cartridge is prevented by the

two sealing rings. It is essential that these rings be in place, and free from cuts or gouges, to insure gas tightness. A gasket is provided to keep moisture out of the chamber; this gasket is not designed to prevent blow-by.

13. When the charge is fired, pressure is built up in the chamber and gas is fed into the tube

through a throttling orifice located between the chamber and the tube. The tube pressure reaches a maximum soon after torpedo movement begins and decreases gradually to zero as the torpedo clears the muzzle.

Firing mechanism.

14. The firing mechanism is designed for either percussion or electric firing, depending on the type of primer used. The firing pin, which is insulated, is wired to an electric circuit. When the striker bolt is in firing position, it forces the firing pin against the primer, completing the circuit from the control station. The primer may then be fired by hitting the striker knob or by closing the electric circuit with the switch provided at the control station.

Tripping latch.

15. A projection to engage the starting lever is welded onto & small door over an access hole cut in the tube. This is the tripping latch. The door is held against its seat by four dogs. Guide strips extending aft from the tripping latch to the breech center the torpedo so that the latch and starting lever line up properly. As these guide strips engage the boss on the upper rudder, they also guide the rudder until it is clear of the latch.

Torpedo stop.

16. Torpedo stops are provided to keep the torpedo in place until firing, at which time they shear. This assembly provides for two shear pins to fit into the torpedo guide stud holes. With the rudder located in the before-mentioned guide strips, and the tail hard against the breech door, the stop pins should fit into the two forward holes of the four holes which formerly held the torpedo guide stud.

Access openings.

17. There are, beside the above openings, two charging and access holes cut in the tube and covered by small plates. One

is for Mark VIII and one for Mark XIV. There are in addition openings for setting speed and depth on a Mark XIV torpedo. These openings are modifications according to Bureau of Ordnance specifications.

Training gear.

18. Each tube is equipped with its own training gear. This equipment permits the tubes to be trained inboard so that no part of the tube structure extends over the rail. When action is expected, the tubes are trained outboard, by hand.

19. The training gear consists primarily of a handle-operated corrosion-resistant steel screw

which rotates within a swivelling cut made fast to the tube forward support. A stop is provided on each screw which serves to fix the training angle.

20. It is essential that the forward tube be fully trained outboard before the after tube is fired.

Training stops.

21. At the muzzle end, the tube carries two lugs drilled with locating holes. A fixed bracket, also drilled, is mounted on the deck. A removable pin is provided for attaching the tube to the bracket, either in the outboard (trained) position or in the inboard (stowed) position. The purpose of the stop is to relieve the training screw of any load caused by lurching of the torpedo tube in rough water. The pin should invariably be in place when the boat is under way.

22. When preparing to shift the tube by means of the training screw, make certain that the pin has been removed. Bring the holes into exact alignment by means of the screw before attempting to enter the pin. The pin should never be forced into place, and will enter easily when the parts are correctly lined up.

23. For loading, the tube must be trained to an extreme inboard position, and in this condition the locating pin will not be in use.

Loading gear.

24. One complete set of gear is provided on each boat to facilitate loading torpedoes into the tubes. This gear consists of three dollies, a height gage and a torpedo strap. The tubes are loaded one at a time, the same loading gear being used for all of them.

25. The dollies are fitted with rollers and jack screws so that the torpedo may be set on them, adjusted to line up with the tube bore, and rolled into the tube. The height gage gives the height to which each dolly should be adjusted. It is applied by dropping into the gaging hole near the center of the dolly. The strap is provided to lower the torpedo onto the dollies.

26. In the loading procedure, each of the three dollies is to-be set on the deck, forward of the tube, in the positions laid out for them and adjusted to the proper height. The loading position of each tube is clearly defined by scribed marks on the forward tube support and the Z guide bars.

Preparation of impulse charge.

27. The regulation charge is 24 ounces of sodium nitrate powder similar to Austin 2-C. Loaded cartridges will commonly be supplied from a depot, ready for use. The following procedure of loading is outlined in case it should be necessary to load cartridges in an emergency.

28. Cartridge cases which have been used in firing should first be washed in a strong solution of cleaning agent similar to Oakite, and dried completely before inserting primers. The loading is to be carried on in a dry atmosphere, not over 50 percent humidity. Powder should be exposed to the air for as brief a period as possible. After loading the case with the specified weight of powder, cover with a cork (or pyralin) wad $\frac{1}{4}$-inch thick which has been freshly dipped in melted paraffin. Press down by hand with a tamping tool. Cover with a layer of melted paraffin 1/8-inch thick. Store unused powder and also loaded cartridges in an airtight container.

29. **It is imperative that every effort be made to keep the powder absolutely dry. Refrain from handling the powder by hand as it will pick up considerable moisture from the hands**.

30. The regulation powder charge (24 ounces) produces an ejection velocity in excess of 40 feet per second, causing the torpedo to clear the deck with a margin of 5 to 6 inches and to dive at the correct angle to insure a successful shot. Should any shot appear to be unduly slow or not to clear the deck by the margin indicated, every item of the charging and loading procedure should be reviewed and checked in comparison with the instructions contained in this pamphlet. Where the Mark

VIII 3D torpedo is used, the regulation charge should **under no circumstances** be exceeded. To do so would expose the torpedo to probable failure by collapse of the afterbody.

Loading and operation.

31. Train tube to loading position, as indicated by scribed lines on Z-bar and tube forward support. To load the after tubes it is necessary to have the forward tubes in loaded position also; this allows room for the torpedo between the forward tubes and the deck house.

32. **Flush the bore of the tube thoroughly throughout its length with light lubricating oil, Navy Dept. Spec. 2110 (SAE #10). Also flush torpedo liberally before loading. Both the tube and the torpedo should be clean before flushing**. After removing the torpedo stop assembly, and raising the tripping latch, the tube is ready for loading.

33. Place the loading dollies on the deck forward of the tube at the positions indicated. Adjust the dollies to the proper heights as given by the height gauge, and to the midpoint of their transverse adjustment.

34. Swing breech door aside.

35. Using the strap provided, lower the torpedo onto the dollies. Fasten a nose line to the nose of the torpedo and take a turn around a cleat.

36. Push torpedo into tube until it is near the loaded position. Make certain that the upper rudder enters the guide strips installed in the top of the bore. If necessary, the torpedo may be raised or lowered, and shifted inboard or outboard, with the jack screws in the dolly assembly. Good alignment will enable the torpedo to be pushed into the tube easily.

37. When the torpedo is **within a few inches** of loaded position, before closing the door, release the propeller lock. Tightly clamp the breech door shut. **Then push the torpedo the remainder of the way into the tube until it bumps the door**.

38. It is essential that the breech door be firmly closed before the torpedo is brought into contact with it. Should the torpedo accidentally slide to or beyond the loaded position when being pushed in, pull it forward to permit the door to close easily. An attempt to back the torpedo forward by means of the breech nuts will invariably result in gas leakage and a poor shot.

39. Likewise, once the door is closed, it is equally necessary to push the torpedo in the full distance against the door. If this is not done, the tripping latch will not engage the starting lever. **The location of the stop pins in the torpedo does not give a reliable indication of the loaded position**.

40. When the torpedo is in loaded position (tail piece against breech door) the torpedo stop pins will fit into the two forward holes of the four holes which formerly held the guide stud.

41. Train to stowed position, insert training stop pin.

In loading impulse charge.

42. Place the cartridge in the chamber. It is preferable to grease the cartridge in order to allow it to enter correctly. If the fit is excessively tight or is loose, the reason should be investigated. Before attaching firing mechanism, make sure that the striker knob is in the retracted position. Enter the firing mechanism in the position indicated by arrow. Start engagement of threads and with a strong quick torque on the handles, lock the breech. The breech nut should jam against the cartridge rim while also making light contact with the weather gasket. When ready to fire, turn striker knob 90° and release, allowing striker bolt to bear upon firing pin. This will bring the firing pin into position either for percussion or electric firing, depending on the primer used. If the breech nut is not hard against the cartridge, the firing pin may not reach the primer. In this event, the charge could not be fired electrically and might not fire by percussion.

43. Caution.--Forward tubes must be fully trained outboard when aft tubes are to be fired, to avoid contact of torpedo with forward tube structure.

44. Tube muzzles should have grease packed around the head of torpedo to keep water out.

45. The bore of the tube should be cleaned with varsol or paint thinner and slushed with

slushing mixture, as soon as possible after firing. This should be done as a precaution against corrosion, as well as in preparation for reloading.

46. Clean all loose powder residue from combustion chamber walls. Ascertain that the chamber orifice is clean and completely free of any obstructions in the throat.

Check list for loading and operation.

47. The above procedure, for loading and operating are summarized here to be used as a check list.

1. Train tube to loading position.
2. Ascertain that tube is clean.
3. Slush tube and torpedo liberally.
4. Remove torpedo assembly.
5. Raise tripping latch.
6. Place loading dollies in positions indicated.
7. Adjust dollies to proper height.
8. Lower torpedo onto dollies.
9. Secure nose line to nose and take a turn with it around a cleat,
10. Remove the wedge which should be behind the starting lever of the torpedo, and set the distance gear off zero. Open stop wide and turn back one-eighth turn.
11. Push torpedo into tube within a few inches of loaded position; making certain rudder enters guide strips. (12) Remove the propeller lock.
12. Tightly clamp breech door.
13. Bump torpedo against door.
14. Release stop assembly.
15. Secure stop pins and tube.
16. Close tripping latch.
17. Place impulse charge in chamber.
18. With striker knob in retracted position, lock firingchamber mechanism.
19. Lower striker knob in firing mechanism, and tube isready to fire.
20. Thoroughly clean and slush tube as soon as possibleafter firing. Clean firing chamber and orifice.

Care and preservation of tube structure.

48. The light materials used require special care to preserve them from corrosion and thus to maintain necessary strength. Although all the pinned joints are made in galvanized steel or iron, and in anodized aluminum, they must be kept well greased to forestall chemical attack.

49. Exposed steel surfaces which cannot be painted should be coated with a suitable grease. This applies particularly to the breech door swing bolts, and tripping latch stem, the chamber, and all the pins throughout the complete assembly.

50. Grease should be applied to pressure fittings throughout the assembly at intervals of 1 week.

51. as should be patched. Outside iron and steel parts are to be painted with quick-drying marine primer before applying the outer coat of gray. Aluminum surfaces should be coated with zinc chromate primer and painted with aluminum paint, before applying the gray paint.

52. Zinc blocks attached to forward Z-bar guide strips should have good metallic contact with the surface of the strip, and should remain unpainted. The blocks are to be renewed at intervals after substantial deterioration has occurred.

53. If, for any reason, the weather gasket is removed and replaced, ascertain that the contact between the gasket and the firing mechanism does not prevent tight contact between the block and the cartridge. This is important as the gasket is only to keep moisture out of the breech and is not designed to prevent blow-by.

Chapter 7. MARK 19 TORPEDO TUBE

SECTION A. MARK VIII, MOD. 3 C AND 3 D, MARK XIV AND MARK XV TORPEDOES

1. The Mk. 19 tube is a stationary tube firmly mounted on the deck with the required angle of tube train. This eliminates the necessity of training out the tube before launching of torpedoes.

2. This tube has several points peculiar to it. It has a slot for the guide stud. This is not a T-slot. It is a flat slot and the torpedo must be fitted with a submarine-type guide stud--that is, a flat guide stud. The slot goes only to the stop pad.

3. The tube has no breech door. It has a screw plug about 6 inches in diameter for access to the tail. This should be open when loading and putting on positive lock. After lock is on, it can be set up.

Note: Tubes of later manufacture will have breech doors.

4. This tube also has rollers. The rollers are mounted on eccentric pins. The pins are locked in the desired position by washers carrying small lugs which ride in holes in the castings. The torpedo must be in the tube before these can be adjusted. The eccentric pins are turned until the desired "height" is obtained. The pins should carry a scribe mark to show whether they are in the "up" or "down" position. If the rollers are in the fully down position the stop mechanism

will not engage. They must be slightly raised. There are four rollers. Usually they will be at different heights, since the center line of the rollers is not uniform and the tube may sag.

5. Compressed air replaces the powder impulse charge used in launching from other tubes. A pressure of 230 pounds per square inch is used in launching Mark VIII-3C and 3D and Mark XIV torpedoes, and of 240 pounds per square inch for launching Mark 15s and 15--1s. The flask may be charged from the air flask of the torpedo, from the boat's compressor, or from a transportable pressure flask, through charging valve on flask.

After charging, the pressure will drop due to cooling. An allowance of from 5 to 6 pounds should lie made for this; and, if the tube is not to be fired within 12 to 16 hours, an additional 5 to 10 pounds should be carried. The average leakage over a period of 24 hours is approximately 10 pounds.

6. The stop mechanism for this tube is contained in the stop mechanism housing mounted at top center on the tube at the position of the guide stud on the torpedo air flask. Two pads for securing this mechanism are provided, one for Mark VIII and Mark XIV torpedoes and the forward pad for Mark XV.

Torpedo Tube Train Angles

Boat type	Train angle	Gyro angle for standard 1° unit of spread
Elco 80'		
Port forward tube	$8^1/_2$ L	8 R.
Starboard forward tube	$8^1/_2$ R	8 L.
Port aft tube	$12^1/_2$ L	11 R.
Starboard aft tube	$12^1/_2$ R	11 L.
Higgins		
Port forward	12 L	$11^1/_2$ R.
Starboard forward	12 R	$11^1/_2$ L.
Port aft	12 L	$10^1/_2$ R.
Starboard aft	12 R	$10^1/_2$ L.
Huckins		
Port forward	10 L	$9^1/_2$ R.
Starboard forward	10 R	$9^1/_2$ L.
Port aft	$12^1/_2$ L	11 R.
Starboard aft	$12^1/_2$ R	11 L.

The stop lever is held in place ahead of the stop on the torpedo by a replaceable breaking link, when the tube is ready for firing. A positive lock is provided aft to prevent possible shearing of the link before you are ready to fire. This lock must be released when the tube is fully ready for firing.

7. The air is released into the after section of the tube upon firing by either local or bridge control, by means of a direct

hydraulic tube and two pistons which open the release valve in firing.

When the main valve and route valve are' open, air is banked up above the main valve piston seating the piston and isolating the air in the flask. When the release valve is thrown, this pressure is vented, permitting flash pressure to unseat the main piston and to pass into the tube, forcing the torpedo forward.

8. The access holes in the tube consist of the following: breech plug, oil-filling plug, tripping latch, depth setting, speed setting, two stop- and charging-valve holes, and the stop-mechanism flange.

9. In using Mark VIII-3C and 3D arid Mark XIV torpedoes the stop mechanism should be put on the after pad. The stop and charging valves for Mark VIII and Mark XIV torpedoes will be under the after stop and charging access hole.

The oil pot filling hole for Mark VIII-3C and 3D will be under the pad in the center of the tube farthest aft. The tripping latch and depth-setting holes are the same for Mark VIII, Mark XIV, and Mark XV torpedoes.

SECTION B. PREPARING MK. 19 TUBE FOR FIRING

1. Take off positive lock, until the threads are disengaged from the split sleeve in the back of the stop mechanism housing.

2. Open route valve by turning counterclockwise until handle is down against packing gland nut.

3. Operate extractor control once or twice, thereby popping the release valve to assure proper operation of hydraulic control.

4. Back off the main valve stem as far as possible.

5. Tube is ready to fire by throwing extractor control over.

If packing gland and route valve are tight, this tube could be held ready for firing indefinitely, but care must be exercised in not moving the hydraulic control, which has only a short distance to go in firing the torpedo.

SECTION C. SAFETY PRECAUTIONS

1. Never start preparing the tube for firing without completely backing off the positive lock on the stop mechanism.

2. Never try to load the torpedo without lifting the stop lever clear of the tube and lifting the tripping latch off the tube.

3. After each firing, the firing valve should be checked before recharging, since firing will often jerk the neoprene piston washer out of its recess. Also the cylinder must be absolutely clean to insure proper operation of valve.

4. The exactor control hydraulic system should be checked frequently for presence of air. This is evident when the transmitter handle will not stay in the after position. This indicates leakage and calls for checking valve assembly.

5. In installing and adjusting tension link, take care that no pressure is exerted in tightening tension link adjusting nut as it will strain the cutaway section of the tension link, and cause it to part prematurely.

6. Check packing glands on main valve and route valve daily for leakage.

SECTION D. LOADING

This tube was designed to be removed from the boat for loading as on a dock or tender. The tube is then replaced on the boat. In calm water with a good crane operator the tube can be loaded without removal. With inexperienced personnel this is not advisable initially. With some experience the danger decreases.

The following steps should be taken in loading the torpedo tube on a dock or tender:

1. Disconnect hydraulic line at the bottom of the exactor control receiver on the side of the firing valve.

2. Remove the eight mounting bolts at the forward and after bracket pads.

3. Put on the three-legged sling, the long leg going aft to the after lifting pad just aft the stop and charging valve access hole; the two short legs going forward to the lifting pads on each side of the forward bracket pads.

4. Hook on with the crane and remove the tube from the boat and set in either wooden

chocks or on a set of mounts on the dock.

5. Lift the stop mechanism lever clear of the tube and into the stop mechanism housing. This is done by pushing down lever handle (part No. 78) until part No. 80 can be put under the forward end of lever handle to assure its staying up until after the torpedo is in position in the tube.

6. Remove the tripping latch from tube.

7. Remove the breech plug.

8. Attach loading winch to the breech of the tube.

9. Unreel wire rope on the loading winch and pass through tube to be hooked onto the tail of the torpedo.

10. Raise the torpedo to the proper height and pull into the tube with the loading winch until the torpedo is in position. The torpedo is allowed to go approximately 1 inch past its neutral position thereby making it easier to remove the wire rope from the tail of the torpedo.

11. Insert breech plug and bring torpedo to its neutral position.

12. Remove the wedge from the tripping lever and put on tripping latch.

13. Remove catch from stop lever handle and bring stop lever down in front of the guide stud.

14. Remove tension link adjusting nut and insert tension link into the adjusting nut.

15. Replace the adjusting nut and insert opposite end of tension link in the stop lever yoke.

16. Insert positive lock (part No. 84) by screwing clockwise until stop lever is hard against the front of the guide stud and clamp with locking screw (part No. 88).

17. Bring up tension link adjusting nut fingertight and lock by screwing down locking screw (part No. 92) firm against tension link adjusting nut.

18. Pick up torpedo tube and return to mounts on boat, letting the forward bracket pads come into place first and then letting the tube down where the after bracket pads come into place.

19. Insert forward mount bolts and pull elastics top nuts down tight.

20. Put on chaffing plate with rubber cushion between the two chaffing plates. Insert mount

bolts through the mount bracket pad in the chaffing plates. Put on jam nuts, bring them down handtight then put on the elastic stop nuts, jamming the elastic stop nuts with the jam nuts, thereby leaving the mount free to work fore and aft as the deck of the boat works under the tube.

Chapter 8. .50 CAL. BELL AIRCRAFT MOUNT

1. The Bell Aircraft twin cradle for .50-caliber machine guns is a flexible, lightweight, scarf-ring type mount equipped with a hydraulic system to absorb recoil shock. It is designed to be fired by either or both hands. It is manufactured in accordance with Bell Aircraft Corporation drawing 03-038-075.

2. The cradle frame is made up of four parallel bearers on which are assembled front and rear trunnion slides. Four shock unit assemblies (two for each gun) are attached, at their forward ends to the rear trunnion slides. At the rear they are attached to the cradle back plate support.

3. Deflector assemblies are bolted to the bearers and support a yoke and chute assembly serving both guns. Bolts holding outer ends of deflector brackets to bearers also hold continuous feed rear brackets in place.

4. The cradle back plate houses trigger and safety mechanism, including trigger-synchronizing adjusting screws. This back plate is easily removed by loosening knurled nut on bottom of cradle back plate support, and the two knurled screws at the top of the hand grips.

5. The mount for the twin cradles is housed in a barbette or stand whose circumference is 44 inches. The stand itself contains a roller ring or base built around the inner diameter--the brake band--and carries thereon a roller path. The base of the mount fits inside and next to the brake band at the top portion of the stand. In so fitting, the roller path is encased by the mount base or ring. To provide easy and smooth operation and to anchor the mount there are 24 bearings mounted in the base ring of the mount and moving in the roller path. These consist of one horizontal and one vertical roller mounted on a small plate. The horizontal one rolls against the side of the V-shaped roller path and prevents other than circular motion in the horizontal plane. The vertical roller rides against the bottom surface normally and supports the mount. However, if the mount moves upward from

shock, the roller rides against the top surface and thus anchors the mount. The small plate on which the rollers are mounted is secured to the bottom ring of the mount by two screws. It should be pointed out that if it becomes necessary to lift the mount it is necessary to first remove these bearings.

6. The mount has a train of 360° but may be secured in any position by a hand-operated brake. This brake is located just above the base of the mount, being attached thereto, and next to the brake band. It is just to the left of the gunner. Its operation consists merely of moving a hand lever to the ON position. This movement operates two eccentric cams. The motion of the cams pushes out a brake bar which in turn, by means of springs, pushes outward on the brake shoe. The brake shoe rests against the inside of the brake band preventing further movement of the mount. It may be applied in any position of the 360° train. In addition the mount may be locked in one definite position by inserting four securing bolts into four equally spaced threaded holes in the top of the scarf ring. These bolts fit into threads in the roller path which are in line with the holes of the scarf ring.

7. The twin guns may be elevated to an angle of 85° and depressed to an angle of 5°, the angle of depression ceasing when the guns come to a rest against the top of the stand. However, certain sections of the stand are higher than others. These elevated sections are so placed in order to prevent the guns being fired on any part of the boat. When not in use, the guns are locked in a vertical position by means of a securing spring bolt attached to the mount and setting into a bar between the two guns.

The training of the mount is operated by the movements of the gunner. Directly in back of the guns, and attached to the inside of the mount, is a back rest. The gunner, having his back placed therein, automatically turns the mount to the right or left by his own corresponding movements.

Functioning of Hydraulic Shock Units

1. The purpose of the hydraulic shock unit is to reduce recoil shock produced by gun fire. This is accomplished by combining

the functioning of an hydraulic piston with the reaction of a specially designed recoil spring.

2. When firing, with gun in level position, the major portion of the recoil shock is absorbed by the action of the hydraulic piston--the spring serving to return the gun to normal position after recoil.

3. Firing at a declined angle, recoil is counteracted by the hydraulic piston and weight of the gun.

With the gun in an inclined position, the spring offsets the weight of the gun and recoil shock is absorbed by the hydraulic piston.

Maintenance of Mount

1. Upon delivery of mount, it should be immediately painted and all bare surfaces should first receive a coat of red lead.

2. Once every quarter, the brake should be taken down and thoroughly cleaned.

3. Springs in the trigger mechanism should be taken down and cleaned whenever necessary.

4. Link deflector should be checked for proper size.

5. Bearings should always be thoroughly greased. A supply of bearings should be kept on board to replace any breakage that may occur.

Chapter 9. DEPTH CHARGES

Description and Operations

1. **Depth Charges Mark VI (Plate 1).**--The depth charge Mark VI contains a 300-pound cast TNT main charge with a 3.5-pound booster charge and is of the same size as the depth charges Mark II, Mod. 2, and Mark III. Each depth charge consists of a galvanized steel case, Mark VI, having a central tube within which are assembled the pistol Mark VI with percussion detonator Mark I, Mod. 1, the booster extender Mark VI, and the booster can Mark VI. The depth charge Mark VI may be distinguished from the depth charges Mark II, Mod. 2, and Mark III by the annular groove located near each end of the case Mark VI. The depth charge Mark VI will fit the depth charge release tracks Marks I and III and may be used with the depth charge projector Mark I (Y-gun), the same as depth charge Mark II, Mod. 2, or Mark III but the pistols and booster extenders Mark VI are not interchangeable with similar components Mark II, Mod. 2, or Mark III.

Detailed Description

2. **Case Mark VI.**--The depth charge case Mark VI is fabricated from sheet steel rolled to shape and welded along a longitudinal seam, forming a cylinder 17.625 inches outside diameter by 27.625 inches long. Near each end of the case a bead is rolled, forming seats for the pressed sheet steel heads, which are spot welded and also edge welded to the case. A steel flange fitted with a pipe plug is welded to each head for filling purposes. A forged steel flange is welded to each end of the seamless central tube and to the center of each head, forming the seats for the pistol and booster extender. The central tube is made heavier than in previous depth charges to eliminate distortions due to filling and handling. No holes, other than the filling holes, enter the explosive space, eliminating sources of exudate leakage. The U-bolts, provided in the heads of

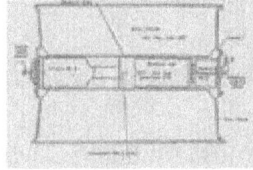

Figure 21.--Depth Charge Mk 6.

previous depth charges for handling purposes, have been eliminated from the Mark VI cases, as experience has indicated that the charges can be handled by slings or barrel clips. The entire case is hot galvanized inside and out, after fabrication. Blank covers are provided to seal the central tube during shipment or whenever the pistol or booster extender are removed.

3. **Pistol Mark VI**.--(a) The depth charge pistol Mark VI embodies, in principle, the general design features of the pistols Mark II, Mod. 2, and Mark III. All parts except the springs are made of nonferrous materials and are generally more rugged to withstand handling and testing. The pistol Mark VI is not interchangeable with pistols Mark II, Mod. 2, or Mark III.

(b) *Operations*.--With the index pointer set for the depth desired, and with the knob of the safety cover knocked off, water will enter through the inlet valve parts, filling the space within the bellows and bellows extension. As the charge sinks, the hydrostatic pressure increases, overcoming the resistance offered by the firing spring and causing the hydro piston and stem to move inward, toward the detonator end. As the piston and stem continue this movement, the spring-engaging collar located at the outboard end of the piston stem will contact the depth setting spring, the instant of contacting depending upon the index pointer setting. For the 30-foot setting, the depth setting spring is not contacted, all resistance to pressure being offered by the firing spring, release plunger spring, and inherent resistance of the bellows. The piston stem eventually contacts the end of the release plunger, compressing the release plunger spring, allowing the lock balls to recede into the space formed by the reduced diameter of the release plunger. As the lock balls recede, they disengage the countersunk end of the guide tube bushing, allowing the entire firing plunger assembly to move forward under the impulse of the compressed firing spring, until the firing point strikes the detonator. When the index pointer is set to SAFE, the spring adjusting bushing is raised to such a position that, when pressure is applied within the bellows and the piston moves forward, the spring engaging collar will contact the rim of the spring adjusting bushing before the plunger lock balls are released, thus preventing the pistol from firing.

(c) Due to the necessity for compressing the depth-setting spring slightly when setting the index pointer to SAFE, more force must be exerted upon the index pointer than can readily be exerted by hand or fingers. A depth setting wrench is provided to permit convenient setting of the index pointer to all indexed positions.

(d) The pistol has eight indexed settings stamped upon the face of the carrying flange, namely, 30, 50, 100, 150, 200, 250, and 300 feet, respectively, and SAFE. The index pointer has two accurate slots through which pass the machine screws which engage tapped holes in the index carrier. This arrangement allows calibration of the depth setting mechanism to be made during tests without disturbing the index pointer dial setting.

(e) The pistol-carrying flange is a bronze forging drilled for eight machine bolts and threaded for the attachment of cooperating parts. A thin, hard gasket is used between the case and the pistol flanges, to eliminate troubles formerly experienced due to canting of the mechanisms in the central tube of the case when the securing bolts were set up unevenly.

(f) The pistol bellows is larger than those used in previous pistols, in order that a 30-foot setting might be obtained when the same strength of firing spring is used. Due to the increase in size of bellows, the depth-setting spring and associated sleeves are heavier than those of the pistol Mark III. The depth-setting sleeve engages the adjusting bushing through a single-thread screw having a pitch of 0.90 inch.

(g) The firing plunger locking balls rest against the countersink of the replaceable guide tube bushing, allowing restoration of the guiding surface in case of excessive wear. The method of securing the detonator is different from that of the earlier depth charges, necessitating the use of a pin wrench for assembling. The centering flange at the end of the guide tube provides a flat surface against which the booster can move about when in armed position.

(h) A new feature is the inlet valve, intended to protect the pistol against countermining. Normally, this valve is kept off its flat seat by a spring, but under the influence of a suddenly applied abnormal pressure, the valve is intended to seat, preventing

entrance of water into the bellows space during the interval that the abnormal pressure acts.

(i) A light brass screwed cover is provided to protect the water entrance parts during storage, while a similar cover, having an extension knob, is provided for use only when the charges are located in the release tracks. This knob is intended to be wiped off by the wiping plates on the release tracks, exposing a hole in the cover and permitting the entrance of water into the bellows space.

(j) Instructions relative to routine inspection, tests, overhaul, and repair of pistols Mark VI are contained in part II of this pamphlet.

4. **Booster extender Mark VI.**--(a) The booster extender Mark VI is, in general, similar to the booster extender Mark III insofar as its operation is concerned. All parts except the extender

springs are of nonferrous materials. Forged bronze flanges have been substituted for pressed steel and a thin hard gasket is used instead of the former thick rubber gasket. The extender mechanism is not permanently attached to the booster can, as in the older mechanisms, but is provided with a flanged collar for engaging a socket on the booster can when assembled in the depth charge case. The booster extender Mark VI is not interchangeable with booster extender Mark II, Mod. 2, or Mark III.

(b) *Operation.*--When the safety fork is removed from the booster spindle, the bellows, assembled under compression, will elongate approximately 0.25 inch, causing the booster spindle to move inward, opening up a passage for the entrance of water around the reduced outer portion of the booster spindle. This inward motion is permitted by the necked portion of the booster spindle in wake of the locking balls. As the charge sinks, the increase in hydrostatic pressure overcomes the resistance of the extender spring and bellows until the locking balls enter the enlarged bore of the spindle guide. With the balls thus released from the engagement with the shoulder of the booster spindle, the extender bellows is free to extend its full travel, under the influence of the existing hydrostatic pressure, forcing the end of the booster can against the centering flange of the pistol. At this time the detonator is housed within the detonator envelope.

(c) Two safety forks are furnished with each booster extender Mark VI. One fork is plain, for use during transportation and storage, while the other is knobbed, for use when live charges are installed in the depth charge release tracks. (See par. 33 (b) of ordnance pamphlet No. 721, Depth Charge Release Gear Mark III.) With either safety fork in place on the booster spindle, the extender bellows is compressed and the booster spindle practically fills the bearing hole in the spindle bushing, immediately under the fork. This combination prevents the entrance of foreign matter into the bellows space. A hole is provided near the end of the booster spindle to allow the use of a spindle retracting tool when assembling the safety fork.

(d) The booster extender will function, causing the booster can to move into engagement with the detonator, when the depth charge has reached a depth of between 12 and 15 feet.

(e) Instructions relative to routine inspection, tests, overhaul, and repair of booster extender Mark VI are contained in part II of this pamphlet.

5. **Booster can Mark VI.**--(a) The booster can Mark VI contains approximately 3.5 pounds of granular TNT, and consists of four parts, the can itself, the detonator envelope, and the head and the socket attached to the head for engaging the flanged collar on the booster extender mechanism Mark VI. The booster can Mark VI is not interchangeable with booster cans Mark II, Mod. 2, or Mark III.

(b) Six inverted dimples pressed in the booster can are used for centering the can in the central tube of the case.

(c) The head is locked mechanically to the booster can, after loading by means of four pressed lugs which engage in corresponding "bayonet slugs" pressed into the can near its open end, to relieve the strains otherwise imposed upon the soldered joint during handling. Air and watertightness of the joint between the can and head is effected by the use of low melting point solder applied with steam heated soldering irons at the loading depots.

(d) The booster can Mark VI is designed to permit the loading and handling apart from the inert booster extender mechanism.

(e) Instructions relative to routine inspection, test, overhaul, and repair of booster cans Mark VI are contained in part II of this pamphlet.

6. **Stowage of depth charge components aboard ship**.--(a) *Pistol stowage box*.--Depth charge pistols Mark VI, when not assembled in the depth charge cases, are to be stowed in the pistol stowage box furnished for that purpose. When stowed, the plain inlet valve cover cap should be in place, the firing plunger in the "cocked" position and the index pointer set at "30". The pistol stowage box is fitted with notched battens so arranged as to provide stowage for a maximum of 12 pistols, together with the necessary knobbed safety covers. Less than 12 pistols may be stowed, depending upon the allowance issued for the individual vessels. The pistol stowage box should be kept locked and in a safe, dry place.

(b) *Booster stowage can*.--Booster extender mechanism and booster cans, when not assembled in the depth charge cases, are stowed together in booster stowage cans. When stowed in the stowage cans, the plain safety fork should be fitted to the booster extender, and the knobbed safety fork placed on the centering ring.

(c) *Detonator stowage box*.--Percussion detonators Mark I, Mod. 1 (65 grain) will be supplied in wooden stowage boxes. Each wooden box contains a total of 12 detonators, 6 of which are packed in each of two copper boxes. The wooden stowage boxes will be stowed in the lockers provided for that purpose in the vessel.

7. **Service tools**.--Each vessel equipped for launching depth charges Mark VI will be furnished a set of the following tools packed in a canvas set:

> Depth setting wrench.
> Detonator holder wrench.
> Extender testing tool.

8. **Safety features and results of tests**.

(a) A depth charge pistol, Mark VI, when set on SAFE, sustained a pressure of over 600 pounds per square inch before the pistol bellows were ruptured. This pressure corresponds to a depth of approximately 1,350 feet in sea water.

(b) A depth charge pistol, Mark VI, when assembled in a depth charge case, and dropped so that the booster end of the case landed upon timber laid over concrete, functioned as follows:

Depth setting	Height of fall	Result
30 feet	6 feet	Fired.
300 feet	15 feet	Fired.
Safe	24 feet	Did not fire.

(c) A booster extender, Mark VI, with the safety fork in place, sustained a pressure of 600 pounds per square inch before the booster spindle pulled through the safety fork. This pressure corresponds to a depth of approximately 1,350 feet of sea water.

(d) A loaded booster can and booster extender, Mark VI, without safety fork, when assembled in a depth charge case, and dropped so that the pistol end of the case landed upon timber laid over concrete, functioned when dropped in a distance of 2 feet, allowing the booster can to assume its "armed" position.

(e) From the foregoing, the necessity for protecting a loaded and primed depth charge against dropping on end is evident. However, if the pistol fires, the booster can will not be in the armed position, and the detonator will explode in the "safety space" provided. On the other hand, if the booster can reaches its armed position, due to a blow or drop, the pistol will not fire. The safety cover and safety fork should invariably be in place whenever live, primed depth charges are handled.

9. **Effect of underwater explosions**.--On plate 9, O. P. 747, are shown the relations existing between the weight of charge, the distance from charge to hull, and the relative damage expected to be inflicted upon submerged and surface vessels. The data shown are the results of experiments conducted by the Bureau of Ships.

Effective radius

30 feet   Fatal damage.
50 feet   Serious damage.
90 feet   Moderate to slight damage.

10. Sinking rates of depth charges.--The rates at which depth charges sink depends upon the condition under which they are launched, the average sinking rate in disturbed water, as in

a ship's wake, being less than charges launched in still water. The approximate average sinking rates are as follows:

Conditions of launching	Sinking rate (feet per second) Mark VI (300 lb.)
In still water	9 feet.
In disturbed water	6 feet.

11. **Weights of depth charge components.**--

	Pounds
Case, Mark VI empty	90.0
Case, Mark VI, loaded, unprimed	390.0
Case shipping covers	2.0
Pistol, Mark VI	17.5
Booster extender, Mark VI	7.5
Booster can, Mark VI, empty	1.7
Booster can, Mark VI, loaded	5.2
Detonator box, with 12 detonators	1.3
Pistol stowage box, empty	50.0
Booster stowage can, empty	2.0
Depth charge, Mark VI, loaded and primed	420.0

Testing, Overhauling, and Repairing

12. General description of testing sets and tools.--(a) With these testing sets air pressure can conveniently be applied to those working parts of pistols and booster extenders which, in service, would be subjected to water pressure. Thus it is possible to discover leaks if they exist and to check the pressure, and therefore the depth, required to operate the booster extender or to fire the pistol. Besides containing the apparatus for testing the pistols and booster extenders, each testing set also contains certain tools that will aid in the assembly, disassembly, and preparation for use of the depth charge material.

(b) In addition to the above-mentioned testing sets, a tool set is provided for use aboard all ships equipped for launching depth charges. This set consists of three tools packed in a canvas bag. These tools are duplicates of tools included in both of the testing sets.

13. **Testing set, Mark II.**--The depth charge testing set, Mark II, consists of the following parts and tools:

1. Testing set holder.
2. Cover, which is provided with a small pressure gage and an auto tire valve.
3. Clamping piece.
4. Depth setting wrench.
5. Detonator holder wrench.
6. Extender testing tool.
7. Cocking tool.
8. Extender stop.
9. Firing plunger sleeve.
10. Rubber washers (2).
11. Air pump with 6 feet of tubing.
12. Socket wrench.
13. Extra valve stem.
14. Two boxes of valve insides.
15. One box of valve caps.
16. Tool box.

14. **Service tool set**.--The tool set for use on board all ships equipped for launching depth charges consists of the following:

1. Depth setting wrench.
2. Detonator holder wrench.
3. Extender testing tool.
4. Canvas bag.

15. **Care of the testing sets**.--The apparatus and tools comprising the testing sets should be kept in the box provided for them when not in actual use. Attached to the under side of the lid of each box is a list of tools which furnishes a ready reference for checking the contents of the box. Care should be taken when using the tools not to strain them beyond their capacity. The pressure gauge should be compared occasionally with a standard gauge to see that its readings are approximately correct.

Instructions for Testing Pistols and Booster Extenders

16. **General instructions**.--Stations issuing depth charges should test pistols and booster extenders before issuing them to

the service. Tenders should inspect and test pistols and booster extenders that have been in storage for any considerable period before issuing them for use with loaded depth charge cases.

17. **Testing the pistol**.--(a) Remove the inlet valve cover and detonator (if present) ; see that

the detonator collar and detonator holder are in place and set the index pointer at the 100-foot setting. Do not test pistols at a setting greater than 100 unless instructed to do so by the Bureau of Ordnance.

(b) Cock the pistol if it is not already cocked. Use the cocking tool.

NOTE.--A pistol is cocked when the firing plunger is in the ready position. If the firing plunger is not in the ready position it can be returned to the ready position by pushing the plunger inward against the reaction of the firing spring until it locks itself in position. (Use the cocking tool.) The relation of the shoulder on the cocking tool to the centering flange on the pistol will indicate whether or not the pistol is cocked. If the tool is stopped by the plunger so that the shoulder on the tool is flush with the face of the flange, the pistol is cocked. If the shoulder is about 0.75 inch from the face of the flange, the pistol is not cocked.

(c) Clamp the testing set holder in a vise with the larger opening up.

(d) Assemble the following in the holder in the order named:

1. Rubber washer (largest outside diameter).
2. Depth charge pistol.
3. Rubber washer (smallest outside diameter).
4. Cover
5. Clamping piece.

(e) See that all the parts are centered relative to each other and that the cover is resting flat on its washer, then clamp all together by turning the clamping piece to the right until tight.

(f) Attach the pump to the valve in the cover and pump air into the mechanism until a pressure of 30 pounds is obtained.

(g) Observe the pressure gage reading; if it is apparent that the system does not leak, or if the loss is not more than 5 pounds in 1 minute, the pistol mechanism is sufficiently tight.

(h) If the system fails to hold the pressure, the leak may be

in the testing set and care should be taken to see that this is made up tight and that the auto tire valve is not leaking.

(i) If the leak persists the pistol should not be used but should be tagged and laid aside for overhaul. If this test is being made aboard ship, return the pistol to a depot for replacement.

(j) If the pistol proves to be airtight, proceed as follows to determine the depth at which it "fires":

1. Pump air slowly into the testing set until the pistol"fires": The "firing" of the pistol is indicated by a pronounced click caused by the firing plunger striking the detonator holder collar.

2. Note the reading of the pressure gage when this occurs. A pressure of 44.4 pounds per square inch is equivalent to 100 feet of sea water, and a reading on the test gage of not less than 42 pounds and not greater than 47 pounds when the pistol "fires" will indicate a satisfactory pistol.

The gage should be watched closely for the exact reading when the pistol "fires," as it is difficult to stop pumping at this instant, especially if the pistol "fires" on the beginning of a down stroke of the pump.

(k) Disconnect the pump and allow the air to escape by depressing the plunger in the tire valve before the clamping piece is loosened.

(l) Remove the pistol from the testing set. Cock the firing-plunger and replace the inlet valve cover.

(m) If the firing pressure conforms to the figures given above, the pistol is satisfactory. If it does not conform to these figures and the test is being made aboard a ship, the pistol should be returned to a depot for replacement. If the test is being made at a depot, lay the pistol aside for overhaul.

(n) Depth charge pistols should be tested only as authorized, because continued working of these mechanisms will distort the metal bellows and produce unnecessary wear on the plunger-releasing mechanism. A pistol to be used for instruction and drill is availa.ble to all tenders.

NOTE.--The gage on the cover of the testing set should be checked occasionally, especially if the readings taken on a series of pistol tests are consistently high or low.

18. **Testing the booster extender**.--(a) Remove the safety fork from the booster extender, then hook the extender stop, on the booster spindle. This can be easily done by pressing on the booster connecting collar of the booster extender so that the groove in the booster spindle is extended above the face of the flange.

(b) Secure the holder of the depth charge testing set in a vise and assemble the booster extender with rubber washers, cover, and clamping piece exactly as in testing a. pistol.

(c) Pump air into the system until the booster spindle is released from the locking slide and extends to the full travel permitted by the extender stop. If this occurs at a pressure of 4 to 8 pounds per square inch, the action of the booster extender is satisfactory.

(d) After testing the booster extender for the unlocking pressure, continue to pump air into the system until a pressure of 20 pounds per square inch is obtained. Observe the mechanism for leaks. If the indicated pressure on the gage does not drop more than five pounds in one minute, the mechanism is satisfactorily tight. If the test indicates that the mechanism leaks, it should be laid aside for overhaul if the test is being made at a depot. If aboard ship, return the booster extender to a depot for replacement.

NOTE.--When making leak tests and leak is observed, be sure the leak is not in the testing set.

(e) A booster extender to be used for instruction and drill is available to all tenders.

19. *Use of the service tool set aboard ships*.--Three tools are furnished for use on board ships equipped for launching depth charges. These tools are packed in a canvas bag and are kept In the pistol stowage box.

> (a) *Depth setting wrench*.--This is a flat wrench designed to engage the pistol index pointer so that it may be easily turned to any desired setting. The wrench will fit on the index pointer in only one way, that is, with the pointer end (marked "A") in the cut-out part of the wrench opposite the handle. This permits visual inspection of the index when it is being turned to a particular setting.

--222--

> (b) *Detonator holder wrench*.--This wrench is designed to screw or unscrew the detonator holder when detonators are installed in, or removed from, the pistol.

> (c) *Extender testing tool*.--This tool has a twofold use: (1) to aid in removing and changing the safety forks, and (2) to test the freedom of the booster extender after it is mounted in the depth charge.

(1) *Removing and changing safety forks*.--Plain safety forks can be pulled from the booster spindle by engaging the hook on the tool in the hole in the safety fork. After the safety fork is removed from a booster extender mounted in a depth charge, the spindle will spring inward about one quarter of an inch. Use the hook on the extender testing tool to pull the spindle outward so that the safety fork to be installed can be engaged with the groove in the spindle.

(2) *Testing the booster extender*.--Remove the safety fork, engage the hook of the testing tool in the hole at the end of the booster spindle and pull outward. Hold outward on the spindle and swing the body of the tool until the recessed end engages the groove in the spindle. Release the tension on the tool and the booster spindle will retract and pull the body of the tool into the hole in the flange. The hook will now be free; swing it outward to clear the flange. Test the booster for freedom of motion by pushing the spindle inward about an inch. To release the tool from the booster spindle, engage the hook on the tool in the hole at the end of the spindle. Pull outward on the hook and disengage the body of the tool from the spindle by swinging it outward and away from the spindle. The hook can now be released.

Routine Inspection and Overhaul of Depth Charges

20. **General instructions**.--All depth charge material shall be given a. routine inspection and overhaul by depots prior to issuing the material, and by ship's personnel when preparing the material for use. In general this overhaul will consist of cleaning, oiling, and testing the material and the making of minor repairs. Major repairs should be made only by shore

stations which have been authorized to make these repairs and which have been supplied with special tools for the purpose.

21. **Inspection and overhaul of cases**.--(a) Remove the pistol, booster extender, and booster from the depth charge case. Removing these mechanisms will be necessary only on board ships during war, as, during peacetime, they will be carried in their designated stowage spaces.

(b) Inspect the case carefully for leaks of TNT exudate. If any leaks occur they will probably be at the welded seams or around the pipe plugs at the ends of the case. If leaks occur in cases aboard ship, or at shore stations, the Bureau of Ordnance should be consulted for instructions as to disposal.

(c) If no leaks are found, check the diameter and length of the case to see that these measurements are within the allowed tolerances. See that the pipe plugs do not project beyond the plane of the ends of the case.

(d) Inspect the central tube and see that it has no projections or deformations which would prevent the free motion of the booster can or proper assembly of the pistol.

(e) Depots shall provide themselves with a cylindrical plug gage to be used in gaging the central tube of the loaded depth charge cases. This gage shall have a diameter of 4.160 inches (plus 0.003, minus 0.000), and a length of 8.75 inches (plus or minus 0.030), and it shall enter and pass freely throughout the length of the central tube.

(f) Inspect the tapped holes in the flanges at the end of the central tube. If the bolts come out freely when the covers are removed it will indicate that the threads are in satisfactory condition.

(g) Inspect and clean the gasket seats on both ends of the case to insure that the assembly can be made watertight.

(h) Inspect the gaskets and see that they are in good condition.

(i) If a depth charge case does not conform to the proper dimensions or is unsatisfactory for any reason and it is being overhauled by a depot, set it aside for repair or, if being overhauled by a ship, return it to a depot for replacement.

22. Inspection and overhaul of pistols.--(a) Test the pistol as directed in the instructions for testing

pistols. If the pistol passes this test satisfactorily it is ready for service use.

(b) If the pistol fails to function satisfactorily, examine the firing plunger and firing spring. To do this remove the detonator holder locking spring, the detonator holder, and the detonator collar. Set the index pointer at 30 and mount the pistol in the depth charge testing set and "fire" the pistol. Hold a piece of wood at the end of the guide tube to catch the blow of the firing plunger. Remove the firing plunger and the firing spring.

(c) See that the locking balls are in position in the firing plunger and that they are in good condition.

(d) Examine the release plunger for ball indentations by pressing inward on the locking balls with the fingers and at the same time rotating the release plunger relative to the firing plunger. If the release plunger has any ball indentations, they can be felt as the plunger is turned. If the balls are allowed to lie in these depressions when the firing plunger is assembled for service, the pressure required to operate the pistol may be changed.

(e) Set the release plunger in a position where the balls do not rest in depressions.

(f) Clean the inside of the guide tube thoroughly and lubricate it with a light coat of oil.

NOTE.--*All* oiling should be done with a light bodied lubricating oil equivalent to Federal Standard Symbol 2110 (see Bu. Eng. pamphlet, N. Eng. 31). Wet a cloth with oil and rub the cloth over the surfaces to be lubricated. Do not "flush" with oil, but use it sparingly.

(g) Examine the firing spring and see that it is in good condition. Assemble the firing spring in the guide tube.

(h) Assemble the firing plunger in the guide tube. To do this, slide the firing plunger sleeve on the firing plunger, depress the release plunger so the balls can recede, then slide the sleeve over the balls. With the sleeve in place, push the firing plunger into the guide tube and continue pushing the firing plunger until it is in the cocked position. As it is possible to start the firing plunger in backwards, care should be taken to see that the firing point points outward toward the detonator holder.

(i) Replace the detonator collar, detonator holder, and detonator holder locking spring.

(j) Clean the depth markings on the flange so they are clear. See that the two holes in the inlet valve stop are clean and open.

(k) Test the pistol as directed in the instructions for testing pistols.

(l) If the pistol fails to function satisfactorily, examine the assembly to see if the trouble can be located and corrected. If the pistol cannot be made to function satisfactorily, mark the pistol "unsatisfactory" and set it aside for complete overhaul or, if aboard ship, return it to a depot for replacement.

23. Inspection and overhaul of booster extenders.--

(a) Test the booster extender as directed in the instructions for testing booster extenders. If the booster extender passes this test satisfactorily it is ready for service use.

(b) If the booster extender fails to function satisfactorily and the trouble cannot be located and corrected without disassembly, mark the booster extender "unsatisfactory" and set it aside for complete overhaul or, if aboard ship, return it to a depot for replacement.

24.Inspection of booster cans.--

(a) Inspect the booster can for leaks, holes, or any evidence that the TNT charge is wet.

(b) Examine the booster for deformations which might prevent its free movement inside the depth charge central tube. Examine the joint between the can and head and see that it is made up tight and in good condition.

(c) Depots shall provide themselves with a ring gage to be used in gaging the loaded booster cans. This gage shall have an inside diameter of 4.145 inches (plus 0.000, minus 0.003), and a length of 1.0 inch (plus or minus 0.030). The booster cans shall pass freely through this gage.

(d) Inspect the detonator envelope and see that it is in good condition and is securely soldered in the booster can.

(e) If there is any indication that the .booster is defective, set the unit aside for complete overhaul or, if aboard ship, return it to a depot for replacement.

Preparation of Depth Charges for Firing

25. General instructions.--Prepare depth charges for firing only from material which has passed the routine inspection and overhaul indicated in paragraphs 20 to 24, inclusive. Make a check-off list and use it during the preparation for firing.

26. Assembly of the booster can and booster extender in the case.--

(a) Engage the socket on the booster head with the connecting collar on the booster extender. Assemble the booster and booster extender in the case, using a good gasket.

(b) Fit the bolts and lock washers. Use the socket wrench supplied in the testing sets and tighten the bolts uniformly so as to make a good watertight joint between the booster flange and the case. It is a good plan in bolting up a joint of this kind to tighten all bolts until a light tension is taken on each. Then tighten one bolt a little more and then the one next to it, and so on, progressing around the flange in one direction until the bolts are all uniformly tight.

(c) Test the booster extender for freedom of motion. To do this remove the safety fork and engage the extender testing tool with the booster spindle. Push the tool inward about one inch and observe if the spindle and booster move without pronounced binding. The spindle has a certain natural resistance to motion due to the reaction of the spring and the friction of the locking balls. If there is binding or resistance in excess of this natural resistance, examine the assembly for the cause, which should be located and corrected before proceeding with the assembly.

(d) Put a plain safety fork in place. Use the hook on the extender testing tool to retract the booster spindle so that the fork can be entered in the groove in the spindle.

27. **Assembly of the pistol in the case.**--

(a) Inspect the holes in the inlet valve stop, to insure that they are clean and open.

(b) Set the index pointer on SAFE. Use the depth setting wrench as it will facilitate setting the index pointer.

(c) Release the detonator holder locking spring and remove the detonator holder and detonator collar. See that the pistol is cocked. If it is not cocked, cock it, using the cocking tool.

(d) Mount the detonator in position between the detonator collar and detonator holder. Replace the detonator holder locking spring. The point of this spring should show on the inside of the guide tube between the detonator holder and the end of the tube. If the detonator holder interferes with the point of this spring it indicates that the assembly is not correct. Determine the trouble and correct it before continuing the assembly.

(e) Assemble the pistol in the case, using a good gasket.

(f) Fit the bolts and lock washers (see the instructions contained in paragraph 26 (b) relative to tightening the bolts). (g) Install a plain inlet valve cover.

28. **General instructions.**--The complete overhaul and repair of depth charge material is to be undertaken only by authorized shore stations.

Chapter 10. DEPTH CHARGE RACKS

1. The depth charge rack holds one Mark 6 depth charge. The rack consists of a base which bolts to the deck, and on which are mounted two tracks. A double securing strap passes over the depth charge, holding it to the tracks on which it rests. A quick release mechanism secures the strap at the inboard end.

2. The base of the rack is made of sheet steel. At each end of the rack base is a flange with bolt holes by which the rack is secured to the deck. Mounted on each end of the rack base is a single track, made of angle steel, with the toe of the angle down and in. The depth charge rests on these two tracks, and is prevented from sliding fore and aft by the upright legs of the angles. The tracks slope downward and outboard. The inboard end of the tracks curves sharply upward to form a shoulder against which the depth charge is secured.

3. The securing strap secures the depth charge to the rack. The strap is a single galvanized steel cable, both ends of which are connected by a triangular link. The strap is held on the outboard side of the rack by two adjustable screws and pulleys, one at each end of the rack. The straps pass over the depth charge and the triangular link is held by the quick release mechanism. The purpose of the adjustable screws and pulleys as the outboard securing points for the strap is to tighten the strap around the depth charge. (See figs. 22 and 23.)

4. The triangular link is secured by the release hook of the quick release mechanism. The release hook is tilted inboard by the toggle lever in order to release the link and securing straps. Until the depth charge is to be released, the release mechanism is locked by a safety pin which passes through the toggle lever. A safety fork prevents the safety pin from backing out accidentally. All parts are brass or noncorrosive metal. The safety pin and fork both have a short chain to secure them to the rack to prevent their loss.

5. To secure a depth charge in the racks, the adjusting screws which serve as outboard securing points for the securing strap

are slacked off. The charge is placed in the racks, the securing strap passed over the charge, and the triangular link caught by the release hook. The safety pin locks the release hook in place, and the safety fork is clipped over the end of the safety pin. The adjusting screws and pulleys are now tightened to remove all slack in the securing straps.

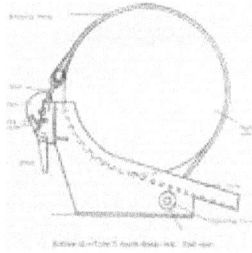

Figure 22.--Type C depth charge rack. End view.

6. To release a depth charge, the safety fork must first be removed, then the safety pin. Then by pulling the toggle lever inboard, the release hook is moved inboard so that the triangular securing strap link is released, allowing the depth charge to roll overboard.

7. A lanyard clip is welded to each end of the rack. A lanyard may be secured to the safety fork or safety cover on the depth charge and secured to one of these clips. By this means the safety

--230--

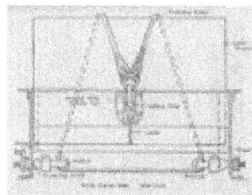

Figure 23.--Type C depth charge rack. Inboard side.

--231--

---

fork and safety cover may be removed automatically as the charge rolls off the rack, making it unnecessary to remove them by hand.

8. The quick release mechanism, and adjusting screw and pulley mechanism, are made of brass or noncorrosive materials. However, they must be kept clean and in good working condition. They should not be painted. The rack itself is steel, and must be protected by a coat of paint to prevent corrosion.

--232--

Chapter 11. SMOKE SCREEN GENERATOR, MARK 2

1. The purpose of the installation is to provide means for laying smoke screens utilizing chemical smoke mixtures.

Description

2. **General.**--The generator is carried on the stern of the boat, with all piping and accessory equipment secured to the carrier rack. It consists of one 35-gallon tank secured to an emergency release carrier, which in turn rests upon rollers in a carrier rack. The carrier is secured to the rack by a latch. Appropriate piping conducts CO_2 from a CO_2 bottle attached to the carrier rack to the tank. The smoke mixture is discharged from the tank through piping and out of two nozzles. The CO_2 serves only as a source of pressure to force the smoke mixture out the nozzles as a spray. Maximum operating pressure of the generator is 150 pounds per square inch.

3. The 35-gallon GENERATOR TANK is fabricated from sheet monel metal, joined by welding. Within the tank are baffle plates to add strength and minimize surging, and a discharge tube which empties the tank as completely as possible by taking the liquid from the low end. On the outside of the tank are two reinforcing bands, which locate and restrain the tank in its mounting; a filling fitting; a flange for the smoke line connection; a pipe-threaded CO_2 inlet tube; and two pad eyes.

4. The tank is mounted in two SADDLES which are welded to the emergency release carrier. Each saddle contains a pair of rollers, upon which the tank may be rotated into its proper position. The reinforcing bands locate the tank in a fore and aft position on the saddles.

5. The tank is secured in place upon the emergency release carrier by the TANK ANCHORING SLINGS. The slings are secured to cable anchor brackets on the carrier by clevis bolts.

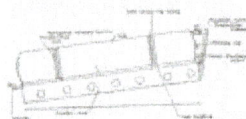

Figure 24.--FS smoke screen generator.

6. The EMERGENCY RELEASE CARRIER is in effect a skid upon which is mounted the generator tank; the discharge piping and nozzles; and a part of the CO_2 pressure lead. A latch on the forward end of the carrier rack secures the emergency release carrier in place. The latch lever is fitted with a toggle-pin which restrains the lever so that the generator cannot,,be jettisoned unless the toggle-pin is first removed. The purpose of the emergency release carrier is to allow the generator tank to be jettisoned in case it has been hit.

7. GENERATOR CO_2 piping may be traced on the diagram. Starting at the CO_2-bottle, the

generator piping consists successively of a CO_2 bottle and valve; a section of copper piping from there to a variable reducing valve; a length of piping from the reducing valve to slip joint, and then to the inlet valve on the tank. The maximum working pressure on this system is 120' pounds. The slip joint serves as a connection between the stationary piping secured to the carrier rack, and the piping which is secured to the emergency release carrier and tank.

8. GENERATOR SMOKE LINE may be traced on the diagram. The line leads from the after, lower end of the tank to the forward end of the tank; out through the outlet valve; then aft below the tank to the two spray nozzles over the stern.

9. SPRAY NOZZLES are intended to emit the smoke mixture in finely divided form, the resulting spray to form a comparatively wide cone. Nozzles are made adjustable, in order to obtain the optimum spray, but the adjustment once determined is not intended to be altered in service except to reestablish the original setting. The nozzles should be pointing aft and up at an angle 0f about 45° above the horizontal.

10. Filling caps are provided for each tank. They are intended for use only when tanks are to be filled with smoke mixture, or when, having been discharged, tanks are to be flushed with water. Under normal operating conditions, a filling cap should never be opened unless the tank is known tohave been completely discharged, and then only while observing all safety precautions noted in paragraph. 17.

11. The CARRIER RACK is the frame in which the emergency release carrier is normally mounted. It is designedly slanted outboard (i.e. toward the stern) at an angle to permit

jettisoning the generator by gravity. It contains eight rollers whose axes are horizontal and approximately athwartships, upon which the emergency release carrier rests, and six rollers with vertical axes to restrain the emergency release carrier from sidewise movement.

12. The RELEASE MECHANISM permits the generator to be jettisoned in case of an emergency, such as rupture of a full tank by gunfire or by collision, or in case of fire near the generator. Jettisoning may be accomplished by first removing the toggle pin from the emergency release lever, and then pulling the lever forward, away from the tank. Gravity will cause the emergency release carrier to roll aft on the carrier rack rollers and over the stern. The slip joint in the CO_2 piping automatically disconnects when the release carrier moves aft.

Care

13. In general, the care of the smoke screen generator equipment involves inspection and maintenance as required to insure that the equipment is at all times in serviceable condition. Periodic inspection should be performed to check up on the following points:

(a) That all working parts are properly lubricated.

(*b*) That all working parts are in operable condition.

(*c*) That no leak either of air or smoke mixture exists.

(*d*) That no parts are corroding.

(*e*) That there is no accumulation of paint, dirt, or other material on an emergency release carrier inboard of any of the rollers mounted in the carrier rack, or between the holding-down keys on the emergency release carrier and their mating parts on the carrier rack, which might possibly impede the jettisoning of the generator in case of an emergency.

(*f*) That all paint is in good condition.

14. Corrosion of the generator tanks, and of the piping, valves, nozzles, etc., carrying smoke mixture, is hot expected to develop under normal conditions except after considerable periods, since these parts are made of monel metal. CO_2 piping and valves, rollers and axle pins, and cast parts are brass or bronze, and therefore are not expected to corrode seriously under normal conditions. The cables of tank anchoring slings are corrosion-resisting steel. The carrier rack, emergency release carrier,

and saddles are fabricated from common steel and therefore corrosion is normally expected to develop upon any part of the surface not properly protected by paint. Protection of the CRS cables of the slings is to be accomplished by the use of graphite lubricating grease. All of the materials of the smoke screen generator except monel metal may be expected to corrode rapidly if exposed to FS Smoke mixture.

MOUNTING

15. The mounting of a generator, after original installation, should proceed as follows: The emergency release carrier is to rest upon the rollers which are mounted in the carrier rack, the carrier latching hook being engaged in the carrier latching eye and secured therein by a toggle-pin. The discharge tube, which passes through holes in the cradle, may be loosely in place. Before proceeding further, the proper lubrication of all rollers and other operating parts should be checked. The tank is now placed upon the rollers of the cradle which are part of the release carrier, the rollers being at the center of the reinforcing bands, and the tanks are rotated upon the rollers until the rollers engage the machined recesses in the bands. The tank anchoring slings are now checked for proper protection against corrosion and are installed so that the cables straddle the reinforcing bands of the tank. Make up the CO_2 and the smoke discharge pipe connections. Tighten tank anchoring slings.

To dismount a generator, proceed as above but in the reverse order.

16. The FILLING OF TANKS will be performed on board a tender or ashore. Filling requires

the provision of a sling arrangement such as indicated on plate III. The object is to transfer smoke mixture from the standard 55-gallon shipping drum to a generator tank without spillage and with the minimum of exposure of the smoke mixture to the atmosphere. The computed internal volume of the generator tank is 35.9 gallons, but its charge is only 32 gallons, to allow for expansion. The weights involved are about as follows:

	Pounds
Generator tank (empty)	125
Shipping drum (full)	900-1000
Filling equipment	16

The following procedure is suggested for filling:

(*a*) Secure slings, the drum and tank lying on deck or on a platform, the bung of the drum being up.

(*b*) Remove tank filling cap and install filling gage, **first making sure that the filling gage float is free and will register when the tank is filled.** Keep the float stem oiled lightly where it protrudes through the filling gage retaining nut.

(*c*) Make sure that the air and discharge stop valves on the tank and the plug cocks in the filling and vent hoses are closed.

(*d*) Make sure that the gasket of the filling and drain drum connection is in place and in good condition and is coated with soft deflocculated graphite lubricating grease.

(*e*) Remove the screw cap from the bung of the drum and install the filling connection on the drum. **Loosen the screw cap cautiously and allow the drum to vent, if necessary, before removing the cap entirely.**

(*f*) Connect the filling and vent hoses to the generator tank first making sure that the ball check valve has been removed from the air-line stop valve. (The drum may be rolled over to facilitate these connections.)

(*g*) Hoist drum and generator tank so that the tank stands vertically and the drum hangs with its axis horizontal, with the bung down, **taking care that no strain is put on the filling or vent hoses.**

(*h*) **Open the two stop valves of the generator tank.**

(*i*) Open the plug cock in the filling hose **cautiously**. If any water is present in the tank, a reaction of some violence may be expected, and smoke may be emitted from the orifice around the stem of the filling gage on the tank. If a reaction occurs, close the plug cock immediately.

Do not open again until all reaction ceases, and then with the same caution as before.

(*j*) **Open the plug cock in the vent line cautiously**.

(*k*) Permit the liquid to flow while watching the filling gage vigilantly. "When the filling gage stem starts to rise, shut the plug cock in the filling hose immediately. Failure to do so may result in the entrapment of smoke liquid in the filling line between the generator tank stop valve and the filling line plug cock, and in its subsequent spillage. Also. the tank should never be filled beyond the 32-gallon limit, which the gage is designed to indicate, as sufficient space must be left for possible

--238--

Figure 25.--FS generator. piping diagram.

--239--

expansion of the liquid in ease the filled tank is later subjected to a considerable rise in temperature.

(*l*) After an interval of a few seconds, close the vent hose plug cock. Disconnect the vent hose from the generator tank, leaving the tank valve open to vent the tank. Cautiously break the joint between the filling hose and the generator tank, allowing any liquid which may be entrapped to drain into the tank. After completely disconnecting the filling hose, close both generator tank valves.

(*m*) Remove filling gage and replace the tank filling cap, making sure that its gasket is in place and in good condition, and coated well with soft deflocculated graphite lubricating grease. If the filling gage is not to be used again immediately, immerse in sodium bicarbonate solution, rinse in fresh water, and wipe dry.

(*n*) Remove any smoke mixture which may be present on the tank connections. As much as possible should be wiped up with dry cloth or waste (discarding immediately). Sodium bicarbonate solution may then be applied, taking care that none is allowed to remain where it may later contact smoke mixture, since such contact will produce a relatively insoluble white precipitate. Lower the generator tank. Lower the shipping drum, with the bung up, disconnect the filling and vent connection from the drum, and replace the screw cap on the drum. Wash the drum around the bung with sodium bicarbonate solution followed by water. If the filling equipment is not to be used again immediately, open both plug cocks and wash thoroughly. Sodium bicarbonate solution may be used if entirely removed afterward by rinsing with water.

(*o*) In partially filling a tank from a partly empty drum or in completing the filling of a tank from a second drum, the same procedure should be followed as when completely filling a tank from a single drum, except that any water present in a tank will be spent by the first-smoke mixture entering.

17. The following PRECAUTIONS are to be observed while filling tanks from drums or while otherwise handling smoke mixture:

(*a*) The standard smoke mixture is FS, a liquid compound of sulphur trioxide and chlorosulphonic acid. It combines immediately and violently with water (even with atmospheric

moisture), the products being sulphuric and hydrochloric acids in the vapor state. In general, then, the precautions are those necessary in the handling of strong, fuming acids, with the additional requirement that moisture must not be permitted to contact the smoke mixture except (as when cleaning up spillage) in such large quantities as will immediately complete the chemical reaction, dissipate the resultant heat, and dilute and flush off the resulting acids.

(*b*) All personnel handling FS will wear acidproof clothing or aprons, gas masks (since the smoke, although nontoxic, will burn the respiratory system if breathed in high concentration), rubber gloves and rubber boots. Personnel not so protected will stand clear and to windward. Every precaution should be taken to prevent liquid FS from contacting any part of the body.

(*c*) If FS liquid does get on any part of the body, it will immediately start to combine with body moisture and will cause a severe burn unless **immediately** removed. Since the application of water intensifies the reaction, as much as possible of the liquid should be wiped off with dry waste or cloth if available. Then flush off immediately and thoroughly with a large quantity of water, followed by washing with a weak solution of sodium bicarbonate in water. The application of grease in any form before thorough cleaning as above will cause the burn to be progressive and to penetrate into the body tissues.

(*d*) If liquid FS in any but the smallest quantity gets on any garment, remove the garment immediately. **Do not apply water while the garment is on the body, as severe burns may result.** Wash the garment with a hose or rinse it in a large container of water; then soak it in a saturated solution of sodium bicarbonate, afterward removing the carbonate solution by a fresh water rinse.

(*e*) Except as noted in the two preceding paragraphs, spilled FS liquid should be immediately drowned by hosing, taking care to avoid the droplets which may be spattered around by the reaction of FS with water. If this wetting-down is performed in an area used for filling operations, the area should be dried before any further tanks are filled.

(*f*) FS liquid in drums should be stowed under shelter and not adjacent to any boiler, radiator, steam pipe, etc. FS of itself is not a fire hazard, but when spilled on other material

constitutes the same hazard as concentrated sulphuric acid, in addition to its fumes. While in store, a drum should be vented occasionally by loosening **but not removing** the bung screwcap while the bung is up. If considerable pressure has built up in the drum tested, all drums should be vented. This venting should be performed in the open air, by personnel protected as prescribed in paragraph 17 (*b*).

(*g*) Filling operations should be conducted in the open air, preferably under cover, but in all events in a dry location protected from spray. The drums should not be exposed to direct sunlight before opening, since a vapor pressure may be built up which will result in a dangerous spurt of FS when the bung is opened. The location chosen for filling operations should he such that the wind blows away from any adjacent personnel or material (including ship's structure).

(*h*) Since the smoke-producing reaction of FS occurs with water, generator tanks and all filling equipment should be thoroughly dried before commencing filling operations. The agency performing the filling operation is charged with the proper washing of generator tanks with fresh water, and with their subsequent thorough drying, which should be accomplished by moderate heating. Generator tanks, as received from the vessels rising them, should have been thoroughly flushed with fresh water.

(*i*) Filling equipment, after use, should be thoroughly washed in fresh water whenever it is not to be used again within 1 hour. After each washing, it should be thoroughly dried by moderate heating.

(*j*) Filling hose should be periodically subjected to hydrostatic test at 50 pounds per square inch in order to detect any progressive deterioration which may occur over long periods.

(*k*) Shipping drums, if still serviceable, may be re-used. As soon as emptied, they are to be thoroughly washed out, dried, and returned to store.

(*l*) No attempt should be made to salvage the liquid in a leaky or otherwise defective generator tank. If practicable, discharge the tank as when laying a screen; if not, dump tank and contents overboard in deep water. If the defect is a minor one affecting only a tank fitting or attachment, the tank maybe salvaged, but no attempt should be made to salvage a tank having a structural defect.

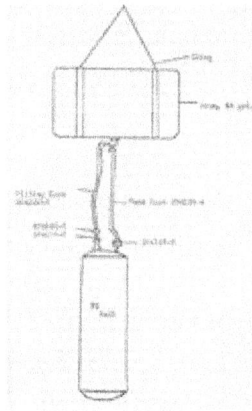

Figure 26.--Refilling FS tank.

18. **Operation of generators.**--To lay a smoke screen the following operations are performed:

(*a*) Check to see that the reducing valve is **closed**, (i.e. valve handle backed all the way out--no pressure on valve spring).

(*b*) Open overboard discharge valve wide.

(*c*) Open CO_2 cylinder valve.

(*d*) Open reducing valve to 40 pounds pressure.

(*e*) Open inlet valve wide.

(*f*) Open CO_2 pressure to 75 pounds. If screen is not heavy enough, increase pressure, but never over 120 pounds. The optimum pressure will usually be in the range of 75 pounds to 90 pounds.

To shut off generator whether tank is empty or not empty: (*a*) Close CO_2 inlet valve on tank.

(*b*) Close CO_2 valve on CO_2 bottle.

(*c*) Close overboard discharge valve.

19. (*a*) It is not desirable to retain a partially discharged tank indefinitely. If left with such a tank after a screening operation, and if it appears that no further screening operations will be conducted for some time, the tank should be completely discharged at the first opportunity in the same manner as in laying a screen, and should then be opened and washed out as described below.

(**b**) Upon the conclusion of a screening operation, empty tanks should be washed, as soon as opportunity offers, by inserting a fire hose nozzle into the "filling hole" of a tank filling as far as possible, **with very little pressure,** and then draining the tank. This should be repeated three times. As this is not practicable aboard an MTB, it should be done in an open area away from boats and buildings. This necessitates removal of the tank from the carrier and the disconnecting of the lines to the tank. This operation should not be undertaken unless the nozzleman is protected as required by paragraph 21 (b). When water first enters the tank a considerable reaction is to be expected; therefore **proceed with caution** and **avoid spattering**. The discharge line and nozzle must be flushed out thoroughly

(c) Upon conclusion of a screening operation, the entire boat's structure adjacent to tanks should be washed down with a hose. If practicable, the tanks should be washed out or re-

moved first, since some emission of smoke or spattering of liquid, or both, may be expected during washing.

20. **Smoke-screen tactics.**--See MTB Tactical Bulletin.

21. As the atomized FS smoke mixture leaves the nozzle of the generator, it combines with the moisture of the air to form finely divided fog particles. The heat developed by this chemical reaction causes the smoke screen to rise. Normally the screen will rise from 200 to 300 feet, forming a solid screen from the water to this height. One tank of smoke mixture may be expected to give a screen about 3,000 yards long. A number of shorter screens may be obtained, the number depending on the length of the shorter screens.

Chapter 12. FM SMOKE GENERATOR

GENERAL

The FM or "Elco" smoke generator consists of a steel bottle of the type in which commercial gases are contained. It has a single threaded opening at one end, which is controlled by a valve. This valve is part of the bottle assembly, and the wrench that opens it is furnished with the original bottle (or generator) of smoke. This wrench has a hinged handle so that a steel protective cap may be screwed onto the bottle over the valve assembly with the wrench attached when the generator is not in use.

To spray the smoke liquid from the generator, a smoke pipe is furnished. This pipe is about two feet long and is bent slightly. On the lower end it carries a fitting to connect the pipe to the nipple on the generator valve assembly. A hinged wrench for this fitting is clipped to the smoke pipe. At the upper end the pipe is threaded to receive a single nozzle.

Four nozzles are provided, and are quickly interchangeable. They are marked for 3 min., 5 min., 8 min., or 12 min.; the time the smoke will last in a continuous screen, using the respective nozzle. The 8 min. nozzle is for use under average condition and the 12 min., nozzle is for night use. If the weather is very windy either a 3 or 5 min. nozzle would produce a better screen.

INSTALLATION

The generator is carried athwartships on the stern of the M. T. B. There are two small wooden cradles secured to the deck, and the bottle is secured to the deck by two flat steel straps which pass over it.

NOTE.--The valve end of the bottle must be slightly lower when installed. The exhaust line leading from inside the bottle to the valve is a short, curved pipe that extends to the side of the bottle just below the valve. Also, it is necessary to install the bottle with the nipple fitting for the smoke pipe pointing straight up, so that the exhaust line opening is at the lowest part of the bottle.

PRINCIPLE OF OPERATION

The smoke-producing liquid in this generator is carbonated when the bottle is filled; thus it is under pressure and will be faced out of the bottle when the valve is opened. No additional source of pressure is required. This generator is built on the principle of a seltzer bottle. It can not be refilled except by the manufacturer so a new bottle of smoke must be installed when one is emptied.

The liquid that produces the smoke is titanium tetrachloride, which, when sprayed into the air, combines with the moisture in the air to form hydro-chloride acid and titanium hydroxide, thus forming smoke. The liquid is very corrosive on steel or flesh. Burns from FM are to be treated in the same way as FS burns.

OPERATION

To lay a smoke screen the smoke pipe must be attached with the appropriate nozzle covered with a rubber cap to keep salt water out. The valve in the bottle is opened fully. To stop smoking, the valve is closed and a rubber cap placed over the nozzle to replace the one blown off when the valve was opened. Only use as much smoke as is needed for the occasion. Save the rest for another time.

CARE

As soon as possible after laying a screen remove the smoke pipe and flush it out thoroughly with water. Wash down the deck and generator with water.

PRECAUTIONS

Avoid getting the liquid on the skin or clothing. It burns like a strong acid. Treat burns the same as FS burns.

Keep nozzles, smoke pipe, and valve assembly clean and lightly oiled. Be careful not to crossthread brass couplings. Do not force valve closed beyond normal tightness. The liquid in the upright smoke pipe will cause a streamer of smoke after the valve is closed, leading one to believe the valve is not seated. Forcing the valve will score the valve seat, thereby causing it to leak.

APPENDIX 2

Notes on Torpedoes

1. Included in these notes are certain check-off lists for preparation and upkeep which are the result of the operating experience of several squadrons.

2. It will be found that certain parts of the torpedo are subject to more deterioration under motor torpedo boat operations than in other types of vessels.

3. Among the first of the above casualties is corrosion from continuous wetting and entrance of water in the tube around the head. This can be remedied by packing around the head tightly with heavy grease and also by slushing the inside of the tube with a mixture of a heavy grease and hot running oil. This forms a sort of bond and tends to prevent water entrance. If the grease used around the head is a heavy grease and is continually repacked, in a short time it will be impossible for water coming over to wash it out.

4. Due to continuous dampness there is considerable trouble with corrosion of exploders, wet boosters, and detonators. These should be inspected at least once every week. Exploders must be kept in good condition.

5. Gyros are subject to considerable vibration and hence damage. Pivots and bottom bearings become grooved and pitted or scratched. Gyros also pick up considerable moisture, and corrosion proceeds rapidly if not noted and checked promptly. They should be checked at least every other week.

6. The usual leaks that develop are predominantly those due to vibration. Stop valves and starting piston plugs should be checked every few days for leaks. The next most common leaks are forward air flask bulkheads and starting pistons. It cannot be stressed too highly that all leaks must be located and stopped as soon as they are indicated. In this connection, torpedoes should be gaged every other day and a running record kept. They should be gaged

at the same time each day to have com-parable

temperatures and therefore pressures. Any big drop must be investigated immediately.

7. Limited storage facilities and operating conditions make the conditions of impulse charges at all times subject to considerable doubt. They should be inspected weekly for bulging or swelling of wadding indicating excess moisture.

8. Appended are recommended check-off lists.

Routine Upkeep of Torpedoes

A. Three times weekly.

1. Gage and boost air flasks as necessary. Gage at same time each day. Keep running record.

B. Twice weekly.

1. Open tripping latch and inspect for leaks around starting piston plug.

2. Inspect for leaks around charging check and stop valve.

C. Weekly.

1. Raise tube tripping latch.

2. Open tube door and put on propeller lock.

3. Remove flat nose piece from warhead and install nose ring.

4. Train tube in line for loading and place three dollies on scribe marks on deck.

5. Close stop valve and place wedge behind starting lever.

6. Attach tackle to nose ring and haul torpedo out of tube.

7. Break igniter lead.

8. Remove propeller lock and turn propellers 50 turns.

9. Operate depth mechanism from 0 to 50 and return to required setting.

10. Refill oil tanks.

11. Take out igniter and inspect combustion pot. Excessive alcohol and water is a sign of

leaks.

12. Open stop wide and turn back one-eighth turn. If excessive "carry over" occurs, drain pot. If a blast goes through, it may be necessary to relock gyro also.

13. Reinstall igniter, make lead.

14. Reload torpedo in tube.

D. Bimonthly.

1. When making weekly check, remove exploder, detonator, and booster, and check for evidence of moisture.

2. Check gyro for rust, excessive oil.

E. Monthly.

1. Remove torpedo from tube as in weekly routine.

2. Disconnect and remove igniter, note condition of end seal.

3. Remove one afterbody, and tail drain plug and drain.

4. Turn torpedo 180 degrees draining combustion flask on way over.

5. Remove exploder mechanism and detonator:

(*a*) Remove holding screws and cover plate over exploder mechanism base.

(*b*) Remove holding screws and exploder mechanism with detonator attached.

(*c*) Remove detonator from exploder mechanism and place in safe stowage space.

6. Remove booster from casing and place in safe stowage space.

7. Replace cover plate and holding screws.

8. Turn torpedo right side up.

9. Remove air, fuel, and water check valve plugs, work and oil check valves, replace plugs.

10. Remove strainer plugs; remove and clean air, fuel, and water strainers and replace; replace strainer plugs.

11. Remove port hand hole plate.

12. Remove safety stick and throw starting lever to rear by hand. Rotate starting gear index spindle several revolutions, insuring that starting piston seats. Replace starting lever wedge.

13. Operate depth setting mechanism from 0 to 50 and return to required setting.

14. Work horizontal rudders a few times up and down by hand, using one hand on each rudder, with the same amount of force on each.

15. Work vertical rudders by hand using same method.

16. Remove propeller lock, turn propellers by hand at least 50 times. Listen for unusual sound. Check action of pallet and slide to see that pallet does not engage pallet pawls while in neutral position with gyro locked.

---

17. Replace propeller lock.

18. Oil and grease power plant.

(*a*) Fill oil tanks (B).

(*b*) Remove grease packing screw from end of after propeller shaft, use grease gun and fill till bearing will take no more (G), replace grease screw.

(*c*) Fill bearing in afterbody with oil (B).

(*d*) Fill grease cavity in forward propeller with grease (G).

19. Remove gyro clamp plate cover and unlock gyro by hand.

20. Remove gyro bottom head.

21. Remove, inspect, and oil gyro. Note that balance nut is tight.

22. Lock and unlock spinning mechanism, by hand and by rotating spinning shaft.

23. Turn gyro index full range right and left. Note that index inside pot lines up with outside setting.

24. Remove propeller lock and turn propellers till cam pawl is in extreme forward position.

25. Install gyro and gyro bottom head, lock gyro, replace clamp plate cover and gasket.

26. Replace port hand hole plate, afterbody, and tail drain plugs.

27. Gage and boost airflask as necessary.

28. Fill fuel and water compartments.

Preliminary Adjustments for Mark VIII-3C and 3D Torpedoes.

These adjustments assume that the torpedo is in good condition mechanically (not in need of major overhaul) and is to be prepared for further firing.

Preliminary.

1. Overhaul the tail; remove tail cone; clean and lubricate all parts therein; examine propellers and remove dents; test exhaust valves for condition of springs; see that sinking gear is removed (installed for war shot) ; reinstall all parts and cone.

2. Turn propellers over by hand to see if shafting is properly assembled and that all parts turn freely; put propeller lock on.

3. Verify condition of exercise head (fill and blow down on deck) ; secure in place on flask and make the air blow connection.

4. Fill oil tanks, oil cups, oil tail bearing, and prime oil pump.

5. Rotate distance index till starting piston seats, noting position near zero when starting piston seats (listen for the click when the distance trip releases the stop plug).

6. Remove atmospheric chamber under diaphragm of depth mechanism. Examine diaphragm for condition, replace if necessary (depth spring should have no load during this operation) ; reinstall atmospheric chamber.

7. Place safety wedge behind starting lever.

8. Remove fuel- and water-filling plugs.

9. Install charging line (use safety strap) and charge torpedo to 1,500 pounds; remove charging line and close stop valve.

10. Remove, examine, and clean air strainer.

Prepare for test of rudder throws.

11. Connect low-pressure testing line in line from charging valve to air strainer body, tool No. 223 in strainer body.

12. Set up on reducing valve speed screw (speed ring in place).

13. See that transportation screw is in place, remove afterbody hand-hole plates, gyro clamp plate and strainer; disconnect steering engine air leads; put in a few drops of gyro oil in the air nipple to oil the engines; reconnect the air leads.

14. Open stop valve and with low pressure air (400 pounds gage) proceed as follows:

(*a*) Check alignment of horizontal rudders with zero lines on cone.

(*b*) Remove transportation screw.

(*c*) Level torpedo.

(*d*) Remove test plug from atmospheric chamber in depth gear. Place 16-pound weight on depth spring (screw rod to nut and hang weight on it).

(*e*) Turn depth index until marking on depth engine valve stem indicates mid travel.

(*f*) Move pendulum fore and aft a few times and note if valve comes to rest in proper position.

(*g*) If depth index does not read "ten feet" set it by disengaging spring sleeve from socket. Upon completion be sure spring sleeve fully engages socket again; turn spring slightly if necessary.

(*h*) Set depth index on zero and remove test weight.

(*i*) Replace test plug and make sure the washer is in good condition.

(*j*) Swing the pendulum by hand all the way aft and all the way forward. Read the up and down rudder throws when the pendulum is against its stops and adjust the horizontal rudders so the throws will agree with the record book 1U 4 D for this torpedo.

(*k*) Move the gyro steering engine valve and read the rudder throws using tool No. 44; the throws should agree with the record book.

(*l*) Note that air is blowing through the top bearing extended over the gyro pot, for the air sustained gyro.

15. Close stop valve, remove testing set with tool No. 223.

16. Replace charging valve plug and washer, also air strainer and plug.

17. Replace water compartment filling plug.

Prepare to test for proper gyro control.

18. Crack stop valve.

19. Put in transportation screw and turn torpedo upside down.

20. Note that gyro outside setting socket is on zero, also gyro pot itself.

21. Now release the spinning gear and turn the pot 90° right and 90° left from the outside setting socket to insure there is no interference in the afterbody; return to zero and check again for aid position.

22. Remove bottom plate on gyro pot. Clean and dry inside of pot.

23. Lock and release spinning mechanism to limber it up.

24. See that cam pawl is in the extreme forward position and install gyro (if the pawl is not forward, cautiously remove propeller lock, turn propellers until it is, and replace propeller lock).

25. Lock and unlock gyro by hand a few times. Each time carefully examine the finger trip to see that it is against the pot wall; if not, the gyro is not fully locked, so release the spinning gear and turn it by hand about $1^1/2$ revolutions clockwise viewed from aft, when it should be possible to fully lock the gyro (as indicated by the finger trip being against the pot wall).

26. Place gyro engine valve in approximately mid position by hand. Remove propeller lock cautiously and turn propellers

--253--

by hand, watching the gyro engine valve meanwhile. If the valve moves, the gyro pot is not properly indexed for a straight shot. It should be properly centered' by the outside setting socket, noticing the resulting discrepancy. Report this to torpedo officer.

27. Take advantage of this opportunity to examine all piping in the afterbody for leaky condition.

28. Replace air screen and clamp plate. Be sure nothing has been accidentally left in afterbody and put on hand hole plates.

29. Turn torpedo right side up and put on a second propeller lock. Lash both securely.

30. Sling and hoist torpedo so it can be turned at will in the air while the gyro engines are running on the test to follow.

31. Fix centering marks on deck for noting creep of gyro on test to follow (remember that the ship itself may swing during the test.)

32. Remove safety wedge from behind starting lever and with stop valve closed and distance index off zero, throw starting lever to the rear. Open stop valve smartly, thus spinning gyro.

33. Close stop valve and remove propeller locks.

34. Keep clear of propellers and open stop valve sufficiently to operate vertical steering engines and main engine by air.

35. Swing the torpedo in azimuth and note operation of vertical rudders by the gyro as the torpedo is swung from side to side.

36. When satisfied with the test, close stop valve and put on propeller locks and lash securely.

37. Remove transportation screw.

38. Open stop valve sufficiently to operate depth engine.

39. Tilt torpedo alternately above and below the horizontal about 3°. Rudders should begin to move with $1/20$ inclination.

40. Close stop valve and replace safety stick behind tripping latch.

41. Lower torpedo on truck or rack.

42. Put in transportation screw and turn torpedo upside down.

43. Remove gyro, replace bottom plate, air screen, and clamp plate.

44. Remove plug from afterbody siphon (install for war shot).

45. Turn torpedo right side up and replace fuel and water filling plugs.

46. Remove and oil all check valves and test operation by hand.

47. Slack up on speed screw.

48. Remove fuel and water strainers and blow through by mouth. Now do the same with a strainer known to be good; a clogged strainer will be detected at once by this method.

49. Check up on all joint screws to see they are properly set up.

50. Set up on after propeller shaft locking nut.

51. If exercise head is fitted with screwed torch pot rings, see that ones for use with torch pot are drilled for wiring.

52. Check up on securing of all accessible studs, nuts, and fittings.

With the above adjustments made, the torpedo is now ready for final adjustments.

Final Adjustments Mark VIII-3C and 3D Torpedoes

1. Propeller lock on.

2. Distance gear on zero.

3. Remove fuel and water filling plugs.

4. Charge to required pressure.

5. Fill head (exercise shot).

6. Drain air flask.

7. Cock air-blowing device, and test air-blowing head device for tightness (exercise shot).

8. Cock air-blowing device, open flask stop, and secure mechanism in head. See air-blow device washer properly on seat and follower ring screwed down tight (exercise shot).

9. Drill torch case ring for wire, do not use wedge. Insert torches in place, puncture top $1/8$-inch hole (exercise shot).

10. Oil reducer.

11. Note speed ring. Set up on speed screw.

12. Examine air strainer--do not oil.

13. Crack stop valve.

14. Roll torpedo 180°.

15. Examine fuel and water strainers.

16. Oil and work check valves.

17. Renew diaphragm (note diaphragm should be renewed before every shot).

18. Replace drain plug and transportation screw.

19. Remove cover plate, air screen, and bottom plate, wipe inside of pot clean and dry.

20. Note gyro index on zero.

21. Inspect pallet pawls, see that they are clean and free.

22. Lock and release spinning mechanism.

23. Turn propellers by hand until pawls are in the extreme forward position when gyro is installed.

24. Install gyro, lock gyro, remove hand hole cover, place gyro engine valve in mid position; turn propellers by hand and watch engine valve; if valve moves, gyro is not correctly placed for straight shot. (Put gyro in position by angle setting device so pallet blade is in mid position; i.e. when it goes back and forth without shifting valve from mid position).

25. Unlock and lock gyro to insure locked gyro; enter hand hole plate and push locking bar home as far as possible. See afterbody siphon pipe and oil pipes clear of spinning gear for curved shot. Take out gyro.

26. Secure gyro cover with air screen and bottom plate in place.

27. Inspect gasket and replace hand hole cover.

28. Turn torpedo upright.

29. Fill oil tank and cup and prime oil pump.

30. Fill water compartment partially.

31. Fill fuel tank.

32. Advance fuel to sprays and replace fuel plug.

33. Fill water compartment, and replace water filling plug.

34. Dummy igniter out.

35. Turn torpedo 90° left; drain combustion pot.

36. Turn torpedo upright.

37. Set depth index.

38. Set distance gear off zero.

39. Crack stop valve.

40. Above completed, haul torpedo to dock. Put on warhead.

41. Inspect and install igniter and make connection.

42. Sinking attachment on. Replacement screw in.

43. Put in gyro. Lock and set angle.

44. Place dollies on deck and set by height gage if available. Otherwise by eye and adjust as torpedo is set in place.

45. Set torpedo on dollies. Put nose line on and take turn on cleat. See that tripping latch is open.

46. Push torpedo in tube till propellers are even with tripping latch.

47. Put in exploder, etc., as per warhead check off list.

48. Push torpedo into tube, being sure tail bearing slides into guide. Stop torpedo when it still has about six inches to go.

49. Take off propeller lock. Close tube door.

50. Push torpedo in till it bumps door.

51. Put in stop pins.

52. Take out safety stick. Close tripping latch.

53. Open stop valve wide and turn back one-eighth turn.

Preparation of a War Head for a War Shot

NOTE.--Before installing war head on the torpedo, it will be necessary to remove the following parts from the forward end of the air flask: (a) Pipe and clip from blow valve to exercise head.

1. Before installing war head on torpedo, turn upside down and thoroughly clean out the exploder housing with kerosene, allow to dry thoroughly.

2. Thoroughly clean gasket seats so gasket will seat on clean metal. This is of great importance!

3. Turn war head right side up and install on air flask, torpedo being horizontal, using only the screws provided with the war head.

4. Replace nose ring by flat nose piece provided, and set up securely.

5. The torpedo being otherwise ready for inserting in tube, take exploder mechanism from box and carefully examine base plate seat to make sure it is absolutely clean.

6. Inspect exploder mechanism to insure all parts are in efficient operating condition and place the mechanism in the unarmed condition. In the unarmed condition, the firing pin guide is cocked (tongue gripped by triggers), and the upper surface of the arming screw is flush with the upper surface of the arming screw nut, bench marks in line. The safety posts of the arming screw should make near contact with the trigger plate and should positively prevent separation of the lower legs of the trigger when the above condition exists.

7. Remove live detonator from detonator box and be extremely careful in handling the detonator so that it will not be dropped or struck. This is vital, and the safety of the ship is seriously involved in this and subsequent steps of preparation.

8. Remove container from detonator and inspect to see that the safety chamber and detonator are clean and in condition for satisfactory operation. Wipe off parts with clean dry rag as necessary. A drop of gyro oil should be wiped on detonator holder threads and no lint or other foreign particles left on any of the mating parts.

9. With detonator holder assembled in safety chamber and top face of detonator holder flush with top face of safety chamber (bench marks in line), attach assembled detonator to arming screw nut with screws provided in exploder box (glass jar). Use screw driver from exploder box so screws will not be injured. (Note particularly that guide posts of exploder mechanism are inserted through holes in rim of detonator holder.)

10. Remove tetryl booster from its container and storage box and see that casing is clean and free from foreign matter.

11. Take assembled exploder mechanism (fiber washer in place on exploder mechanism base) and securing screws to the war head and place booster on top of safety chamber, holding by hand so it will not fall off.

12. Insert these units upward in exploder casing of war head, being extremely careful not to drop them.

13. See fiber gasket properly aligned and while holding the exploder mechanism firmly to its seat in the war head, insert securing screws and set up evenly and firmly all around (this joint must be absolutely watertight).

14. Install cover plate over exploder mechanism base and see that fan is turned so blades do not project beyond lower surface of war head (two of the three blades are staggered in manufacture so this can be accomplished--do not make more than one turn of the fan to accomplish this and always turn fan in direction it will be turned while torpedo is running in water).

15. Load torpedo in tube.

Treatment of Torpedoes After a Run--Mark VIII, Mod. 3C and D

To guard against deterioration, and to insure maintenance of torpedoes in condition for further firing, the following treatment is essential after a run.

1. Hoist in torpedo, place on truck, and close stop valve.

2. Put on propeller lock. Install transportation screw.

3. Remove torch pot from head.

4. Close valve on forward end of flask.

5. Remove air blowing mechanism from head, clean and stow away with tension on spring released.

6. Drain afterbody and tail cone, and leave out drain plugs.

7. Remove handhole plates in afterbody.

8. Fill oil pot, tail bearings, and afterbody oil cup, prime oil pump by turning propeller.

9. Remove fuel and water filling plugs.

10. Remove igniter and set depth at zero.

11. Turn torpedo upside down (drain water from exercise head, and fuel and water from their compartments; also drain the combustion pot from the igniter opening). Install dummy igniter.

12. Remove gyro clamp plate cover, and remove gyro (turn propellers as necessary to get cam pawls forward of cam so gyro can be withdrawn).

13. Dry out and oil with gyro oil the top bearing in gyro pot.

14. If gyro has been flooded, immerse in gasoline and blow off with dry air. Put a few drops of gyro oil on wheels, side and bottom and top bearings. The gyro should be broken down for careful examination of balls and ball races as soon as practicable. If not flooded blow off gyro with dry air, and oil as above.

15. Turn torpedo right side up. Put safety wedge back of starting lever.

16. Charge air flask to about 700 pounds pressure. Install water filling plug. Remove plug to air strainer, and put in a few drops of gyro oil. Replace plug.

17. With an oil gun and using hot running torpedo oil, lightly oil steel parts of gyro mechanism

and distance gear.

18. Close stop valve, remove safety wedge back of starting lever, remove propeller lock, and stand clear of propellers.

19. Crack stop valve, and allow engines to turn over and circulate fresh oil through all oil passages in the power plant. Operate horizontal and vertical steering engines to lubricate valves.

20. Close stop valve, put on propeller lock, put safety wedge back of starting lever.

21. Remove water filling plug, and reinstall fuel and water filling plugs.

22. Slack back on speed screw on regulator.

23. Reinstall drain plugs and afterbody handhole plates.

24. Turn torpedo upside down; wipe inside of gyro pot dry. Replace clamp plate cover and washer.

25. Turn torpedo right side up.

26. Drain air flask.

27. Remove and oil check valves.

28. Reinstall fittings in exercise head for storage.

29. Prompt removal of the tail, and cleaning and lubricating of tail bearings, and prompt removal of the main engine from the afterbody and cleaning of salt water from between propeller shafts, are essential. These steps should be taken as soon as practicable after completion of a run, preferably within 36 hours, unless the torpedo is to be run again shortly, and these procedures are therefore impracticable.

Adjustments to Exercise Head Mk. 17, Mod. 2 for Mk. VIII, Mod. 3C and D. Torpedo

	Tool No.
1. Remove air release mechanism	48-141A
2. Connect air blow lead to exercise head, blank off pipe in exercise head, crack air release mechanism stop valve and remove blank	13-141A
3. Attach exercise head to flask, take care not to crush pipe	49
4. Exercise discharge valves by hand, note that they operate and seat properly, and that the springs are not broken.	

5. Fill exercise head with fresh water.

6. Calibrate air release mechanism to prescribed pressure   441; 34

	Tool No.
7. Crack air release mechanism stop valve and blow through piping (note that there is no restriction in pipes)	49
8. Attach air release mechanism to air line in head	141A
9. Cock air release mechanism	441
10. Open air release mechanism stop valve. See valve is seated on its outboard seat	49
11. Test air release mechanism and connection for leaks by immersing in water.	
12. With air release mechanism cocked, secure with leather gasket and cover plate, evenly in place	48
13. If no leaks are found around stem, put on air release mechanism protective cap. See washer in place and vent in cap clear	407
14. Install torch pot in torch case, using leather gasket; secure cover evenly in place.	
15. Tear off seal on torch pot before loading torpedo in tube.	

NOTE.----It is particularly important in preparing the exercise head for firing to be sure that the leather gaskets under the air release mechanism and torch case are tight. If they are not, the head may not blow and the torpedo will be lost.

Steps To Be Taken To Insure Against Cold Shots

Two--connections on line from reducer to air manifold.

Two--air checks' outer seat leaks and sticky valves.

Two--pipe connections (improperly set up, cross threaded, and closed-up orifice).

Two--bulkhead connections to fuel and water delivery checks.

Two--delivery checks (sticky and leaky).

Two--spray connections improperly made, crimped pipe, clogged sprays.

Two--igniter connections improperly made, cross threaded.

One--washer under plug in water compartment, set up tight.

One--reducer oil plug (not set up or cross threaded).

One--leaky syphon bellows in reducer.

POOR PIPE CONNECTIONS, LEAKY VALVES, CLOGGED STRAINERS, RATHER THAN DEFECTIVE IGNITERS, CAUSE COLD SHOTS.

Note.--PROPELLERS SHOULD BE BLOCKED, TAIL VANES TESTED FOR SQUARENESS.

Blowing head connections should be tested for 2,800 pounds pressure. Remove air blowing attachment and apply pressure to air blowpipe. Inspect inside of head for bubbles. An air leak at the nipple inside of head would cause a light head and a short run.

MAINTENANCE OF EQUIPMENT

PT's require considerably more maintenance than other types. Guns are subject to considerable wetting down and consequently greater upkeep. Appended are check-off lists for routine upkeep of guns and miscellaneous equipment.

The lists appended are as follows:

1. Routine upkeep of 50-caliber.
2. Routine upkeep of torpedo tubes.
3. Check-off list for 50-caliber prior to firing.
4. Points to be observed during firing of .50 cal.
5. Points to be observed after firing of .50 cal.
6. Casualty report for ordnance equipment.
7. Routine upkeep of 20 mm.
8. Check-off list for 20 mm. prior to firing.
9. Routine upkeep of depth charges.
10. Routine upkeep of Mk. 2 smoke screen generator.

MOTOR TORPEDO BOAT SQUADRONS

U.S.S. PT _____   Gun No. _____

Check-off list for routine upkeep of .50-caliber machine guns

Between firings, the following steps will be taken to insure maintenance of machine guns in good condition:

Gun covers will be kept on at all times when turret is not in use.

DAILY.

1. Inspect gun throughout without disassembly, for signs of rust or lack of oil. Carry out routine if gun has been wet or shows signs of corrosion.

2. Wipe all exposed parts with heavy oil, if needed.

3. Wipe bore and chamber with heavy oil, if needed.

BIWEEKLY OR AS NEEDED.

1. Disassemble gun.

2. Inspect, clean, and oil all parts using the "Before firing check-off list."

3. Reassemble, wiping all exposed parts with heavy oil and using heavy oil in bore, chamber, and outside of barrel.

Small arms: Rifles and pistols

BIMONTHLY>.

1. Disassemble, inspect, clean, oil and reassemble.

Signed _____
Date _____

--263--

MOTOR TORPEDO BOAT SQUADRONS

U. S. S, PT _____ Tube No. _____ For _____ quarter, 19 _____

Check-off list for routine upkeep of torpedo tubes

WEEKLY.

1. Grease training screw.

2. Clean training ways and lightly wipe with petrolatum.

3. Train tubes through limit of train.

4. Oil and operate dogs on door to prevent frozen threads.

5. Oil and operate wing nuts on stop pin plate.

6. Grease and operate tripping latch.

7. With gun, grease all pressure lubrication fittings:

> On each pedestal (14).
> On each door hinge (2).
> On each tripping latch (1).
> On each train screw bearing (1).
> On each after train screw angle drive (2).

8. Paint all bare spots on tubes to prevent rust.

9. Check electrical firing circuit.

MONTHLY.

1. With torpedoes out of tube. Inspect and clean out impulse chamber and gas passage, grease lightly.

2. Inspect tubes for rust, dive and slush with slushing mixture.

Signed _____

Date _____

MOTOR TORPEDO BOAT SQUADRONS

U.S.S. PT _____   Date _____

Check-off list for .60 caliber machine gun prior to firing

Check-off list to be completed before each firing.

Each part listed to be cleaned, oiled, and inspected to be sure that it is free of burrs or other damage, and is in operating condition.

1. Extractor cam.

2. Switch (works freely, no lateral play, nut pinned in place).

3. Breech lock cam has slight lateral movement, no vertical or longitudinal movement, screw staked in place.

4. Side plate trigger (works smoothly; nut tight and pinned in place).

5. Belt-holding pawl (spring strong, underside clean).

6. Retracting slide (nuts and screws tight, works smoothly).

7. Interior surface of receiver.

8. Feed mechanism (works smoothly).

9. Rear barrel bearing.

10. Cover extractor cam.

11. Cover extractor spring.

12. Cover detent pawl.

13. Cover latch.

14. Bore and chamber (clean and dry).

15. Barrel bearing surface.

16. Barrel extension.

17. Breech lock (double bevel forward and on top, works freely).

18. Firing pin hole clean, use only soft brush.

19. T-Slot (do not use metal object to clean).

20. Belt feed lever cam.

21. Remainder of bolt.

22. Firing pin extension (should not touch face of sears when retracted).

23. Sear (notch in good condition).

24. Sear slide (works smoothly).

25. Sear spring in good condition. Set in straight.

26. Sear stop pin not bent (replace, don't straighten).

27. Sear and firing pin operation.

28. Extractor (sharp edge of lug rounded off).

29. Ejector works smoothly.

30. Ejector spring in good condition.

31. Ejector pin in place.

32. Head space adjusted by bolt method.

33. Oil buffer body.

34. Oil buffer body spring (lock in good condition).

35. Oil buffer tube lock spring and stud in good condition.

36. Oil buffer tube completely filled with oil (USE BUFFER OIL ONLY), no air bubbles. Filling screws, relief valve screw, packing gland plug, and oil buffer tube cap tight.

37. Breech lock depressors (cam surfaces smooth, slight vertical movement only, rivets in good condition).

38. Driving spring rod straight, spring in good condition.

39. Head space tested after gun is assembled.

40. Gun tested for smoothness of operation (by hand).

41. Back plate buffer and adjusting screw hand tight with combination tool.

42. Ammunition inspected for faulty rounds and proper loading in chest.

Signed _____
Date _____

Points to be Observed During Firing .50 Cal.

It is to be understood that these points are to be observed as occasion arises or opportunity permits. Firing is not to be interrupted merely for the purpose of observing them.

1. Clean bore and chamber.

2. Oil working parts and cam surfaces.

3. Tighten back plate buffer adjusting screw.

4. With gun unloaded, pull trigger and inspect face of bolt to see if firing pin protrudes.

(Inspect for broken firing pin.)

5. See that nuts on mount are tight.

Points to be Observed After Firing .50 Cal.

1. Unload gun.

2. Disassemble gun.

3. Clean bore and chamber.

4. Clean all parts.

5. Inspect all parts for breaks, fractures, burrs, wearing, and operation. Use check-off list so as not to overlook anything.

6. Inspect and fill oil buffer tube. If it shows signs of leakage, locate leak and remedy.

7. Reassemble and adjust gun for firing.

--267--

PT _____

CASUALTY REPORT FOR ORDNANCE EQUIPMENT

Unit name or description (Mk. Mod.) _____

Part No. or description _____

Serial No_____

Nature of damage_____
_____

Cause of failure_____
_____
_____

Remedy required_____

Spares on hand_____

REMARKS

_____

_____

_____

Signed _____

Note: This report to be signed by commanding officer or executive officer of PT and turned in to gunnery officer.

---

20 mm. Upkeep

Weekly or as necessary from exposure and as soon after firing as possible.

1. Disassemble entirely and clean.

2. Oil double loading stop very lightly and reassemble.

3. Inspect barrel springs carefully for signs of corrosion or fatigue failure.

4. Examine face piece carefully.

5. Examine hammer for cracks.

6. Assemble breech bolt and check protrusion of striker, pin in firing position.

7. Reassemble complete gun oiling lightly first. If necessary a little heavier oil than recommended may be used *except* in double loading stop.

8. Barrel should not be oiled outside and only with light oil inside.

9. Before assembling barrel in place examine chamber entrance for burrs, dents, etc. This must be a smooth cone.

10. After reassembly check trigger, trigger mechanism parallelogram for movement and for open assembly.

11. Check interlock rod for operation.

20 mm. Before Firing

1. Cock gun.

2. Put on safety.

3. Trip interlock gear by hand.

4. Be sure ammunition is properly greased.

5. Put tension on magazine.

6. Place magazine on gun locking in place.

Depth Charge Upkeep

Weekly:

1. Clean flanges on pistol and booster extender.

2. Take off cap, check inlet holes.

3. Take off safety fork and work booster in and out.

4. Put on safety fork and cap.

5. Run depth setting from 0 through 300 to 30 feet and back.

6. Regrease flanges on pistol and booster extender.

Monthly:

1. Take off booster extender and take out booster can with safety fork on.

2. Take out pistol being very careful that setting is on safe.

3. Inspect detonator for dampness.

4. Wipe off flanges on pistol, booster extender and case.

5. Wipe out central tube and oil lightly.

6. Inspect booster can for loosening of top and bulging. Insert booster and see that it moves freely.

7. Insert booster extender (see that gasket is good) and set up evenly on flange studs.

8. Take off fork and move booster extender spindle back and forth to see that it waves freely.

9. Insert pistol (see that gasket is good) and set up evenly on studs.

Bimonthly:

1. Take out pistols and boosters and test with test set as per BuOrd instructions for use test sets.

Routine Upkeep of F. S. Smoke Generator

Weekly:

Grease bearings of release rollers.

Bimonthly:

Remove and clean nozzles. Replace and check setting at two turns.

Monthly:

Weigh CO_2 bottle.
Check slip joint for tightness.
Clean and test reducing valve and gauge.

--270--

Literally Decoded, Gentlemen, It say, 'Nuts To Us.'

--271--

Transcribed and formatted for HTML by Larry Jewell & Patrick Clancey, Hyperwar Foundation

Motor Torpedo Boat Manual

February 1943

⚓

U.S. Navy

PART III. SEAMANSHIP AND NAVIGATION

Chapter 1. STEERING AND BOAT HANDLING

SECTION A. GENERAL

This important phase of PT operation cannot be stressed too highly. Basically, all naval actions depend upon placing the ship in an area where she may attack the enemy, and maneuvering

--273--

her in that area after arrival. It is the function of good seamanship and navigation practices to place the ship so that she can do the most damage to the enemy with the least damage to herself. In PT boats, the importance of good boat handling is magnified, because of the boat's small size, high speed, and, particularly, its vulnerability to damage by the action of the seas.

Good boat handling largely depends on three factors: (1) Common sense, (2) proper instruction, and (3) experience.

Common sense is something which no amount of teaching will develop, unless the student himself is trying his best. Proper instruction is added to this, and the student goes out to an operating squadron with these two factors as tools. Experience alone will tell whether he uses these tools to become a good boat-handler or just another dock-smasher.

SECTION B. CHARACTERISTICS OF THE PT BOAT AT SEA

PT boats in their present stage of development are a specialized weapon. The ones in current use are the best answer to the question: "Is it possible to build a small ship, extremely fast and still seaworthy, which can deliver a real knockout punch to a capital ship?" It is manifestly impossible to combine all the seaworthiness of a round-bottom sailing ship with the speed of a Miss America. Some designers chose to emphasize speed. Their boats performed brilliantly as long as the sea was calm, but simply could not take rough weather. Others built boats that could take the worst weather in their stride, but could not make speed enough to close the range on an aircraft carrier. The Navy's PT boat is one that (a) can outrun anything that floats and carries weapons big enough to sink her, and (b) can make reasonably high speed in bad weather.

Naturally, such a compromise type of boat requires special handling in a seaway. Up to about a 4-foot sea, the PT boat can make her maximum speed on any course.

When the seas increase to about 8 feet, she can still make her maximum speed down wind or across it, in fact on every course except dead into the seas. If the normal course is directly into the wind and sea, in heavy weather, the boat may be injured by

trying to make maximum speed. In addition, the crew will be unable to man their stations properly and may even be injured, thus placing them out of action at a time when all hands are needed. Perhaps most serious of all is the fact that, forcing the vessel at high speed into the seas causes so much spray to come-over the bow that visibility is reduced to a very great degree. This is particularly undesirable, because the very success of a mission, to say nothing of the lives of the crew, usually depend, upon spotting the enemy before being spotted, and hitting him where it hurts, before he can bring his guns to bear effectively. All these considerations point to the necessity for tacking the boat. This means to steer a zigzag course, taking the wind and seas quartering over the bows instead of from dead ahead. Then the boat can resume much of its speed, and visibility will improve notably. Just how much the base course must be altered to do this depends upon the seas and the condition of loading. 30° to 45° is ample under the worst conditions, and usually 20° is sufficient. Another controlling factor is the question: "Which is more important, that I get there fast, or that I go farther?" Naturally, at increased speed on zigzag courses, the boat uses more gas to cover the same distance made good than she does plugging along at slow speed dead into the wind. The course and speed must be chosen with this fact in mind.

If the seas continue to increase, the boat will be able to maintain speed and come closer and closer to steering right into the seas and wind. When the sea gets to about 20 feet and greater, she can still steer down wind or across it, and she can even steer into it very well, using only a turn or two of the wheel at the crest of each sea, to momentarily slant her bow into the next sea at a favorable angle. Doing this first to the right, then to the left, and so on, will permit the boat to make good practically a straight course, dead aweather, at good speed.

SECTION C. CHARACTERISTICS OF THE PT BOAT ALONGSIDE THE DOCK

The PT boat has three right-hand propellers, and two or three rudders, each rudder set directly aft of each propeller and in the slip-stream. Even in a single-screw vessel with a right-hand propeller there is a slight torque, or tendency for the vessel to go to-

the left with her engines ahead and rudder amidships. This torque is very noticeable in a PT boat, since all three propellers turn right-handed. This is caused by the fact that the top blade of the propeller is working in water of less pressure than that in which the bottom blade is working at any given moment. This gives the bottom blade a stronger thrust against the water in a sideways direction, and tends to throw the stern to starboard and the bow to port at slow speeds--approximately 1,000 r. p. m. on all three engines. To compensate for this torque it is necessary to give the helm about 3° to 4° of right rudder. As the speed of the boat increases, she begins to rise up and plane on top of the water. This results in "packing" a good deal of water under the boat on which a good deal of pressure exists. The term for this is "impaction," and it results in pressure on the water directly under the after part of the hull, but not extending below the hub of the propeller. At about 1,500 r. p. m. this impaction about equals the water pressure below the hub of the propeller, and the result is that both top and bottom blades of the propeller are turning in water of equal pressure, canceling out the torque completely. Therefore at 1,500 r. p. m. or thereabouts, with all engines engaged, and the rudder amidships, the boat will go straight ahead, with no tendency to turn right or left. When the engine speed reaches approximately 2,000 r. p. m., the impaction increases so much that the effect is to have the top blade of the propeller turning in water of greater pressure than that in which the bottom blade is turning, and thus the torque is now applied so as to throw the stern to port. The result is a tendency of the boat's head to go to starboard, which must be corrected by 2° to 3° of left rudder. The torque effect is less in the newer PT boats.

The torque effects should be borne in mind whenever handling alongside the dock as well as when under way outside.

Another characteristic of the PT boat is her ability to turn in her own length, at slow speed, with one engine ahead and one astern. The rudder, during the maneuver, should be hard over in the direction the handler desires to have the boat turn. Thus, to turn her in her own length to port: starboard engine ahead, port engine astern, wheel hard over left. To turn to starboard everything is put opposite: port engine ahead, starboard engine astern, and wheel hard over right.

Since the wing propellers are offset from the centerline, a comparatively quick turn right or left can be made by using just one engine ahead, and the rudder hard over in the direction you want the bow to turn. Thus, to turn left, put your wheel hard left and go ahead on your starboard engine. Customarily, only the wing engines are used when maneuvering alongside the dock, while the center engine is left idling, in neutral, as a stand-by.

Going ahead on the port engine, with rudder hard over left, makes the boat go practically straight ahead for a length or two. With the starboard engine ahead, and rudder hard over right, she will have a slight tendency to go to the left.

Backing on the port engine, rudder amidships, the stern tends to go strongly to port. Backing on the starboard engine alone, rudder amidships, it will tend to go to starboard. The rudder, at slow speeds, has very little effect except as a baffle plate for the propeller slipstream to work against and to give the stern an initial thrust to right or left when the engine is put in ahead position. To steer the boat while backing on one engine it is often necessary to use the propeller thrust of the other engine in ahead to slew the stern in the desired direction. In backing, if the wind is strong, the boat will tend to back into the wind regardless of which engines are engaged.

Whenever possible, approach to a dock should be made at a very flat angle. This means approaching the dock so as to be nearly parallel to it when you touch. Many times this is impossible, and the approach will have to be more nearly at right angles to the dock. Backing the outboard engine, and going ahead on the inboard engine if necessary, will swing the boat parallel to the dock just before she touches.

When backing away from the dock, put the rudder hard over toward the dock and go ahead briefly on the outboard engine. This will throw the stern off the dock, without appreciably moving the boat ahead, and then you can go astern on the inboard engine and back clear.

A good landing is always made at comparatively slow speed.

Before making a landing, the engines should all be disengaged to test engine telegraphs, at a safe distance from the dock. This also serves the purpose of insuring that the clutches are not "frozen" in ahead. Reversing the engines should also be

accomplished as a test on their availability, if needed, to stop the headway of the boat.

In this connection every effort must be made to conserve machinery. Excessive use of clutches and engines in jockeying back and forth to make a four-point landing at the expense of engines, clutches, and reverse gears is definitely a damaging operation. A good landing is one that causes a minimum damage to the boat. MTB's are very light and can readily be hauled in by hand once the dock is approached close enough to get a line across.

SECTION D. MANEUVERING TABLE (IDLING SPEED)

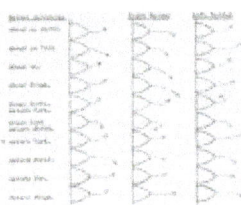

Figure 27.

Arrows indicate how sharply and in which direction ships head will turn.

ON A WINDY DAY, THE BOAT WILL TEND TO BACK INTO THE WIND.

For practical maneuvering, the boat when backing on the port engine alone, will usually back straight for a length or two.

SECTION E. MOORING A PT BOAT

Figure 28.--2-line mooring.

Figure 29.--Breast and spring mooring.

In areas where tide range is over 4 feet this type of mooring will have to be tended. Lengthening the bow and stern leads will provide a mooring which will need little or no attention during use and fall of tide with less than 12 feet range.

Figure 30--Mooring alongside another PT. This mooring can also be used for towing alongside.

--279--

SECTION F. ANCHORING A PT BOAT

Three factors enter into the art of anchoring a PT in a snug and seamanlike manner. They are: (a) Proper tackle, (b) selection of good holding ground and lee, and (c) intelligent use of gear. These factors will be considered singly.

1. **Proper tackle**.

PT's are equipped with two anchors of the patent type the Northhill, weighing approximately 25 pounds, and the Danforth weighing approximately 50 pounds. Both anchors, although of different patterns and weights, depend more on design than weight for their holding power. Of the two, the 25-pound North-hill is the better anchor for general duty, although either one is good. The anchor line, or rode, is of $3^1/2$-inch manila, approximately 35 fathoms long, with a thimble spliced into the end. The Samson post, or fore bitt, is used to take the strain of the anchor line which leads out through the bullnose. A 2-fathom shot of chain is always used between the anchor and the manila line, as a precaution against cutting the line, and also to help the light anchor hold down against the surge of the boat.

2. **Selection of good holding ground and lee**.--The boat will ride best to ground tackle if she is in a protected spot, preferably

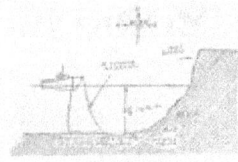

Figure 31.

---

in the lee of a bit of high ground, and away from heavy seas or swells. If it becomes necessary to anchor in an open roadstead, particular care must be taken that the best holding available is utilized.. Mud holds to PT anchors best, with sand, gravel, and rock coming next in that order. (Coral can be made to hold the anchor absolutely fast by jamming it, but injury to the gear is almost certain to occur when getting under way again.)

3. **Intelligent use of gear**.--First, pick your anchorage from the chart or by eye. Note any available bearings on which to approach clear of all dangers. Use your lead all the way in. Assure yourself that you will have room to swing 360° in case the wind changes, and have all your gear laid out on the foredeck clear for running. Approach your selected anchorage from the leeward, if possible, at dead slow speed. Drift slowly up to your bearings or ranges, and when they come on, let go your anchor. Back down on one engine briefly as soon as you have let go, so that your boat will be making slight sternway, enabling the anchor to get a good bite. Pay out enough line to insure that the anchor will not be pulled out by a pull too nearly vertical. (A safe rule is, 5 fathoms of line to every fathom of water at the anchor. You cannot pay out too much line, unless it puts you into dangerous proximity to rocks or shoals.)

When you are sure your anchor is firmly set, secure your engines and recheck your bearings or ranges on the beach, so that you can tell if you drag. Frap the manila line with old rags, canvas, or other chafing gear where it passes through the bull-nose. Every watch or at least every six hours freshen the nip at the bull nose. That is, slack out or take in a foot or two of your anchor line, and re-frap it with chafing gear, so that no one spot has to take all the strain and chafe over a period of time.

If you feel there is danger from a sudden blow or if you do not trust your gear overmuch, let go another anchor alongside your bow, on a slack line about two-thirds as long as the anchor line to which you are riding. Secure the inboard end of this new and slack line to a different cleat or bitt, and coil down the slack on deck, stopping it off with cut yarns, if your boat is pitching or rolling badly. In case the anchor line to which you are riding drags or carries away, the second anchor will automatically take hold, and save you from dragging or drifting into danger.

In general, once your Northill--called the right bower--is set, and if you have plenty of scope in your anchor line, you should be able to ride out anything short of a hurricane. Above all, care for and inspect your anchor gear frequently and well. Your boat's safety and the success of a mission may depend on it.

SECTION G. ADDENDA TO ANCHORING A PT BOAT

1. Boats operating in tropical areas, where coral bottoms are to be found in almost every anchorage, have reported that neither of the present anchors on PT's can be expected to stand up in continual use under such conditions. The relatively light flukes catch in coral, and when the time to get underway arrives, the anchor is so hard and fast that it can only be pulled clear by main force--"steamed out." This results in a bent or broken anchor.

Also, these boats report that for anchoring in the above coral conditions, in deep water especially, the 2-fathom shot of chain mentioned in the text is insufficient to prevent cutting and chafing of the manila anchor line. Five or six fathoms are recommended.

2. Steps are being taken to procure 75-pound Navy standard anchors for boats operating in coral seas. The length of the chain shot will be increased to 5 fathoms.

Towing another PT boat.

Standard towing equipment includes a fitting on each side of the clime close to the water line with a bridle and quick-releasing hook. In towing it is important that adequate line be payed out to obtain the most comfortable riding compatible with the particular circumstances.

If possible the towing vessel should tow at a speed that will permit the PT to capitalize on as much of her planing as possible.

A secondary method of towing is to use one end of the 30-fathom anchor line of $3^1/2$-inch manila, two or three round turns are taken around the 20 mm. gun mount and the end made fast with a bowline to its own standing part. The other end of the line is passed or drifted to the boat to be towed where it will be made fast at the bow either to a towing pennant or directly to the Samson post. The strain must be taken up gradually. For a protracted tow in heavy weather, it may be best to shackle

--282--

two anchor lines together, thus doubling the length of the tow, and allowing both boats to ride easier.

SECTION H. CONCLUSION

Always bear in mind that the sea is bigger and more powerful than anything that floats. Remember that the good seaman is one who yields to the sea when necessary, and opposes her with headwork rather than hull construction. The PT boat has been described luridly with respect to its riding qualities as a cross between a bucking horse and a streamlined pile driver. It is true that careless people can get hurt aboard one, but you will soon discover that she is a real boat, capable of performing well in any situation, and one that can get right out there and deliver the goods.

Chapter 2. DEAD RECKONING

A. Dead reckoning.--If the navigator had no means of observing celestial bodies to determine his position, he would still be able to calculate his approximate position at a given time by keeping track of all his courses and distances sailed, and noting the points at which they placed him. This process is called dead reckoning, and may be solved either by use of computation and table or by plotting. If computation is used, middle latitude sailing is ordinarily employed. However, the navigator generally uses plotting sheets to solve his dead reckoning problems, and this is the only method we will consider here.

Plotting sheets for any latitude may be obtained from the Hydrographic Office. Using the plotting sheets for the approximate latitude in which the ship is located, it is only necessary to lay off, from the last well-determined position, the courses and distances run successively. The resultant point is called the dead reckoning position, and is labelled D. R., followed by the time and date.

Since any good navigator takes frequent celestial observations for position, the use of dead reckoning today has been reduced to plotting a short run between observations, or to keep track of the ship's movements during periods of poor visibility when observations are impossible.

Because the dead reckoning problem is based primarily on courses steered and distances run, the dead reckoning position may be in considerable error due to poor steering, failure to compute distance correctly, or currents in the ocean. Steering and computation errors admit of no set rule to compensate them, but currents, when known, can be offset quite feasibly. An explanation follows.

B. Currents.--The difference between current effect and wind effect, insofar as the navigator is concerned, is so slight that when both strength and direction of either leeway or drift

due to current are known, the same diagram will solve the problem involved. Two cases are possible:

1. Given course and speed: To find the course and distance made good through a current of known set and drift.

2. To find the course, at a given speed, that will allow the ship to make good a given course, through a current of known set and drift.

(In the above cases, set and drift of current might be replaced by set and drift resulting from wind effect. In such instances, the problem would be one of leeway, but would be solved precisely the same.)

Case 1--To find course and speed made good.--A ship steams on course 211°, speed 12 knots, through a current whose set is 075°, and whose drift is 3 knots.

See figure 32.

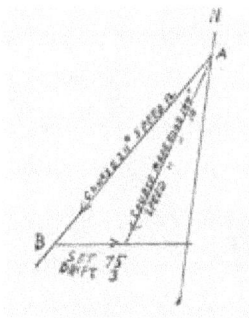

Figure 32.

Lay off on your chart or plotting sheet the true course steered from a point A on a Meridian NS, to a point B which is 12 miles distant, along the course line, from A. Point B is the location

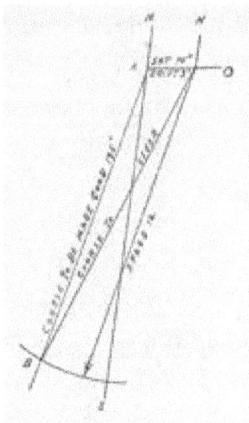

Figure 33.

at which your ship would have arrived in 1 hour, had there been no current. Now, from point B lay off a line in the direction of the set of the current (075°) for a distance equal to the drift of the current (3 miles), call the end of this line point D. Now

connect point A and point D. The length of the line AD is the distance made good (10 miles), while the direction of line AD is the course made good (199°).

Case 2.--To find course to be steered to make good a given course over the ground.

As in case 1, the ship's speed is 12 knots, and the set of the -current is 075°, drift 3 knots. To find course to steer to make good a course of 195° see fig. 33.

From a point A, on the meridian, NS, lay off a course of 195° for an indeterminate length. From A lay off another line, AD in the direction of the set of the current and for a length equal to the drift of the current. From point D swing an arc of 12 miles (your speed), so that it intersects your course line of 195°. Call the intersection B, connect the points D and B. Then the line DB represents the course to steer to make good a course of 195°.

(In cases 1 and 2, all courses are considered to be true, and measured from the meridian NS clockwise through 360°.

Chapter 3. CHARTS AND COMPASSES

SECTION A. CHARTS

Charts are extremely accurate maps of portions of sea and coast areas. Each, chart contains particular information as to the peculiarities of the bottom, depth of water, lighthouses, lightships, location of buoys, wrecks, Coast Guard stations, and other information that will be of aid to the mariner. It indicates the obstacles to be avoided, and the best courses to follow when making passages. To understand the chart thoroughly, it. is necessary to understand something about its construction.

The earth being globular in shape, the representation of its surface on a flat piece of paper is necessarily of artificial construction. The construction of a chart, on a fiat piece of paper, to represent the earth, whose surface is round, requires the use of a scheme known as a projection, in which curved surfaces appear to be flat. All projections have some errors, but the most common, or Mercator projection, is sufficiently accurate in lower latitudes to be used for navigation. The polyconic projection is used to a lesser extent, particularly by the United States Coast and Geodetic Survey.

An explanation of the Mercator is briefly this: The earth is imagined as a ball which has been placed inside a large cylinder and caused to swell until its surface coincides with the surface of the cylinder which encloses it. By cutting the cylinder along a meridian and opening it out into a flat surface, we have a representation of Mercator's chart. All the meridians on a Mercator chart are parallel, straight lines, and the degrees of longitude are all equidistant. The latitude parallels are everywhere at right angles to the meridians, and therefore the rhumb line or the course of a ship can be shown on this chart as a straight line. For navigational purposes, the Mercator chart has a great advantage over the polyconic chart. However, in the Mercator chart, the degrees of latitude are all unequal, being increased in length from the equator toward the poles.

Tables of meridional parts go with this chart, which give the length of run as minutes of longitude at the equator. With the aid of these tables, it is possible to construct a Mercator chart.

Charts are divided into two classes; general charts and plans.

Plans are used primarily in survey work, while the navigator uses general charts. General charts are those that take in a large part of the ocean, the entire ocean, or a considerable part of the coast line and its rivers and waterways. They are divided into sailing charts, for use in offshore navigation, and charts of the coast. Charts of the coast are for use in coastwise navigation when the vessel, during most of the time, will be in sight of land, and can fix her position by buoys, landmarks, lights, and soundings. The numbers in water areas on a chart indicate depths of water.

The charts have markings which stand for such different things as lighthouses, lifesaving or Coast Guard stations, anchorages, buoys, and light ships, etc. The various kinds of bottom are indicated. Every chart has a key to the markings and symbols. A few of the chart symbols are represented below.

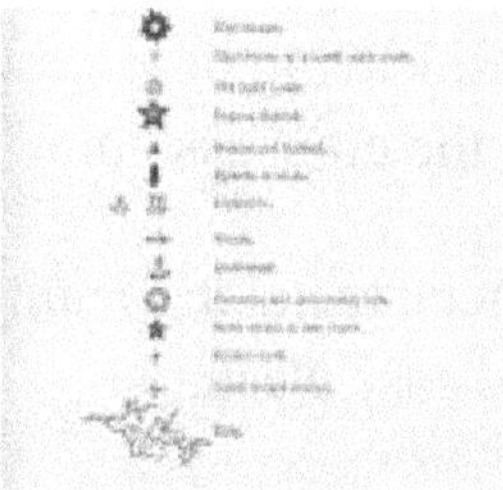

Figure 34.

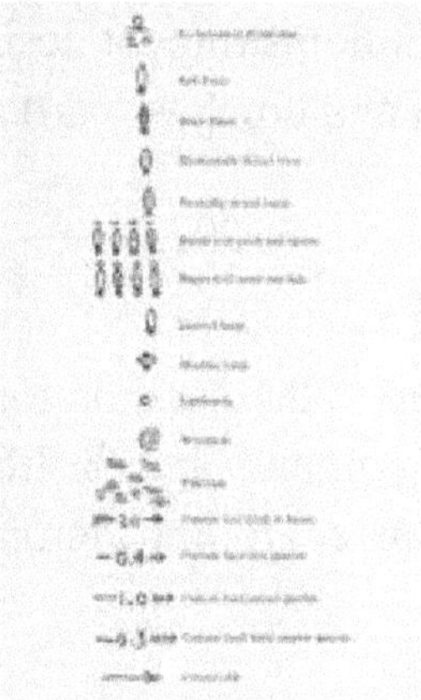

Figure 35.

These markings are found on the charts of the Atlantic and Pacific seaboards, and of adjoining coastlines, such as Nova Scotia, Newfoundland, Mexico, the West Indies, and Central America, which are published by the United States Navy Hydro-graphic Office and the United States Coast and Geodetic Survey. The markings of these two publishers of charts are almost the same, but they differ in a few instances, and they have a large variety.

On general charts great curves are laid off. These curves represent the 10-, 20-, 30-, and 100-fathom curves. They are of great value when navigating along the coast.

SECTION B. THE PIONEER AIRPLANE COMPASS

This is a small, compact, liquid compass secured to the top of forward bulkhead in the cockpit directly over the wheel where best seen by the helmsman. The dials are slightly luminous so as to be seen clearly for night steering. The liquid in the compass is composed of highly refined kerosene oil. The lubber's line in this type of compass is on a small glass plate directly facing the helmsman, and is vertical rather than horizontal, Unlike other compasses it indicates the swing of the stern, rather than the bow. To lower reading of compass (from 250°,to 230°), turn wheel to left; to increase reading (250° to 270°), turn wheel to right. With a little practice this will be readily understood.

Suggestions.--To prevent bubble when compass is exposed to direct rays of sun, build small wooden screen to go over the compass, leaving one end open so that the compass may be seen to steer by, and in this way protecting the compass liquid from overheating and leaking.

Care.--Do not place any iron or magnetic metal in vicinity of this instrument while under way. Cover when not in use. Keep face and case clean.

SECTION C. OBSERVER COMPASS

Instructions for Use and Care

The observer compass is a precision-built instrument designed especially for obtaining distant shore bearings. The magnetic element and compass card are especially "dead beat" so that any

unsteady motion of the ship transmitted to the hand or compass will not disturb or interfere with its accuracy. Construction of the compass and flashlight is entirely of brass or bronze so that there is no local magnetic disturbance. Do not attempt to use the observer compass close to iron or steel fittings.

The hinged-prism mounting is made rigid so that the prism cannot be put out of alignment and change its focal length. Should the image in the prism become indistinct it is probably due to dirt or water lodged between the prism and its bracket. To clean the prism, simply remove the screw from the chromium V-piece and the bracket, clean the prism, and replace it. Notice the alignment before setting the screw down hard to make sure that the alignment is correct.

The compass bowl is equipped with a corrugated expansion chamber to take care of contraction and expansion of the liquid, and there is also a very large and capable bubble trap. As the compass is filled with a high-grade aircraft compass oil, it sometimes develops a bubble due to cold weather. Should this occur, it is only necessary to tip the compass upside down and then level it slowly. This will put the bubble in behind the bubble trap where it will not be visible nor disturb the magnetic action of the compass card.

Care should be taken when removing and replacing the instrument in the carrying case. This case is designed to protect the prism from being knocked out of place, as well as removing the possibility of vibration reaching the jewel and pivot. It is recommended that the carrying case and compass be stowed in a flat or horizontal position. This prevents wear and tear on the jewel and pivot.

Should it be necessary to insert a new bulb in the flashlight, first remove the batteries, then unscrew the flashlight tube. The bulb may be replaced in its reflector. If the occasion arises where a spare complete flashlight is needed, simply unscrew the three small screws on either side and the forward side of the compass.

To use the observer compass, it is necessary to hold it at eye level (at convenient distance from the eye), and get the object on the prism at the same time, holding the lubber line in line with the chromium V-sight. The compass should be held approximately level when observing these bearings. The intensity

of the light which shines through the compass is sufficient to illuminate the section of the chart on which you may be plotting the bearings.

The compass itself may be used as a spare or telltale by fixing its carrying case to a vertical bulkhead. With the compass in the case, it is usually necessary to turn the flashlight on to read it.

The compass is over $9^1/2$" all, $3^1/2$" outside diameter. The carrying case is of mahogany and nicely fitted. Its dimensions are 11" long, $4^1/2$" deep and 4" wide.

Care.--Place in case on board built for it. See that case is securely fastened. Wipe carefully to remove any water and see that glass and prisms are always clean. Secure in its locker, made especially for this instrument.

SECTION D. THE SPHERICAL COMPASS

(Kerosene--Highly Refined)

It is located in the pilot house. It is used as a checking compass with the Pioneer on the bridge or as a steering compass when vessel is being conned from the pilot house.

Care.--Same as for Pioneer compass.

SECTION E. VARIATION

The influence on the compass needle due to magnetic attraction of earth or influence outside of the ship in called Variation. It is the angular difference between true North and Magnetic North. Its value for any locality is found on compass nose on chart of that area, and varies for different localities.

Figure 36.

SECTION F. DEVIATION

Error caused by magnetic substances such as iron and steel on board the boat itself is called Deviation. It exists to a greater or lesser degree on every boat. Moreover, deviation on any boat is not constant; that is, it is different in amount for every different heading of a boat or ship. Cards are made up for each compass on board, showing the deviation on different courses.

To correct a course for deviation and variation, the following diagram should be memorized.

In the preceding diagram, the arrows indicate the direction in which the corrections are to be applied, i.e., whether the course is being corrected to obtain **true** or **compass** course. The letters stand for the following quantities:

C--Compass course.

D--Deviation.

M--Magnetic course.

V--Variation.

T--True course.

To find deviation of compass.

There are several methods commonly used, for example, by azimuth of the sun, and by reciprocal bearings of a stationary object on the shore, such as a church steeple, mountain peak, etc. The compass error can be checked on any heading by known bearings such as ranges on coming into harbors, or by known bearings of any object or objects on shore.

In calibrating the compass, it is best to previously lay off on the chart, from prominent objects, ranges which will give magnetic headings not more than 15°-20° apart, obtaining sufficient ranges to cover the circle of 360°. Then the boat is taken out, and her head put on the various ranges, noting on a card (Napier's diagram) any differences between the charted range and the actual heading by compass when on the range. Such differences, if they exist, constitute the deviation of the compass on that heading. These deviations are arranged in a column,

--294--

opposite their respective headings, and using any two adjacent headings it will be possible to obtain the deviation for any intermediate heading by interpolation. A card of such interpolations should be made up, giving deviations for headings every 15° from 0° to 360°.

This deviation card must be checked at regular intervals, and always when any alteration involving sizable quantities of metal on the boat is involved. It is necessary to calibrate the compass with all metal objects in their standard stowage spaces, and with the boat in her normal sea condition.

--295--

Chapter 4. PUBLICATIONS AND RECORDS

SECTION A. PUBLICATIONS

Tide Tables

The tide tables contain the time of high and low water, the range, etc., of all principal ports of the world, also the tides of all navigable rivers in the United States. They are published by the Coast and Geodetic Survey.

Light Lists

Light lists contain information regarding the characteristics of all light and lighted buoys, also characteristics of fog signals and stations equipped to sound them, as well as stations fitted to sound submarine bells and the characteristics given. Radio beacons also are listed. Each publication shows on its cover the area covered. They are published by the United States Lighthouse Service.

Current Tables

The current tables contain the time of slack water, minimum ebb and maximum flood, also velocity of the current for all the principal ports of the world. These tables are of particular assistance to a ship's captain or navigator planning to go alongside a pier or dock in any port in the world. They are published by the Coast and Geodetic Survey.

The Coast Pilot

The Coast Pilot is published in several volumes and contains information regarding the entire coast line and navigable sounds, rivers, and harbors of the United States. There are five volumes for the Atlantic coast, one for the Pacific coast, two for the coast of Alaska, one for the Hawaiian group, and two for the Philippines. These volumes are published by the Coast and Geodetic Survey.

Chart Catalogues

There are three chart catalogues: for the Atlantic, Pacific, and Asiatic stations. The catalogues contain index charts from

which can be found the portfolio numbers covering all the areas of the world. By referring to the correct portfolio the desired chart of any locality in these areas can be found. They are published by the Hydrographic Office.

Nautical Almanac

The Nautical Almanac contains information regarding the sun, moon, stars, and planets, of value to the navigator for fixing the ship's position when out of sight of land. Published by Naval Observatory, Washington, D. C.

Chart Correction

1. Chart corrections are made from a publication called "Notice to Mariners," which is published weekly by United States Coast Guard and United States Hydrographic Office, jointly. This contains all important corrections to charts, and notes changes in aids to navigation which have occurred since the publication of the charts in general use at the time of issue.

Two copies are sent weekly to ships and stations, or to anyone requesting them. Notices to mariners requiring immediate dissemination are sent out by radio, under three classes of security: (1) Plain, (2) Restricted, and (3) Confidential or Secret.

2. Each notice should be read carefully. Charts to be corrected first are listed in bold-face type at bottom of notice. These charts are largest scale (detailed) of the area containing correction.

Upon completion of corrections on charts designated, a note should be made in the lower left-hand corner of each chart, stating date of notice.

3. Next, corrections should be made in the United States Light List, and if any new lights or buoys have been established, the notice should be cut out of the issue, and placed in the proper place in the Light List, and U. S. Coast Pilot.

The bottom of each notice shows the charts and publications to which the corrections pertain, as in the following example:

H. O. Charts, 1061, 611, 1013, 981.
U. S. Coast Survey Charts, 290, 294, 1215, 1218.
U. S. Light List, Atlantic Coast (North) 1942, page 70 or No. 345. 1-348.
U. S. Coast Pilot, Section B, 1940, page 105.

These references should be checked off the list as soon as the corrections have been made to all the publications aboard.

SECTION B. THE LOG

The log is the only complete official record of the ship during her commission. It is imperative that the log not only be complete, but also accurate and clear. Because of many routine inspections required to be entered in the log, it also serves as an important check on whether or not they have been made. The boat captain is responsible for the accuracy and completeness of all entries, by whomsoever made.

PT boats use the district craft log which is simpler and less detailed than the standard deck log. It is better to enter events as they occur so that nothing remains to be done but to verify the columns and sign the remarks. It is required that the ship's log shall be a careful, detailed, and accurate record of current events, since it is frequently used as evidence before courts and boards, and is consulted in many cases which come up years later. The smooth log is the ship's deck log. Therefore, officers should take pains to collect all the data required and to enter them into the log, using the proper phraseology.

There must be no erasures in the rough log. In civil courts, the rough log and the quartermaster's notebook are considered better evidence than the smooth log. Any erasure in them opens to question their competency as evidence.

The quartermaster has charge of the preparation of the log. By the regulations he is required to carefully examine the log book to see that it is prepared in accordance with instructions, and to call the attention of the watch officer to any inaccuracies or omissions in the entries. The quartermaster is responsible to the boat captain for seeing that the entries in the log are in proper form, but the officer of the deck is responsible for the entries during his watch and, unless directed by orders of the boat captain, he is not compelled to make changes in any entry he may have made.

The regulations require that the smooth log shall be signed by the boat captain and submitted to the squadron navigation

officer for his approval monthly, or when requested by the navigator, or called for by executive officer or commanding officer.

Every boat captain and quartermaster should frequently read "Directions for Keeping the Ship's Log," and "Extracts from the United States Navy Regulations, 1920, Relative to the Log," both of which are in the front of the rough Deck Log Book (N. Nav. 330). Extracts from "Instructions for Writing the Log," Watch Officer's Guide, will be found in Appendix II of this book.

Chapter 5. AMERICAN BUOYAGE SYSTEM

Buoys--Entering Harbor (Channel) From Seaward

On RIGHT-HAND side of channel (starboard) are **Conical** or **Nun-shaped buoys**, painted **Red** with **Even** numbers (2, 4, 6, 8, etc.). **Red** or **White** lights are placed on starboard side of channel.

On LEFT-HAND side of channel (port) are **Cylindrical**, or **Can** buoys, painted **Black** with **Odd** numbers (1, 3, 5, 7, etc.). **White** or **Green** lights are placed on port side of channel.

Obstruction buoys--Painted **Red** and **Black**--horizontal bands. May be passed on either side.

Bell buoys.--Flat-topped float with skeleton framework supporting a **Bell**.

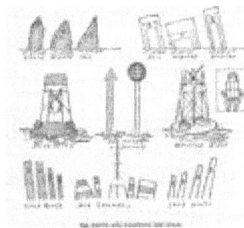

Figure 37.--Conical or nun shaped buoys: even numbered and red. Cylindrical or can buoys: odd numbered and black.

Gong buoys.--Have flat top with skeleton framework supporting a series of four gongs of varied tone.

Whistle buoys.--Are conical with whistle on top.

Fairway buoys.--Are painted **Black** and **White**--Vertical stripes, and may be passed on either side, close to, as they indicate deep water.

White buoys.--Are anchorage buoys, designating anchorage grounds.

Spar buoys are long slender buoys of wood. They may be used with the other types of channel buoys in which case they are painted red or black, depending on the side of the channel.

White lights may be either side of channel for entering vessels-- but colored lights are only on sides indicated above.

Lighthouses

Character of lights.--To avoid confusion, lights are given distinct characteristics. These are indicated by abbreviations as follows:

Lights which do not change color	Characteristic phases	Lights which show colors in various combinations
F.=Fixed	A continuous steady light	Alt.=Alternating.
Fl.=Flashing	A fixed light varied at regular intervals, the duration of light being always less than that of darkness.	Alt. Fl.=Alternating flashing.
F. Fl.=Fixed and flashing.	A fixed light varied at regular intervals by 1 or more flashes of greater brilliance or different color, or both. A flash is preceded and followed by a diminution of light or an eclipse.	Alt. F. Fl.=Alternating fixed and flashing.
Gp. Fl.=Group flashing.	Showing at regular intervals groups of flashes.	Alt. Gp. Fl. -A1-ternating group flashing.
Qk. Fl.=Quick flashing.	Shows not fewer than 60 short flashes per minute.	
I. Qk. Fl.=Interrupted quick flashing.	Shows quick flashes for about 4 seconds followed by a dark period of about 4 seconds.	
S-L. Fl.=Short-long, flashing.	Shows a short flash of about 0.4 second, and a long flash of 4 times that duration, this combination recurring about 6 to 8 times a minute.	

Occ.=Occulting	A steady light totally eclipsed at intervals. The period of darkness exceeds the period of light.	Alt. Occ.=Alternating occulting.
Gp. Occ.=Group occulting.	A steady light totally eclipsed by a group of 2 or more eclipses.	

Chapter 6. PILOTING

SECTION A. INTRODUCTION

As long as man has been going to sea, one of his major concerns while afloat has been the determining of his position. He has always been trying for the best possible answer to the question: "Where am I now, and where do I go from here"? The answer to this question we call navigation or the art of guiding a ship from place to place on the earth's surface. Navigation is a general term, covering all branches of the art. It can be broken down into the following branches:

(*a*) Celo-navigation, or nautical astronomy. This is the art of finding the ship's position on the earth's surface by the use of observation of celestial bodies, such as the moon, sun, stars, and planets. This art is at its best offshore and is not in general use along the coast.

(*b*) Geo-navigation, or piloting. This is the art of guiding a ship from place to place, using terrestrial objects for help and guidance. These terrestrial objects may be natural landmarks, such as a mountain or headland, or they may be man-made aids to navigation, such as lighthouses, lightships, or buoys. Depths of water, configuration of the land, tide rips, and other natural features of geography are also employed.

PT boats, with their high speed, shallow draft, short range, and limited navigational facilities perforce are more adapted to piloting than to nautical astronomy. While it is possible to take a sun sight or star sight and work it out aboard a PT, it is usually much more satisfactory and practical to use local aids to navigation. In other words, if a battleship navigator could be called a "star gazer", then a PT navigator should be called a "buoy bumper." This is not an uncomplimentary term, since piloting alongshore calls for just as accurate and skillful work as does nautical astronomy. In fact, an error of 5 miles in a noon observation of the sun while the ship is a thousand miles offshore is not in itself a very serious thing, while an error of even 1 mile

when sailing alongshore in some regions may result in the loss of the ship through grounding on a weather ledge.

This chapter is concerned with means of finding your position in a short time with an acceptable degree of accuracy, and with the methods of checking the position of the ship while moving from place to place.

SECTION B. INSTRUMENTS USED IN PILOTING AND THEIR OPERATION

(1) The Chart

Charts are simply very accurate maps of a region. They contain data on depths of water, currents and tides, location of aids to navigation, shape and configuration of the land, compass data, and local conditions which may be of value or interest. The best ones in the world are published by the Hydrographic Office, United States Navy, and are available free to naval vessels.

(2) The Parallel Rulers

This instrument is composed of two identical wooden rulers usually made of ebony, so joined by a pair of hinges as to be capable of being separated from each other to the limit of the hinges while still remaining parallel at all times to each other. They are used to transfer a selected course to the compass rose on the chart, and thereby enable the navigator to obtain his true or magnetic course in terms of degrees.

(3) Dividers and Draftsman's Compass

There are two similar instruments. The dividers consist of two legs, hinged at the upper ends, and having points at the lower ends. They are used mainly to "step off" distances on the chart, being set by hand from the latitude scale at the side of the chart to the desired distance in miles. The draftsman's compass is identical with the dividers, except that one of its points is a pencil lead, allowing the navigator to employ it for drawing circles of any prescribed diameter, such as, "a 12-mile circle from a lighthouse, indicating its limit of visibility as represented on the chart."

--303--

(4) Protractors and Universal Drafting Machine

These instruments are devices which can be used for the same purpose as the parallel rulers, and may be described briefly as improvements on them. The method of operation is similar, and results are the same.

The protractor consists of a transparent plastic disk, marked off as a compass rose. (Usually it has a smaller, movable disk mounted concentrically on the center pivot with it, used to offset courses for variation.) There is a long plastic arm also pivoted in the center of the compass disk.

To transfer courses, the card is set over the first point of the course, and turned so that its north points in the same direction as the north on the chart's own compass rose. The movable arm is then turned to coincide with the desired course line, and the magnetic or true course read off directly from the compass rose of the protractor.

The Universal drafting machine is a device much like the protractor, except that it is attached to the chart table, and its rose set to coincide with that of the chart. Then the machine can be moved around from course to course on the chart with no further setting necessary.

(5) The Observer Compass

This is the trade name given by its manufacturer to the portable hand bearing compass. Its function is to determine the magnetic bearings of objects in sight. The compass card is reversed, and has a reflecting prism attached to its case. A flashlight is included in the handle for use at night.

In operation, the observer compass is held up at eye level, and turned so that the prism is toward the object sighted, such as a lighthouse or tower. When the sight mark on the prism and the lighthouse are in line, then the magnetic bearing of the lighthouse will be seen reflected in the prism. This magnetic bearing is considered to be free from deviation, since the hand compass is always held well above the metal parts of the boat.

(6) The Sextant

Sextants are used mainly for celestial navigation. However, they are useful in piloting for the measurement of horizontal angles between objects, after which the angles are laid off on the

chart to fix the ship's position. Occasionally, vertical sextant angles are taken to determine the ship's distance off a chartered object.

(7) WSN Speed, Time, and Distance Calculator

This device is as a means of quickly obtaining time, speed, or distance run, when any two of the three are known. It is a transparent plastic rectangle with three scales on it, marked respectively "Time," "Distance," and "Speed." In use, a straightedge is laid across the scales, intersecting the proper scales at the two known points. Then the third factor is read off at the point where the straightedge intersects the third scale. (See fig. 38.)

Example: Given:

Speed: 20 knots.

Distance: 4 miles.
Required: Time 010.
Passage.
Answer: 12 min.

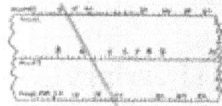

Figure 38.

SECTION C. PLOTTING A COURSE

The job of plotting a course is one on which the safety of the vessel may depend. It should be done properly, and above all accurately.

The steps in plotting a course are:

(1) Select the two points involved on your chart; for example, Lighted Bell Buoy No. 2, from which you intend to sail and Fairway Buoy No. 2A, at which you intend to arrive.

(2) Lay your parallel rulers (or protractor) on the chart, so that they connect the two points (buoys in this case).

(3) Draw a light line connecting the two buos[7]s, and remove the parallel rules. Notice carefully that your course line as drawn does not cross any dangerous spots, such as shoals or ledges, and that it does not pass too close to any other dangers, such as wrecks, points of land, etc.

(4) Replace your parallel rulers exactly on the line you have drawn. Now, holding one of the rulers firmly and moving the other, "Walk" them to the nearest compass rose, being sure that they are not joggled away from their original angle. Stop your parallel rulers with one edge directly on the cross in the middle of the compass rose.

(5) Now note the reading of the outer compass rose where the parallel rulers cut it. This is your true course. To obtain the magnetic course, add or subtract the variation (found on the compass rose) to the true course, adding if westerly and subtracting if easterly variation. Or, you may note the reading of the inner compass rose in points where your parallel rules cross it, and convert the points to degrees to obtain magnetic course. If any deviation exists in your compass for this course, apply it to your magnetic course to obtain compass course.

(b) Label your course line plainly but lightly, as: "C. 179° true," "C. 015 Mag." etc.

(7) Now take your dividers to the side of your chart. Spread the points to a convenient number of minutes of latitude, say 2 minutes on the scale. This distance equals 2 miles on the chart. Step off, along your course line, the number of units between the two buoys, and if you have a

space left over which is less than one 2-mile unit, take this distance between the points of your dividers and carry it to the scale at the side, to see exactly how far it is. When you have determined the length of your course line, label it: "Distance 7.5 miles," "16. 0 miles," etc.

SECTION D. METHODS OF DETERMINING POSITION

(1) Bearings in General

(*a*) Bearings are imaginary lines drawn between objects, an expressed in degrees or points. The bearings we are most con-

cerned with in PT boats are bearings taken of an object from the PT. Such bearings may be expressed as true bearings, magnetic bearings, or relative bearings.

(*b*) True bearing of an object from a PT boat is the angle made at the PT between the Geographic north pole and the object sighted, expressed in degrees, clockwise through 360°.

(*c*) Magnetic bearing of an object from a PT boat is the angle at the PT boat between the magnetic north pole and the object sighted, expressed in degrees, clockwise through 360°.

(*d*) Relative bearing of an object from a PT is the angle at the PT boat between the PT boat's bow and the object, expressed in terms of points (1 point equals Examples of these three bearings are given in the diagram:

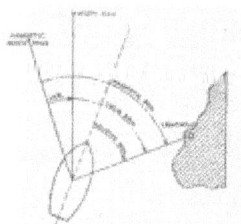

Figure 39.

The bearings taken from the observer compass are considered to be Magnetic Bearings. They can be converted to true bearings by adding or subtracting the variation in the correct direction. Cross bearings from a PT are best taken in this manner. Bow and beam bearings are of course relative bearings, and can best be taken in terms of points on the bow, rather than by compass.

(2) Cross Bearings

1. Suppose you are sailing up a coast line, a few miles offshore. You have in sight two prominent objects, say a lighthouse and a water tower, whose positions are indicated on the

chart. To obtain your position: Sight the lighthouse over your Observer Compass, and note the reading in degrees. This is a magnetic bearing, of the lighthouse from you. Lay out this bearing from the lighthouse on the chart. You now know you are somewhere on the line you just drew.

Now, sight the water tower, and get a similar magnetic bearing of it. Lay this bearing out on the chart, from the water tower. You now know you are on this line somewhere, also: You will notice that the two lines cross on the chart. Since you are on *both* lines (or bearings) somewhere, the only place where you can be is the spot where the bearings intersect. To eliminate the possibility of error, it is always wise, if possible, to obtain and lay out bearings from three objects. This method gives you a good cross, or fix, which must be your position.

Cross bearings may be taken of any visible objects which appear on the chart.

Figure 40.--Cross bearings.

(3) Bow-and-Beam Bearings

Suppose that now you are sailing up a coast line on a steady course, and you have one lighthouse or other prominent charted

object in sight. To get a fix or position, you proceed as follows: Take a bearing when the object bears 4 points on your bow, that is, broad off the bow. Take the time at this instant, and note your speed. Keeping speed and course constant, take another bearing when the object is right abeam, or 8 points, and note the time. Figure out the distance you travelled between the time you took the first bearing and the time you took the second bearing. This distance is equal to your distance off the object when it was passed abeam. (The distance can be figured this way: 60 divided by speed in knots--number of minutes required to go one mile. Then, elapsed time between bearings divided by number of minutes required to go one mile equals distance between bearings.

Example: Elapsed time--8 min.; speed--30 knots. Then: 60 divided by 30 equals 2 minutes required to go 1 mile, and 8 divided by 2 equals 4 miles, which is the distance run.

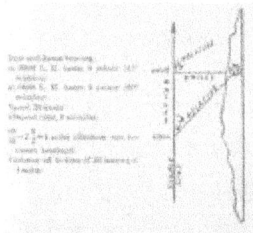

Figure 41. --Bow-and-beam bearings.

The bow-and-beam bearing has several variations. Perhaps the most useful is the 2 point-4 point bearing. This one is worked similarly to the bow-and-beam, except the bearings are taken when the object bears 2 points, or 22 1/2 degrees, relative; and 4 points, or 45 degrees relative respectively. The distance run will be the distance *from* the lighthouse at the time of the second bearing. Notice in the example below, that the distance *run* is *not* the distance from the lighthouse *when abeam*.

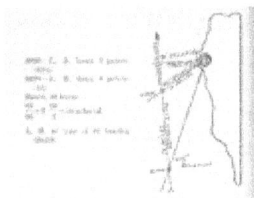

Figure 42. --22^{1}/2°-45° bearings.

There are two advantages to the 2 point-4 point bearing.

First: It gives you a fix *before* you get to the position abeam of the object. Since many lighthouses are placed near shoals or ledges, it is a good idea to know your position before you get to the danger area.

Second: With the data already obtained and assuming your course and speed do not change you can easily *predict* the distance you will be from the lighthouse when you do pass it abeam. This is found by multiplying the distance off the lighthouse at

B by .7. In the example above 10 miles X .7=7 miles=distance you will pass off the lighthouse when it is abeam. This is called the *.7 rule*.

(4) The Running Fix

This is a means of determining your position by two bearings of one object with a run between. The running fix is not absolutely accurate, and should be considered only as an approximation. It should never be used as a departure fix. With only one prominent charted object in sight and your course and speed constant, first take a bearing of the object and note the time and speed. After you have run far enough to change the bearing of the object at least 30°, take another bearing of the same object, and again note the time.

Now figure the distance in miles which you made good between the time of the first and the time of the second bearings. Set your dividers at that distance. Lay out your two bearings on the chart, from the object. Now by the use of your parallel rulers, move the dividers along the two bearings, parallel to your course line, until the points just touch both bearings. The point where the dividers touch the second bearing is your position at the time of the second bearing.

An alternate method of plotting the running fix is to: Lay off both bearings as before. Then, from any point on your first bearing lay off your course line, for a distance equal to the distance run. From the end of this course line, lay off a line parallel to your first bearing. Where this line intersects your second bearing is your position at the time of the second bearing.

Figure 43. --Running fix.

(5) Danger Angles and Bearings

When running along a coastline where a hidden danger such as a shoal or reef exists, it is sometimes advantageous to make use of the danger bearings or danger angles. If one prominent charted object is visible, lay off a danger *bearing* as follows: From the prominent, charted, object in sight, lay off on your chart a line running clear of the shoal on the side on which you wish to pass. Find the magnetic or true bearing of this line, and from your boat, see that you do not get over on the other side of the danger bearing.

Example:

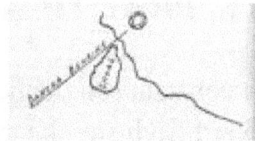

Figure 44. --Danger bearings.

If two prominent charted objects are visible in the vicinity of the dangerous spot, lay off a danger *angle* as follows: Pick a point outside of the shoal or danger well clear of it. From this point on your chart, lay off the angle between the two charted visible objects, and measure this angle. Then, using your sextant to observe the actual angle between the objects, see to it that the angle remains always smaller than the one you have laid off on the chart. (The same procedure can be followed by passing inside the danger, keeping the observed angle always larger than an angle laid off on the chart well inside the danger.)

Figure 45. --Danger bearings.

(6) R. D. F.

The Radio Direction Finder is used similarly to the observer compass. The bearings are plotted in the same manner, although the distances are usually much beyond visible limits. Cross bearings are the most frequent R. D. F. bearings used. Single, dead-ahead, bearings are also favorites, since they give a course from the P T to the R. D. F. station as a "beam" to run on. Bow-and-beam bearings are seldom taken from an R. D. F. station, but are perfectly possible, as is the running fix.

(7) Chain Soundings

Charts are the source of much valuable data for the navigator. One method of determining position relies upon the soundings printed on the chart. The method is: Take a series of soundings, evenly spaced, perhaps 1/8 of a mile apart, and in any constant direction. Lay out on a piece of transparent paper the depths of water obtained, spaced at the proper intervals, on the same scale as the chart you are using. Now lay your strip of transparent paper over the chart in the vicinity of your supposed position. Move the paper around until the soundings on them coincide with the soundings on your transparent strip of paper in the direction of the course line followed while taking the soundings. The ship's position will be the location of the last sounding taken, at the time of the last sounding.

SECTION E. PRACTICAL HINTS

When running in clear weather, keep a constant rough check of your position, such as "I am now approximately 4 miles from Vineyard Lightship bearing about SW," or "Point Judith is one point on my port bow, distance 5 miles." These rough checks will be of great help to you, should fog close in or should you suddenly have to do a series of maneuvers which may make accurate dead reckoning impractical.

Charts of the largest scale available should be used. An error of a fraction of an inch on such a chart may be only a few yards, while on a small scale chart the same error might mean being miles off.

Remember that sound signals in fog are subject to various errors. Regard them always as approximate in estimating distances and directions.

Practice taking bearings, even when you know your position. Besides increasing the accuracy of your navigation, it will inspire confidence in your own work.

Say to yourself at frequent intervals: "Suppose I were booming along as I am now, and suddenly I saw an uncharted red-and-black buoy to starboard, what would I do?" or, "If that tow boat ahead turned sharply to port, what should I do?" and the like. Try always to keep "one jump ahead" of the present situation.

Bear in mind the phrase "**Red right returning**" as a guide in determining how to pass buoys.

There are two things you must always keep aboard your boat: Keep your reckoning, and keep your head.

SECTION F. STORM WARNINGS AND WEATHER SYMBOLS

General

Because of their small size, high speed, and relative lightness of construction, PT boats are vulnerable to violent weather at all times, and dependent upon the weather much of the time. While he can, if necessary, take his boat to sea under any weather

--314--

conditions, the good PT boat captain is at all times properly informed as to the state of the weather and its possible hampering effects on his proposed operations. He knows that ice can reduce his boat bottom to splinters, that bad weather will decrease his visibility greatly, and that seas can slow him down materially. Therefore he takes an unusual interest in weather conditions in his area.

Storm Warnings

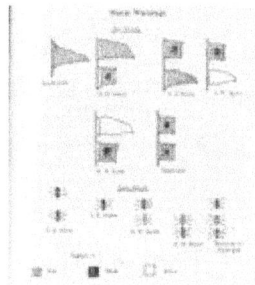

Figure 46.

--315--

Weather Symbols

(Letters to be used in recording the weather)

b--Blue sky, cloudless.
be--Blue sky with detached clouds.
c--Sky mainly cloudy.
d--Drizzling, or light rain.
e---Wet air, without rain.
f--Fog, or foggy weather.

g--Gloomy, or dark, stormy-looking weather.

h--Hail.

l--Lightning.

m--Misty weather.

o---Overcast.

p--Passing showers of rain.

q--Squally weather.

r--Rainy weather, or continuous rain.

s--Snow, snowy weather, or snow falling.

t--Thunder.

u--Ugly appearance, or threatening weather.

v--Variable weather,

w--Wet, or heavy dew.

z--Hazy weather.

Great intensity of any weather feature may be indicated by an underline thus: r., heavy rain.

SECTION G. SEA ANCHOR

The function of a sea anchor is to hold the head of a ship to the sea and enable her to ride out a gale. With small ships it has been used with good results. PT boats do not head into the wind well when riding to a sea anchor, but it will materially lessen the amount of drifting.

Figure 47.--Sea anchor.

SECTION H. THE LEAD

The instrument used in determining depth of water is called the lead. There are several kinds of leads in use. The band lead used on PT boats weighs from five to eight pounds, and is used in coming into harbor, to find the depth of water the boat is in. The lead line is fastened to the lead with a piece of leather or line well tied on; the line is marked thus:

At:

> 2 fathoms with 2 strips of leather.
>
> 3 fathoms with 3 strips of leather.
>
> 5 fathoms with a white rag.
>
> 7 fathoms with a red rag.
>
> 10 fathoms with a piece of leather with hole in it.
>
> 13 fathoms with the same as 3 fathoms.
>
> 15 fathoms with the same as 5 fathoms.

17 fathoms with the same as 7 fathoms.
20 fathoms with 2 knots.
25 fathoms with 1 knot.
30 fathoms with 3 knots.
35 fathoms with 1 knot.
40 fathoms with 4 knots.

The object of taking a sounding is to find the depth of water, and get a specimen of the bottom. The lead may be armed with tallow and made to pick up pieces of the bottom by which the character of the bottom is determined. Comparison of the depth of water and specimens of the bottom with the markings on the chart gives a fairly accurate check on positions found by dead reckoning.

It is used along the coast when any doubt is in mind as to the boat's position or the exact position of lights or landmarks.

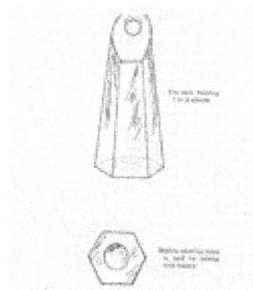

Figure 48.

So What!! Buck Rogers Did That Last Week

Motor Torpedo Boat Manual
February 1943

⚓

U.S. Navy

PART IV. COMMUNICATIONS

Chapter 1. MISSION OF THE COMMUNICATION COURSE

The mission of the course is to qualify all students in the following:

a. Standing proficient communication watches.

b. Thorough understanding of rules and principles of security.

c. MTB standards of visual (blinker and semaphore) and code communications.

d. Operating and maintenance--knowledge of communication and electrical equipment on board.

The degree of proficiency and the amount of knowledge in communications expected of students will depend to some degree on the student's rating. For example, it is intended and expected that officers and radiomen should learn more than a ship's cook and the instruction is designed to give officers and radiomen a more advanced course; however, all other ratings must meet certain minimum requirements in order that a satisfactory standard of communication efficiency may be maintained in operating squadrons.

Chapter 2. SECURITY

Security is the protected condition of naval subjects which prevents or hinders the enemy getting certain information which would be of military value to them.

Inadequate or faulty security of certain information can directly cause battles, ships, and lives to be lost; that is why proper security is so important and necessary.

Study the following rules which will preserve security. After you have studied them, remember to practice them at all times.

A. Make it your policy never to discuss naval or military matters on the beach.

B. Do not reveal naval or military information to your friends "confidentially" or otherwise. Resist the temptation to get attention by putting out "inside'? information. Your friends and relatives, as well as strangers, will naturally be curious to know about motor torpedo boats because they are new, different, and spectacular, and it will be your duty to politely but firmly divulge nothing. Remember that their interest usually is idle curiosity, and no good can come from answering their questions; there is a good chance that a great deal of harm may result.

C. The following are subjects which the enemy would be particularly interested in knowing-- for this reason be particularly careful about guarding their security:

1. Dimensions of the boats.
2. Their speed.
3. Their seakeeping qualities.
4. Their cruising range.
5. Their offensive and defensive power.
6. Their armament.
7. Their engines, propellers, and shafting.
8. Their complement.
9. Future plans and employment.
10. Tactical doctrine.
11. Communication facilities, procedure and frequencies.
12. Disposition and location of various squadrons.
13. Number of men in training.

14. Number of new boats being built and plans of construction.
15. Means of getting boats from one place to another.
16. Ships present in harbor, movement of ships, supplies and task forces, reports from friends on battles and engagements.
17. Unusual events, liberty rules, watches, duties.

D. Do not let military information slip out over the radio. For example, do not disclose speeds, frequencies, recognition signals, codes, whereabouts of boats, etc. Do not "jabber" over the radio. Use standard voice procedure so as to avoid circuit peculiarities. Avoid unnecessary testing and talking over radio. When practicable use visual communication instead of radio.

E. Take every step within your power to guard "classified" matter. There are three types of classified matter. They are:

1. **Secret**. --Secret matter is the most highly protected classification. Compromise of secret matter might endanger the national security.

2. **Confidential**. --Confidential matter is the next highest category after secret. Compromise of confidential matter might be prejudicial to the interests and prestige of the Nation.

3. **Restricted**. --Restricted matter is of such a nature that it's disclosure should be limited for reasons of administrative privacy.

Classified matter on each boat must be properly safeguarded. Secret and confidential codes, charts, letters, recognition signals, operation orders, etc. , must be kept locked up when not in use and handled always with strict accountability. A boat must never be captured with classified matter still on board. It must ut all costs always be thrown overboard or burned.

The compromise of a code or recognition signal may cause many other ships using the same code and signals to fall unsuspectingly into the hands of the enemy.

F. See that your shipmates or friends or relatives do not compromise security. Do not sit idly by while vital information is passed about. Stop such carelessness tactfully if you can; if you can't, stop it by any method that will work.

G. Do not lose your notebook or leave it lying carelessly around. The enemy has brought the war behind our front lines; we must fight him there as well as at the front. Practice security of naval and military information at all times.

Chapter 3. VISUAL COMMUNICATIONS AND CODE

No student will be considered qualified in communications until he can meet the following standards in semaphore, blinker, and code:

	Words per minute		
	Semaphore	**Blinker**	**Code**
Officers	8	8	10
Radiomen	8	8	20
Quartermasters	10	10	10
Others	6	Alphabet	Alphabet

Some systems are more helpful than others in learning semaphore, blinker, and code, and these will be demonstrated in class. However, success is probably 90 percent sweat and 10 percent the system.

Students should use every opportunity to develop their signaling to the point where they can at least meet the above requirements. Classrooms are available at night for practice and study at blinker and code. Semaphore flags can be had by drawing them from the communication office.

For many students the number of classroom hours available for signaling drill will be inadequate. These students must make this up by drill on their own outside the classroom.

Students must familiarize themselves with the following principles used in flashing light (blinker) and semaphore:

Flashing light.--The senior officer embarked in a ship is considered to be the originator of a message unless indicated differently. When using multiple call signs, the responsibility of seeing that other ships get a message lies with the ships lying between the originator and the addressees. In using individual call signs a ship does not relay unless the preamble requires it.

In situations in which answering might reveal the location of naval units, the originator makes "N N N" on a blinker tube (which means do not reply) and then sends the message twice-- thus avoiding disclosure of light in all but one direction and making reasonably sure that the message gets through.

In flashing light procedure, the person receiving gives a short dash after each word received. The sending station should repeat a word until the receiver indicates that he has received the word correctly by giving the short dash. "B," is used to show receipt of a message.

On MTB's, flashing light signals are sent by searchlight (day) , by blinker tube (night) , and by MP (multipurpose) light (day and night). The MP light is probably the best for all round blinker signaling on the MTB's. The method to use in transmitting by flashing light depends upon the particular circumstances at the moment. The number of addressees and their position relative to the originator, the degree of security desired, and the degree of rapidity desired are all factors to be considered. A point to be remembered in connection with this is never to use a high-power system when a lower powered one will suffice. Semaphore should always be used wherever practicable for reasons of security. To illustrate, even the flashes of directive flight may be seen from an aircraft too far away to be seen from surface vessels.

When using flashing light of any kind during daylight hours, or directive light at night, always ascertain that your light is training directly upon the receiving station as though you were trying to illuminate him. If during the transmission, the receiving station makes "W," it means that your light is improperly trained or that it is too weak to receive. In this case make sure that the light is trained properly and is level. If the receiving station continues to make " W," the transmitting station must shift to a higher powered system.

Semaphore.--In sending semaphore always stand erect, feet together, with arms straight. Endeavor to make the characters plainly with a distinctive pause between characters. Always watch your arms, not the receiver, in order to check yourself. When making characters such as "I," "O," "H," "X," and "W," the pivoting of the body at the waist allows these letters to be made more clearly. Never permit your hands to. curl

around the body. Pretend that you have no elbows and keep your arms parallel. Avoid stiffness. A relaxed attitude is best as it is not tiring for long messages.

There are special signs (prosines) used in semaphore. They are:

The answering sign.--Used to answer a caller, when condtions affecting the receiving and sending are bad, to show that a word or item has been received.

The attention sign.--To call a ship or gain attention.

The front sign.--Used before and after each call sign, word, code group, other procedure sign, and between letters of a code group.

The numeral sign.--Used before and after each group of numerals or combinations of numbers and letters in the text.

The semaphore sign.--"SEM" made by flashing light to indicate that semaphore will be used thereafter.

The visual space sign.--Double "I" used to separate code group.

Move signs.--Used in cases where the sender has chosen a poor background, making it difficult or impossible for the receiver to catch the message. These signs are:

    MR--Move to your right.

    ML--Move to your left.

MU--Move up.

MD--Move down.

VA--When using semaphore for an executive signal, "VA" shall be used for the 5-second dash used in other methods.

Chapter 4. RECOGNITION SIGNALS

Recognition signals are used between vessels (and aircraft) to determine mutual identity, i.e., whether friendly or enemy.

Recognition signals are composed of (a) the challenge, and (b) the reply. These signals are usually made either by flashing light, by smoke bombs or flares. Very's stars and flares are usually used in emergencies when flashing light has failed for one reason or another.

Recognition signals must be on every boat before getting underway. These signals are confidential and must either be returned to the Communication Office or destroyed by burning when defunct.

Always observe the following rules with regard to recognition signals:

> (a) Never challenge unless prepared to back it up with instantaneous offensive action.

> (b) When giving a reply to a challenge, give it accurately and promptly. This means always being prepared, i.e. have blinker light and pyrotechnic pistols at hand and the signals for the time clearly in mind. Never, wait until you have been challenged to look up the signal. Such delay may be fatal.

> (c) MTB's may frequently be mistaken for submarines because of their small freeboard and "cigar" appearance. MTB personnel must be particularly alert to identify themselves rapidly to friendly craft.

Chapter 5. RADIO VOICE PROCEDURE

Students should practice radio voice procedure between themselves until they have become familiar with it and it has become second nature. Normally, any embarassment or self-consciousness will be overcome by this sort of practice and when students actually talk into the microphone they will already have gained confidence in themselves.

The following is an illustration of standard voice procedure:

Supposing the PT 61 wants to call the PT 62, the 61 operator says:

"2 from 1 answer"

and the PT 62 operator comes back with

"1 from 2 go ahead."

(Note that the number of the boat being called comes first and that of the caller last.)

The PT 61 operator then gives the message:

"2 from 1" (message) "go ahead."

The PT 2 operator then acknowledges by the following:

"1 from 2 Roger."

Roger means "I have received your transmission." If the PT 61 had given the PT 62 an order, the operator would inform the boat captain and the latter might instruct the radioman to answer with a

"Wilco"

which means "I will comply. "

If an operator wants to tune his receiver, he can call a boat and ask for a "long" or "short test count. " A "short test count" is from 1 to 5 and back to 1; a "long test count" is 1 to 10 and back to 1.

If a radioman wants to know how he is being received he may ask another boat

"How do you receive me?"

and if the answer is:

"I receive you strength five"

this signifies the reception is good. Strength four down to

strength one represents less satisfactory degrees of reception in that order.

When speaking over the microphone do so clearly and distinctly, holding the instrument close to your mouth. Do not shout. Enunciate clearly.

Never say please or thank you on the radio. Never engage in unofficial transmissions. Keep testing and traffic down to a minimum. Be careful not to give away confidential information in talking over the radio.

Radio silence is a condition where absolutely no radio transmissions are permitted. Breaking radio silence is a serious offense.

Radio operators must not send transmissions unless authorized to do so and they must report all transmissions to the boat captain immediately upon receipt.

While it is often convenient to stand radio watches on the loudspeaker, the radio watches should be stood by earphone as weak receptions may not be heard on the loud-speaker.

It is good practice to use "Z" signals whenever possible. "Z" signals are abbreviated signals for certain frequently used messages and they are found in the communication procedure book located near the radio. Students should familiarize themselves with this book.

A complete radio log will be kept at all times and an entry made at least every 5 minutes. Below is an example of a typical radio log.

Date_____ 19_____   Page_____
Operator_____   Freq_____

U.S.S. (name of ship or station)

RADIO LOG

(Time G. C. T.)	Call	Remarks

--329--

Chapter 6. THE RADIO

You should memorize the following data about the radio:

Name.--Navy Model TCS radio telephone and telegraph transmitter and receiver.

Frequency range.--1. 5-12. 0 megacycles (1,500-12,000 kilocycles).

Output.--40 watts Key/CW; 20 watts voice.

Power supply.--Two dynamotors.

Antenna.--Whip type--20-foot vertical.

Instructions for Operating TCS Radio

See that "Radio" switch in engine room is in the ON position. The whip antenna should be in the fully extended position at all times while the radio is being used for receiving or transmitting.

Receiver

1. Set "Band Switch" on appropriate band position.

2. Set "Oscillator Selector" in correct position (Generally "M. O. ").

3. Set "Tuning" control, using proper scale.

4. Set "RF gain" and "AP gain" controls to about position 5.

5. Set "Voice-CW" switch to type of signal being received.

6. Turn "Power" switch ON.

7. After set has "warmed up" readjust "timing" control if necessary, and adjust RF and AF gains for good signal volume.

Transmitter

1. Set "Band Switch" on appropriate band position.

2. Set "Tuning" control to correct frequency. (When using first band, use direct reading. When using second band, divide frequency by two and put result on dial. When using third band, divide frequency by four and put result on dial.)

3. Set "Oscillator Selector" to correct position. (Generally "M. O. ")

4. Place "Emission" switch on Voice or CW as desired.

5. Plug in Key or Microphone as required.

6. *Set "Plate Tuning" on "0", "Coupling" on "5", "Ant. Cond. " on OFF, "Loading Coil" on "0", and Antenna Loading on "O".*

7. Put "Power" switch in ON position and let equipment warm up for about 20 seconds before proceeding.

8. Press Microphone button (or hold Key down) and with other hand turn "Plate Tuning" to right slowly until "Plate Current" meter needle dips to a minimum point.

9. Turn "Antenna Loading" control to the right until a maximum reading is obtained on the "Antenna Current" meter.

10. Check the reading of the "Plate Current" meter; if it is above the first red mark (when using voice), decrease it by decreasing the "Coupling" control. If using CW, reduce current indication to slightly below the second red mark, using above method.

11. If operating on band 1 and no reading is obtained on the "Antenna Current" meter after carrying out above steps, set "Loading Coil" to position 3, further adjusting it to the position where the greatest "Antenna Current" reading can be obtained.

12. When using the third band, if no indication can be obtained on the "Antenna Current" meter, shift "Ant. Cond. " to "Series" and then readjust "Antenna Loading" control, if still no indication set "Ant. Cond. " to "Parallel" and again readjust "Antenna Loading. " One of the 3 positions will be the correct one, and this can only be determined by test.

Remote Control

1. Make all adjustments to receiver and transmitter as given above.

2. Set "RF gain" at 5, and "AF gain" at 10 on receiver.

3. Set "Power" switches on receiver and transmitter to OFF.

4. Insert Microphone (and headphones if desired) in proper jacks in control unit.

5. The receiver and transmitter may now be started and stopped by use of the switches on the control unit. Also the volume of the incoming signal may be adjusted by means of the "Volume" control on the remote control unit.

Location of Faults

Receiver.--Receiver motor generator set will not start:

1. Battery switch in engine room power distribution panel not on RADIO position.

2. Battery fuse on engine room power distribution panel open.

3. Interlock switch open in receiver.

4. Fuse open in motor generator mounting base. Receiver motor generator set will not turn off at receiver: (a) Receiver POWER ON--OFF switch in ON position at remote control unit.

Receiver motor generator set will not turn off at remote control unit: (a) Receiver POWER ON--OFF switch in ON position at receiver.

Steady howl in receiver when tuned to transmitter frequency: (a) Transmitter OSCILLATOR SELECTOR switch in MO TEST position.

Unable to hear boats in company and able to hear distant base station: (a) Receiver RF GAIN advanced too much, causing local loud signal to block receiver completely.

Transmitter.--Receiver motor generator operating but transmitter motor generator will not start:

1. Interlock switch open in transmitter unit.

2. Fuse open in motor generator mounting base. Transmitter motor generator set will not turn off at transmitter: (a) Transmitter POWER ON--OFF switch ON at remote control unit.

Transmitter motor generator set will not turn off at remote control unit: (a) Transmitter POWER ON--OFF switch ON at transmitter.

Notes on the Operation of the TCS Radio

Further instructions for tuning.--When motor torpedo boats are operating together as a unit, experience has shown that difficulties are experienced in radio communication between boats of the operating unit and also between the boats and the base or tender from which they may be operating. These difficulties are experienced even though all boats may have their transmitters and receivers "tuned" to the same frequency. The word "tuned" is used advisedly, for it has been found that personnel are superficial in setting up their transmitters and receivers and because

of this all boats are not operating on the same frequencies. A difference of only a few kiloycles in the tuning of one boat can cause breakdown of radio transmission and reception. Whereas, under most circumstances, the radios are operated on crystal-controlled frequencies, even then differences great enough to hamper communication may be experienced.

A small amount of care and effort in originally setting up and tuning the receiver and transmitter will pay dividends in the long run. All boats should tune their receivers carefully to the exact frequency being used by the senior boat or the base. Calling the senior boat or base before getting under way and definitely making sure that all transmitters and receivers are on the exact frequency is the best way to do this. A method of doing this is for the senior boat to "zero beat" his receiver with the transmitter of the base or tender and then to "zero beat" his transmitter with his receiver. All other boats should then check their frequencies with the senior boat. In this manner the senior boat will be on the exact frequency of the base or tender and all boats will be on the same exact frequency, having checked their equipment prior to getting under way. (The "zero beat" method will be demonstrated in the boats.)

Radio watches must be stood with the headphones. It is the poorest kind of radio procedure to stand a loudspeaker watch. The loudspeaker exists merely for the information of the boat captain. It has sometimes occurred that boats have stood radio watches on the loudspeaker, with the volume turned to a position where the signal being received from the boats in the immediate vicinity is received at a comfortable loudness. The signal of a station calling the boats, then, from a great distance would not be audible over the loudspeaker and communications would break down.

Chapter 7. ELECTRICAL SYSTEM

Description

1. The primary electrical system is a 24-volt direct current installation which is fed by storage batteries and generators. It is a two-wire system employing a grounded negative return; i.e., the negative side of each circuit is connected to the ground system and to each other. This method of wiring is employed so that the voltage of all circuits will be of the same value, regardless of their location in relation to the batteries, thus effectively eliminating any effect which might be caused by the resistance of a conductor.

2. The system is divided into two subsystems known as the "Battle" and "General" systems. When the "General" system is in use, all of the power, white lighting, and navigation circuits may be used. When the "Battle" system is in use, all of the power and only the battle lighting circuits may be employed.

Batteries

The storage batteries are located in the engine room and consist of two banks of 24 volts each. Each bank is composed of two 12-volt, 150-ampere-hour capacity batteries, connected in series so as to furnish 24 volts at 150 amperes per hour. These batteries are of the common lead-acid type, especially constructed for durability. The two banks are known as battery No. 1 and battery No. 2.

Generators

As the electrical system depends on storage batteries for its energy, some means must be provided to recharge these when their energy has been exhausted. This is accomplished by electrical devices known as generators, which convert mechanical energy into electrical energy in quantities sufficient to renew the strength of the batteries.

Four generators are provided. First, the one of the largest capacity which is known as the auxiliary generator. This machine is a gasoline-driven, air-cooled device, capable of delivering 175 amperes of current at 28. 5 volts, or 5 kilowatts. Second are the three main engine generators, each of which is connected to the shaft of one of the Packard engines. These three generators have a capacity of 75 amperes at 28 volts each.

The auxiliary generator performs a function other than that of charging batteries in that it is used to furnish the additional power required for certain electrical machines on the boat beyond the capacity of the batteries.

Voltage Regulators

As the voltage of generators varies with their speed and since we must have a constant voltage of a certain value (28. 5 volts) , we employ a device known as a voltage regulator. This machine is appropriately named in that it regulates the voltage of the generator to a certain value. Each of the four generators has its own independent regulator.

Distribution and Control

In the engine room is an electrical distribution and control board. This board or panel has many electrical cables from all parts of the boat running into it and is equipped with various switches, relays, and indicating meters. It is used to distribute the electrical energy from the batteries and generators to various parts of the boat and various electrical machines in the amounts required. The meters indicate where the electrical power is coming from, going to, amount and condition of.

Forward, in the chart house, is a secondary panel board to be used in conjunction with the one in the engine room. On this panel are switches for controlling the navigation lights, signal buzzers, and a system selector switch, to select either the battle or general system (if installed).

The electrical current is conducted to various parts of the boat by means of various-size cables, which are for the most part run through conduits. These conduits are both round and square of various sizes, dependent on the number of cables running through them.

Junction boxes are located at frequent intervals along the conduits. All conduits are, or should be, watertight and gas-tight. Where the conductors are outside of conduits, they are covered with a metal braid called shielding and all connections to fixtures are watertight and gastight.

All switches and fixtures throughout the system are of the enclosed, gastight type.

Power Machinery

The electrical devices requiring a large amount of power in excess of the capacity of the batteries are only two in number and will be operated only from the auxiliary generator singly NEVER AT THE SAME TIME AND NEVER DIRECTLY FROM THE BATTERIES. These are the air compressor (if installed) and the galley range.

Fuses and Circuit Breakers

All electrical circuits are protected from overloading by fuses or circuit breakers. They are located in several boxes throughout the boat and are of various electrical and physical sizes.

Vent Blower Motor

Air is forced through the boat's ventilating system by means of a fan attached to an electric motor of one-half horsepower capacity. This motor is located in the armory. It consumes approximately 15 amperes at 24 volts, thus necessitating power additional to the storage batteries if the blower system is to be operated for a long period of time.

Galley Range

The heating units of the galley range draw large amounts of current. It requires approximately 63 amperes at 24 volts. It is NEVER operated from the storage batteries alone. This high current must be supplied by the auxiliary generator or the three engine generators working at maximum capacity.

Gas Alarm

The gas alarm is an electrical instrument, employed to take samples of air from either the engine room bilges or the tank compartment and measure its gasoline vapor content. If the air is found to be of sufficient gaseous content, the device automatically lights a red -warning light and sets a siren into operation.

Storage Batteries

Storage batteries are devices employed to store electrical energy in a convenient manner until ready for use. They are designed to withstand severe usage over a period of many months with intelligent care. Certain laws must be observed in order to obtain this long, faithful service. These laws are few and can readily be applied by anyone in the naval service, regardless of their electrical knowledge. They are:

1. Do not attempt to work the battery over its rated capacity.

2. Do not charge or discharge beyond normal limits.

3. Keep plates covered by approximately one-quarter inch of electrolyte.

4. Keep battery tops dry and clean.

5. Do not allow battery to stay in a discharged condition.

6. Keep batteries well ventilated.

7. Keep battery terminals lightly covered with a good grade of grease (preferably vasoline).

8. Keep battery connections tight.

As the electrolyte in a storage battery gives off a highly explosive hydrogen gas under certain conditions, the following precautions, in addition to the maintenance rules above, must be observed.

1. Keep temperature below 115° F. at all times.

2. Allow no open flames or electric sparks near the battery.

3. Keep metal tools from the vicinity of the battery, as they might fall across the battery terminals and produce an electric spark.

4. Keep cell covers on batteries at all times except when taking samples of the electrolyte or adding distilled water.

5. Keep battery well ventilated, especially during charge, in order to dissipate the hydrogen gas into the atmosphere.

The state of charge of a storage battery is determined by means of a battery test set known as a "Hydrometer. " This device measures the specific gravity of the electrolyte, which is proportionate to the state of charge. For the type of battery used aboard the PT boats this is 1. 275 for a fully charged cell. When this reading drops to 1. 200 the battery should be recharged. These readings are considered at 80° F. and must be corrected for other temperatures. The battery test set includes a calibrated thermometer to facilitate this.

Bonding System

The rapid movement of a PT boat through the water causes considerable friction. As friction is the producer of static electricity, then a PT boat becomes quite a storehouse for this electrical charge. The electrical charge is of extreme danger when in the immediate vicinity of gasoline or its fumes, as a tiny spark caused by it may result in an explosion of sufficient force to destroy the boat. In order to control this electrical charge and pass it off safely to the earth, every piece of metal of appreciable size and every frame of the boat are electrically connected to one another and finally to a ground strip of copper along the boat's keel. The water under the keel acts as an electrical conductor to the earth, thereby allowing the static electricity to pass harmlessly to the earth via a path of low resistance.

The elimination of sparks caused by static electricity also cuts down interference in radio reception aboard the boat.

Auxiliary Electrical System

An auxiliary electrical system for use when at a dock has been installed. It is operated by 110 volts A. C. and is used for lighting, cooking, and heating. It serves only the portion of the boat forward of the chart room. It is connected to the shore line by means of a portable cable carried aboard the boat. The system is designed to consume a maximum of 100 amperes at 110 volts. All fuses for the entire system are located in a fuse box inside the steering chain locker in the wheelhouse. This system has its own independent wiring and lighting fixtures.

--338--

Maintenance

The greatest factors in maintaining any electrical system are frequent and thorough inspections. It is much easier to prevent a casualty than to repair the damage after the casualty has occurred. These inspections should be conducted immediately after the boat has returned to its base after being underway for any length of time. The following points should be noted:

1. See that all electrical connections are tight.

2. Note condition and state of charge of the batteries.

3. Inspect all electrical conductors for breaks in their outside shielding.

4. See that all switches work properly.

5. Replace any burned-out fuses, after determining the reason for the fuse being burned out, and correcting the abnormal condition.

6. See that all electrical fittings are in good condition.

7. Inspect the bonding system for any loose connections or breaks.

ALWAYS REMOVE THE VOLTAGE FROM ANY CIRCUIT WHILE REPLACING A FUSE IN THAT CIRCUIT. When in doubt, turn all switches on the engine room panel board to OFF.

Carry at least 300 percent spares for all sizes of fuses and 100 percent light bulbs used aboard the boat.

Chapter 8. RADIO DIRECTION FINDER

The Purpose of a Radio Direction Finder on a PT Boat

The radio direction finder on a PT boat is used to get radio bearings on radio signals. These bearings, like those taken with a pelorus, are used to help determine the position of the boat. I The R. D. F. is particularly useful when navigating out of sight of land and in fog.

Location of the R. D. F. in the 77-foot PT's

The R. D. F. in the 77-foot boats is located in the wheelhouse on the starboard side.

Specifications of the R. D. F. Used in the 77-foot PT's

Name.--Bludworth Standard Arrow.

Frequency range.--280 to 520 kilocycles.

Current supply.--Independent six-volt storage battery charged from the boat's 24-volt circuit.

Antennae.--(a) Rotatable loop located on the starboard side of cab.
(b) Small vertical "whip" located on port side of cab.

Operation of the R. D. F. Set (Bludworth)

Step 1.--Insert headphone plug in phone jack.

Step 2.--Turn battery charging switch to "off" position.

Step 3.--Turn set on by turning masterswitch to "on. " Adjust volume (volume control knob).

Step 4.--Set tuning dial to frequency of signal station desired.

Step 5.--Rotate loop wheel until minimum signal is heard. (a minimum is the point of weakest signal just before a point of silence or null).

Step 6.--Adjust "balance" knob until as sharp a null as possible is obtained.

Step 7.--If the boat is lost and the operator is not certain which side the signal is coming from he will use the sense feature. (It must be realized that radio signals are bilateral, and that if

there is a null of 090°, there will also be one at approximately 270°, etc.; therefore, the operator must either know or determine which side the signal is coming from.) To operate the sense feature, turn the short red pointer, marked with an "S", to the bearing on which there is a null. Depress sense button and listen to signal. Then turn the "S" pointer approximately 180° to the reciprocal bearing. Depress sense button and listen. The bearing on which the signal is loudest will indicate the side from which the signal is coming.

Step 8.--Before a fix can be gotten, it is necessary to get at least two bearings by a repetition of the procedure ju^t outlined.

Operation of Radio Direction Finder
Model DAE

A. Steps

1.
    a. Turn power switch to ON position.
    b. Plug in headphones.
    c. Unlock loop.
    d. Turn dial light switch to ON position, if illumination of tuning scale is desired.

2. Band Switch:

    Band 1--240 to 520 KC.
    Band 2--480 to 1050 KC.
    Band 3--970 to 2000 KC.
    a. Place band switch in position 1, 2, or 3 as required for the desired frequency band.

3. Advance Volume Control clockwise as required.

4. Turn on BFO switch to obtain high pitched tone most convenient for taking bearings. Place "Balancer" on O.

5. Tune in desired signal with tuning knob. Readjust volume control, if necessary, and rotate loop handwheel until signal is clearly heard and identified.

6. To take bearing rotate loop to obtain minimum value of signal, adjusting the Balancer Control to the right or left of O position to sharpen bearing. Correct bearing is NO SIGNAL or NULL position. Use relatively high volume while at or near "NULL" position of loop and balancer.

7. After bearing has been obtained from azimuth scale, refer to calibration chart for corrected bearing, noting frequency band or frequency listed on calibration chart.

8. If general direction or. SENSE of incoming signal is not known, the following must be done after the bearing is taken: lower volume and turn Balancer so that pointer is at SENSE position and hold it in that position against tension. Then rotate the loop several degrees (i.e. about 20°) towards lower readings on the scale and observe whether the signal increases strength. If so, the bearing is correct. If not, the reciprocal of the bearing is correct.

9. When securing unit, turn power switch to OFF position. Lock loop with hand brake.

Plotting Radio Bearings

The following procedure is standard for plotting R. D. F. bearings.

1. When the R. D. F. operator gets a null,, he calls out "Mark" to the helmsman and notes the time,

2. The helmsman calls down the boats heading (reading directly from the magnetic compass) to the R. D. F. operator.

3. The R. D. F. operator then relays the following information to the navigator:

    a. Time of bearing.
    b. Station.
    c. Corrected D. F. bearing.[1]
    d. Ship's head.

Since the bearings gotten on the R. D. F. are bearings relative to the boat's keel, they must be converted to bearings relative to the ship's heading magnetic. To do this the navigator simply adds the R. D. F. bearings to the boat's heading as read from the magnetic compass. If the sum is greater than 360° the navigator subtracts 360°. The navigator will then correct this bearing for errors of deviation, variation, and, if the station is over 50 miles

[1]Corrected bearing: The bearing corrected for the deviation which is caused by large masses of metal and closed loops in the vicinity of the direction finder loop antenna.

away, for mercator distortion, using the proper table in H. O. 205. The resultant corrected bearing will then be a true bearing and can be plotted on the chart as such.

It must be remembered that a fix from R. D. F. bearings gives only an estimated position and as such, therefore, should be marked "E. P. " The D. R. track line is not replotted from a radio bearing fix.

Radiobeacon Stations

The sources of signals which are used by R. D. F. 's on PT boats are. radiobeacon stations and light vessels. Each PT should have on board Hydrographic Office Publications 205 and 206, which list all radiobeacon stations and light vessels of the general area in which operations may be expected. Radiobea-cons are indicated on all charts by O in orange. These stations maintain published schedules during clear weather and operate continuously during periods of poor visibility. In general, the beacons transmit modulated, interrupted continuous wave (MOW) identifying signals of long and short emissions. Those on the coasts of the United States employ very simple signals of one characteristic and the beacons are generally arranged to operate in groups of three, on the same frequency, so as to permit taking three point bearings in rapid succession from three, different transmitters. For instance, at and near the entrance to New York Harbor are Fire Island Light Vessel, Ambrose Light Vessel, and Barnegat Light Vessel. Fire Island transmits 1 minute and is silent 2 minutes; Ambrose the next succeeding minute after Fire Island and is silent 2 minutes; Barnegat the next succeeding minute after Ambrose and is silent 2 minutes; it is evident, therefore, that during the period of transmission, bearings may be taken on three light vessels successively within 3 minutes. During clear weather most groups of three beacons transmit in the order described for two 10-minute periods of each hour. Each hour is divided into 6 periods of 10 minutes each. Period 1 is from the hour to 10 minutes past, etc.

Calibration of the R. D. F.

Magnetic forces which exist in each PT have a disturbing influence on incoming signals. This influence will cause bearings

to be wrong by plus or minus so many degrees. The purpose of calibration is to determine what this error is throughout the R. D. F. compass rose. Briefly this is done by comparing R. D. F. bearings of transmitting station with bearings taken by pelorus. The comparison will reveal plus or minus errors on various bearings which can then be worked into an R. D. F. error table. With this table at hand, corrected R. D. F. readings can be given the navigator. The Bludworth R. D. F. has a mechanical automatic compensator needle which, when properly adjusted to the various errors, will automatically correct the indicator needle so that reading can be direct. The calibration of an R. D. F. on a PT requires considerable preparation and understanding; therefore, it is suggested that PT officers, radiomen, and quartermasters study up on this work by reading paragraphs 30-55 of chapter 30 in M. E. I.

General Remarks

Due to a phenomenon known as night effect, in general, Ri D. F. bearings taken at night, sunset, and sunrise, should be regarded as of doubtful accuracy. For further explanation Of "night effect," consult M. E. I., chapter 30-101.

Operation of the R. D. F. on PT's is not difficult. However, patience and practice are necessary before a new operator will gain confidence and proficiency.

Chapter 9. COMMUNICATIONS PROCEDURE

Communication procedure is the correct method whereby naval communications are conducted.

Naval communications are in the following forms:

(a) **Letter**.--A communication in writing generally expressed with some degree of formality and transmitted by physical transfer in the original state.

Example.--None necessary.

(b) **Mailgram**.--A communication expressed in brief form and transmitted by physical transfer usually in the original state.

Example.--MAILGRAM

    From: BUSHIPS

    To: COM MTB RON FOUR
          091415
          THREE MODEL TCS SHIPPED
          8 JULY.
          MAILED AT WASH. D. C.

                        Authenticated by:

                              (Signature)

(c) **Message**.--A communication expressed in brief form and transmitted by special means to hasten its delivery. The term embraces dispatches, signals, and procedure messages.

1. *Dispatch*.--Any message (other than a signal or a procedure message) in plain language or encrypted.

Example--

>   Z NAM 310400 NAA Q NBA P GR 15 BT
>   JCPOO NDEFG SMKDL
>   ACYEN CYGPM FLTOK
>   SOP--TG GTQMH HEUMP
>   CMWFT ELEPE CAGHT
>   LORSI STOVE JCPOO

2. *Signals*.--A message whose text consists of one or more

visual displays, special sounds etc., the meanings of which are prearranged.

Example.--

>   DIV V COM IM BT
>   SAIL BAKER TACK DOG GEORGE

3. *Procedure message*.--A message whose text contains one or more procedure signs (with or without data) or whose text consists of a repetition of a portion of a message. *Example.--*

>   NAA J NAM
>   ZMQ NR 12/WA DOLLARS 5000

It must be remembered that the science of communication procedure cannot be reduced to a few pages and a complete description of the subject is beyond the scope of this book. Officers, radiomen, and quartermasters should refer to communication instructions for guidance. The points covered below are only the more elementary and are designed to familiarize students with the general scope of the subject.

Procedure Signs--Procedure Signals

Procedure signs (prosines) are single letters or characters, or combinations thereof; i.e., CTZ AR VA, etc. Procedure signals (prosigs) are three letter prosines with "z" as the first letter, i.e.,

ZMA, ZTE, ZCE PROSINES and PROSIGS have certain definite meanings, such as frequently used orders, instructions, requests, reports, etc., and are used to conduct communications more rapidly and accurately. For example, the following is a complete list of PROSINES:

AA	All after.
AA	Blank.
AB	End of transmission.
AS	Wait.
B	More to follow.
C	Correction.
CC	Corrected version follows (used in signals).
D	Deferred.
E (8 or more)	Erase--Error sign.

F	"F" method, do not receipt for.
GR	Group count.
H	Hold for delivery until called for.
IX	Execute. To follow.
IX	Execute. (At termination of 5-second dash.)
IMI	Repeat
J	Verify and repeat.
K	Go ahead, transmit.
KK	Parentheses.
L	General relay sine.
N	Exemption sine.
NR	Serial number.
O	Urgent.
OP	Operational priority.
P	Priority.
Q	Information.
R	ROutine and receipt
S	Signal strength.
T	Specific relay sine.

V	From.
VA	End of schedule.
W	Interference
XE	Slant sine
Y	Acknowledge.
Z	Originator.

Procedure signals are listed in the communications procedure book.

Parts of Message

All naval dispatches and messages are made up of three general parts: Heading, text, and suffix.

(A) Heading

The heading is composed of four parts, namely, the call, preamble, address, and prefix.

The call is used to establish communications and is made up of the call sign of the station called followed by the prosine "V" meaning "from," and the call sign of the calling station.

The preamble immediately follows the call (or call up) and contains routing instructions, appropriate prosines, and the calls of the stations to whom or by whom the dispatch is to be relayed or delivered.

The address in general shows by whom the dispatch was originated and to whom it is to be delivered. More specifically the address sometimes contains addresses for whom the message is only passed for information. Should the dispatch not be intended for some addressees within a collective address, these addresses can be exempted by use of an appropriate prosine. The address also contains the date and time group which is the reference number. The first two digits give the day of the month and the last four digits give the G. C. T. time which is generally the time of origin.

The prefix is that part of the heading containing the precedence of the dispatch as well as the group count of the text. Included in the prefix are sometimes instructions for addressees to acknowledge the dispatch.

Examples of calls (or call-ups)--

090 V A3U AR or 6 V 5 AR

Examples of preambles (underlined):

NEKT V A3U T <u>NAVX</u> (NEKT is to transmit the message to NAVX as indicated by the specific relay prosine T)

03A V A3U NEKT <u>T NAVX</u> (03A is the collective call for a group of ships. NEKT who is included in this group is designated to transmit this message to NAVX as indicated by the specific relay prosing T).

Examples of address (underlined):

03A V A3TJ T <u>NEKT Z A3U 192305 03 A</u> (This address shows the prosine Z indicating the originating station A3U, followed by the date and time group and the call sign of the station addressees.)

Examples of the prefix (underlined):

<u>C5QVA3TJ</u> Z F5L 132300 NAVX <u>P GR 34 BT</u> (This prefix contains the precedence sine and the group count. In the example, the precedence is PRIORITY and the group count is 34. Action addressee N-AVX is ordered by F5L to take priority action on the message).

--348--

Example of heading.--

<u>A3UVF5L</u>   <u>T</u>   <u>ZF5L172345 NAVX</u> <u>PGR12BT</u>
Call-up Preamble Address   Prefix

(B) Text

The text contains the idea or information which the originator desires to convey to the addressee (S).

(C) Suffix

The suffix is always a prosine or combination thereof and/or call signs. As all transmissions must end with a prosine or a combination thereof, this is known as the suffix.

Example.--

C2P V F9Z T Z NARC 231800 A3U D GR 3 BT
<u>Your 221935 AFFIRMATIVE. /K</u>
       TEXT   SUFFIX.

Executive method.--In order to make up signals that "will be executed at certain time or upon signal, the "execute to follow" signal is used. The **execute to follow** prosine is IX and its use is illustrated in the following examples:

> 3 V 7 IX BT FIRE THE RED ROCKET K

This shows that the dispatch will be acted upon when the controlling or originating station "executes" the signal. When the originating station is ready to execute the signal, he makes the following: 3 V 7 IX (*5 sec.*) k. Upon cessation of the 5-second dash the signal is executed.

NONT.--The voice procedure equivalents to the above examples are:

> 3 V 7 EXECUTE TO FOLLOW BREAK (OR SIGNAL)
> FIRE THE RED ROCKET GO AHEAD

and then:

> 3 V 7 STAND BY TO EXECUTE (5-SECOND. PAUSE) EXECUTE (GO AHEAD
> (ADDED IF RECEIPT IS DESIRED))

--349--

Three types of communication procedure are:

(a) **Normal procedure.**--In this method a transmitting station calls the station for whom the message is intended and delivers it. However, as is often the case, the addressee is not in direct communication with the originating station when it becomes necessary for the message to be relayed by other stations. Stations which usually handle much relayed traffic are generally shore stations who send schedules and clear great amounts of this traffic. Normal procedure **always** includes a **time and date group** and a **group count**.

(b) **Abbreviated normal procedure.**--When the addressee and the originator are in direct communication, the call-up may serve as the address, e. g., NEKT V A3U 022300 P GR 22, etc. In this example NEKT is to take action on A3U's dispatch. In abbreviated normal procedure NEKT can receipt thus: V NEKT R. For since NEKT is in direct communication with A3U it is permissible to drop the call sign of the station called since this is understood.

(c) **Abbreviated procedure.**--Abbreviated procedure is readily recognized by the omission of one of the following things in the heading: The date group, the time and date group, or the group count. Example: C5L V A3U BT _____. In this example the time and date group and the count have been eliminated. (Note. It is desired to use at least the time group whenever possible for easy reference to the dispatch.)

Prosines used to indicate precedence of naval dispatches are:

1. **"O"**. This prosine means the dispatch is of "URGENT" precedence and must be treated

with the utmost speed possible. A maximum delay of 5 minutes is permissible in taking action. The urgent prosine is used with contact reports, or contact signals when the enemy has been sighted or contacted and/or in dispatches about contact.

2. **"OP"--Operational priority**.--This prosine ranks immediately below the urgent precedence in matter of speed of action required. Its use is confined to dispatches relating to operations of Fleet units.

3. **"P"--Priority**.--Denotes a precedence allowing a maxi-imum of 20 minutes in handling or taking action on a dispatch-bearing this prosine.

4. **"R"--Routine**.--This classification of precedence is for dispatches which require only normal speed in handling. In the use of routine precedence the prosine "R" is usually omitted and the absence of any prosine indicating precedence is assumed to mean routine.

5. **"D"--Deferred**.--The lowest precedence assigned to messages in normal naval form is called deferred, and indicates a delay in action can be allowed until the beginning of office hours on the morning following the origin of the dispatch. Office hours are arbitrarily assumed to be 0800. The prosine "D" is usually assigned to messages of lesser importance.

Call Signs

1. **General**.--There are two main types of calls, namely, radio and visual.

2. **Radio call signs**.--(a) Three-letter calls of which the first character is the letter "N" are assigned to all naval shore radio stations.

(b) Four-letter calls of which the first character is the letter "N" are assigned by international law to all naval vessels. This call, in addition to being their radio call, is also their INTERNATIONAL CALL.

(c) Four-letter call signs which are pronounceable, such as MUSK, PAUK, etc., are assigned geographical locations, offices ashore having no radio communications, geographical areas, and groups of any of the aforementioned; offices having no radio and Naval activities without radio.

(d) Call signs made up of letter-numeral-letter combinations are assigned to commanders of fleet or ship units, to groups of commanders, and to groups of ships. These calls are known as collective calls.

Examples.--

 C 5 Q is the call of commander battleship division three.

O 3 A is the call of battleship division three.

(e) Means are provided for encrypting any of the above calls.

(f) Secret calls of various combinations of characters can be compounded for use with all ships, stations, and offices.

(g) For information on tactical calls, see section (e) under "Visual Call Signs. "

3. **Visual call signs**.--(a) *General.*--There are three types of visual calls, namely: Ship, commander, and collective calls, the latter consisting of combinations of the former two types.

(b) A ship's call consists of the ship's class call letter and her call number in one, two, or three digits. All vessels and aircraft are assigned a class call letter to indicate the type. For example, B stands for battleships, R for aircraft carriers, D for destroyers, etc.

(c) Collective calls consist of the letter "F" and a numeral designating a specific group. By placing the letter "F" between the numerals, the commander of that group is formed. To illustrate, 22 stands for Battleforce (F22) and the. commander battleforce call is made by inserting the letter "F" between the two numerals. Thus we get 2F2. To illustrate further, "AP" means transports and "F7" means Base Force. Then APF7 is the call for transports of the Base Force.

(d) When it is desired to call a type commander of a fleet or force, the complete call is formed in this manner: place the class letter of the type designated and the alphabet letter "F" between the two numerals of the organization. For those calls below "10" the numeral "Zero" is used as the first element of the call sign.

(e) *Tactical calls.*--Different task forces of the fleet are assigned numerical task forces, groups, or units. A letter is provided for commander and collective calls, and which letter of the alphabet is used depends upon the geographical area in which the fleet is operating. The division of the task organization is the FORCE. Forces are subdivided into task GROUPS, and, in turn, task groups are subdivided into task UNITS. By placing the letter of the group between the first and second numbers, the commander call may be formed. The numbers preceding the letter of the organization form the collective call. To illustrate,

let us assume that "U" designates the Atlantic Ocean. Then:

0U1 is the call of commander task force one.

U1 is the call of task force one.

1U2 is the call of commander task group 1.2 (commander task group 2 of task force 1).
U12 is the call of task group 1.2 (task group 2 of task force 1).

IU12 is the call of commander task unit 1.1.2 (commander of task unit 2 of task group 1 of task force 1.)

U112 is the call of task unit 1.1.2 (task unit 2 of task group 1 of task force 1.)

(f) To indicate numerals greater than 9 the character "X" is placed before the number to be raised and performs the operation of adding 10 to that number. For instance:

X9 means 19 and **X1** means 11.
1XU23 is the call of commander task unit 1.10.3.
U1X23 is the call of task unit 1.12.3, etc.

Chapter 10. INTERNAL COMMUNICATIONS

Because MTB's are relatively small craft, the problem of internal communications is far from being as complex as it is on a battleship, for example.

It is important, however, that there be efficient communications between the bridge and the engine room, the bridge and the fantail (20-mm. and depth charges) and between the bridge and the torpedo tube stations.

The principal method now used for getting word from the bridge to the various other stations on the boat is the SOUND POWER phone system. Sound power phones may be used effectively in relaying orders to the engine room, to the depth charge, or 20-mm. station. As the name of these phones indicates, they are powered by sound and not by batteries.

Another means of communication between bridge and engine room is the buzzer; There is a buzzer button in the cockpit and one in the engine room for attracting the attention of the bridge. The buzzer system is most frequently used for communicating standard orders, such as stand by to shift clutches, secure from shifting clutches, start engines, secure engines, etc. These signals should be standardized, but certain boats use variations that they have found more practicable; students therefore should familiarize themselves with the standard and special signals on boats they are on.

There are other methods of internal communications which can be used to advantage under certain circumstances. They are:

1. Hand signals
2. Flag signals
3. Using a pistol shot as a signal.

4. Installing siren for Fire or general quarters.
5. Installing a howler on fantail for dropping charge signal.

Whatever system is used on any particular boat, it is important that student find out the systems used when on a patrol or on board for duty.

If a boat is to be able to fight effectively as a unit, its internal communications must be efficient and reliable. The man on the fantail must have no doubt as to when to drop the depth charges; so also with the men standing by the torpedoes to fire by percussion.

Conclusion

While the mission of the communication course is to qualify students for PT duty from a watch-standing viewpoint, it must be realized that in the short period of 2 months it will not be possible to observe all students individually in their abilities to act as radiomen.

On reporting to their respective squadrons, graduates should continue with practical instruction and above all the development of an understanding of sound communication principles.

Look Skipper - No Hands

Transcribed and formatted for HTML by Larry Jewell & Patrick Clancey, Hyperwar Foundation

Motor Torpedo Boat Manual
February 1943

⚓

U.S. Navy

PART V. HULL CONSTRUCTION AND ENGINEERING INSTALLATION, ELCO 77-FOOT MTB, ELCO 80-FOOT MTB

Chapter1. ELCO 77-FOOT MTB

(A) The 77-foot MTB's were built by Elco Naval Division, Bayonne, N. J. They are 77 feet over-all length with a beam of 20 feet. The boats are a V-bottom, hard chine design with a draft ranging from $2^1/2$ feet forward to $4^1/2$ feet aft, and have a loaded displacement of approximately 46 tons. A hard chine design has very little V-shape on its bottom whereas a soft chine boat has a considerable V which gives a sharper entrance into the seas. The hard chine design gives greater speed due to the fact that it causes the boat to plane but it also causes the boats to be

extremely wet in choppy or very rough weather, particularly at slow speeds. The wetness of this type and its lack of sea-keeping qualities has resulted in our later, more modern designs which have a softer chine.

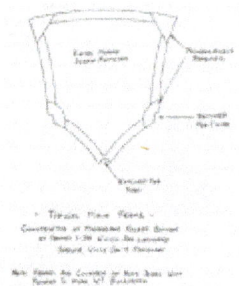

Figure 49.

The first step in the construction of an MTB is the assembly of the prefabricated main frames on a building jig which is a double 12- by 12-inch wooden base extending the entire length of the boat. The frames are built of wood braced with plywood

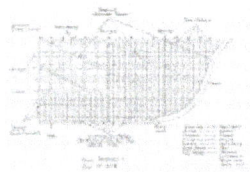

Figure 50.

angles. The bottoms of frames 1 to 34 are laminated of spruce, white oak, and mahogany; the upper part of frames 1 to 34 and the entire frame from 35 to 69 are made of mahogany. All the frame joints are secured with marine glue and screws. Bulkheads are merely frames, properly braced and covered on both sides with fir plywood. They are, for all practical purposes, watertight.

The spruce keel, to which is spliced to an oak stem, is put in place and secured with brass bolts. The chine, which is the hull member forming the joint between the bottom of the hull and the sides, is made of spruce and also bolted on. Spruce diagonal frames on the hull sides and longitudinal battens on the bottom are notched into the main frames and fastened with brass screws. Intermediate frames between the main frames are similarly installed in the three forward compartments. The hull is now ready for planking.

(B) The planking is in two layers both made of mahogany boards 6 inches wide. Both layers above the chine are 3/8 inch thick; on the bottom, the inner layer is 3/8 inch, the outer layer $7/16$ inch. The two layers are laid on diagonally opposite to each other with sheets of airplane fabric laid in marine glue in-between. The

Figure 51.

planks are fastened to the main frames below the water line with monel screws and above the waterline with brass screws. The fastenings to the diagonals, battens, intermediate frames and securing the planks to each other where there are no frames are copper nails riveted over burrs.

(C) When planking is complete, the hull is turned over and the inside work begun. Longitudinal girders made of mahogany covered with plywood run from bulkheads 1, 2, and 3 back to the stern and give the boat a great deal of its stiffness. Cedar clamps or battens are screwed to the inside of the frames on the

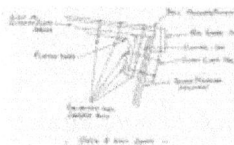

Figure 52.

sides of the hull and run from bulkhead No. 1 to the stern. The main deck frames are notched, spruce deck longitudinals are screwed in place and a 5/8-inch mahogany plywood deck is put on. The deck is secured to the hull with plywood knees between each frame. The knees are bolted to the deck and to the covering board on top, and to the planking, gunwale, and guard clamp on the sides. An oak rub strake outside the gunwale and an oak chine guard make the outer hull work complete. (See illustration.)

(D) The gasoline tanks are mounted on padded frames and secured in place with padded metal straps. Each tank is provided with its own separate fill pipe and each one vents immediately below the gunwale on the outside of the hull. The engines are

mounted on bed frames which are secured to the longitudinal girder. Shims are provided for aligning the engines properly.

(E) The canopy is framed with spruce with all corners and angle joints made of mahogany and fastened with screws and glue. The frame is covered, inside and out, with light plywood which is secured with glue. The voids between frames are filled with rubber insulating material. For convenience in removal of tanks and engines, the canopy is made in three sections, each of which can be removed. The forward or pilot-house section contains the sheet aluminum cockpit and the controls. The midship section contains the gun turrets which are plywood except for a thin metal shield on the top. The after, or engine-room section, is very easily removable and is fitted with a hatch large enough to permit the passage of a reverse gear, V-drive or auxiliary generator. All canopy joints are covered with tape made of airplane fabric to make them watertight and metal clamps are used to hold the two sections together.

(F) A great amount of deck cracking was experienced in the 77-foot MTB's due to the fact that the deck did not have as much flexibility as the hull. This weakness was eliminated by the installation of a hollow fir "strongback" which is a longitudinal stiffener on the deck from forward of the pilothouse to the lazarette hatch on both sides of the canopy. A tendency for the canopy to crack was likewise eliminated by the "strongbacks" and a slightly heavier construction and modified design of the canopy.

(G) The boat's fire-fighting equipment consists of several small hand CO_2 extinguishers and an automatic Lux CO_2 system. The two tanks in the Lux system are located in the starboard officer's stateroom with heat actuators in the tank room and engine room which will cause the system to discharge upon a sudden increase in temperature. A manual control is provided on the deck immediately forward of the canopy hatch.

(H) Scuppers are provided to drain water on deck or overboard from the ports, clear-view screens and cockpit. However, the main drainage employs the use of hand bilge pumps and automatic bilge bailers. There are two hand bilge pumps, one under the ladder leading down into the crew's living compartment and the other on the forward starboard side of the center engine. The forward pump may be used to pump either the crew's

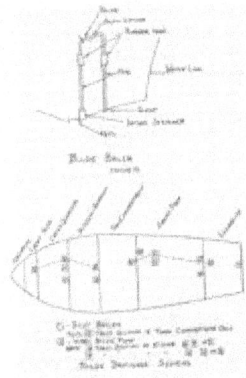

Figure 54.

---

head, crew's quarters, and officer's quarters; the after pump may be used for either the tank compartment, engine room, or lazarette. Bilge bailers utilize the suction created by the motion of the water over a scoop in the bottom of the boat while underway to pump water from the bilges. They are entirely automatic in operation and commence pumping at a speed of about 12 knots. There are six bilge bailers located as follows: one in the lazarette, two aft in the engine room, one forward in the engine room with a suction in the tank compartment, one in the officer's quarters, and one in the crew's compartment.

(I) The power plant of the Elco 77-foot MTB consists of three 1,350-horsepower Packard 4M2500 engines. The engine itself can be studied thoroughly in the Packard Operations Manual. The engineering installation has been developed by the boat builder and requires considerable study to understand completely.

(J) The cooling water and lubricating oil in the engines are cooled by use of a heat exchanger in which the cooling medium is sea water. The heat exchanger is a metal cylinder divided into two sections with 50 to $75^1/4$-inch outside diameter copper tubes inside through which salt water flows. The oil and water flow over the tubes, each in its separate section, and are cooled by a constant flow of sea water. Thermostats bypass the heat exchanger in the oil system until the temperature reaches 140°-145° F.

Sea water is supplied to the heat exchanger by an inlet and outlet scoop under the bottom of the hull. There are two scoops for each heat exchanger and each of them is equipped with a valve, the controls for which are located on the inboard side of each wing engine. In normal underway operation, the outlet scoops are opened wide and temperature is controlled by varying the opening of the inlet scoop. While idling at the dock, however, water is circulated through the heat exchanger by the engine saltwater pump, the intake for which is located in the outlet side of the heat exchanger. To insure the pump pulling water through the heat exchanger, when idling or maneuvering at the dock, it is necessary to close the outlet scoop and open the inlet scoop wide.

The lubricating oil system utilizes a separate 30-gallon tank for each engine equipped with a gage glass to indicate the oil level. Only 24 to 26 gallons of 1,100 (S. A. E. 50) oil are put in the tank. Oil is pumped from the engine by the scavenger pump through an

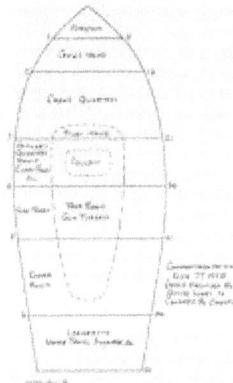

Figure 55.

on-edge type oil filter (which must be cleaned daily by turning the handle once), cooled by the heat exchanger, and then back to the oil tank.

The water system of each engine is provided with an expansion tank which is installed higher than any part of the engine. A gage glass shows the amount of water in the tank. The main purpose of the expansion tank is to provide a level for the water system although it does replace water lost through leaks, evaporation, etc. Cooling water after it has been through the engine, does not return to the expansion tank. It is cooled by the heat exchanger and goes directly back to the engine.

As the engines are installed in the boat, the two wing engines are apparently installed backwards, the reverse gear being towards the bow of the boat. To drive the propeller shafts which run aft, a gear box called a V drive is used. The V drive consists of two cone-shaped gears with roller bearings at each journal. The engine drives one gear which drives the other which, in turn, drives the propeller. Cooling is accomplished by use of water jackets through which sea water is pumped by the engine salt-water pump. A separate oil tank for each V drive is located in the bilge under the unit. Oil is put in the housing of the V drive itself and its level is determined by a bayonet type gage on the filler plug. Lubrication is furnished by an oil pump driven by the unit itself.

(K) The 2-inch Monel propeller shafts go through the hull through a unit called the stern tube. The stern tube is a bronze casting with a flax-packed gland on the inboard end which keeps the water out of the hull. A packing nut tightens or loosens the packing. Cooling is obtained by circulating salt water with a small scoop. A bronze bushing is lubricated by a permanently installed grease gun.

There are eight bronze struts bolted to the bottom of the boat, three for each wing engine shaft and two for the center engine shaft. Each strut is equipped with a rubber bearing which is a pressure fit. When a bearing becomes worn enough to permit shaft vibration, the whole bearing must be replaced.

The three propellers are bronze and keyed to the shaft with a bronze key. Great care must be exercised in the installation of propellers to be certain that they are all the way "home" on the taper and not riding the key or off center.

Chapter2. ELCO 80-FOOT MTB's

(A) The 80-foot MTB's are constructed similarly to the 77-foot boats in that transverse frames are prefabricated and placed upside down on a building jig. There are 69 frames and the transom spaced differently depending on the load to be carried. The bottoms of the frames from the bow aft to the tank compartment are laminated of spruce, white oak, and mahogany. The remainder of the frames and the upper part of the forward frames are made of mahogany with a narrow white oak capping on the inner side.

After the frames are in place, longitudinal battens are let into the main frames from the bow to the forward end of the tank compartment where they are scarfed into a solid layer of mahogany planking which extends under the entire tank compartment. Battens are similarly scarfed into the after end of the tank-compartment inner planking, but from that point to the transom the battens run on top of the frames with spruce spacers in between forming a solid flat foundation for the planking from the forward end of the tank compartment to the stern

Secondary transverse frames and topside diagonal frames are similar to the 77-foot boats except that secondary frames are found in various parts of the boat where strain is excessive as well as in the forward three compartments. In the place of longitudinal deck battens, two longitudinal clamps are installed from bow to stern on either side of the deck openings for the superstructure. In addition, all the deck space between the superstructure openings has a longitudinal clamp running on the keel line. An 8-inch coaming is installed above the deck from the forward end of the superstructure to the after end of the engine room hatch This construction replaces the deck strongbacks installed above the deck on the boats of MTB Ron Four. Diagonal wooden pads and stainless steel webbing under the torpedo tube foundations complete the deck framing.

Intercostal plywood knees which were used to tie in the deck and hull on the 77-foot MTB's have been discarded. Both

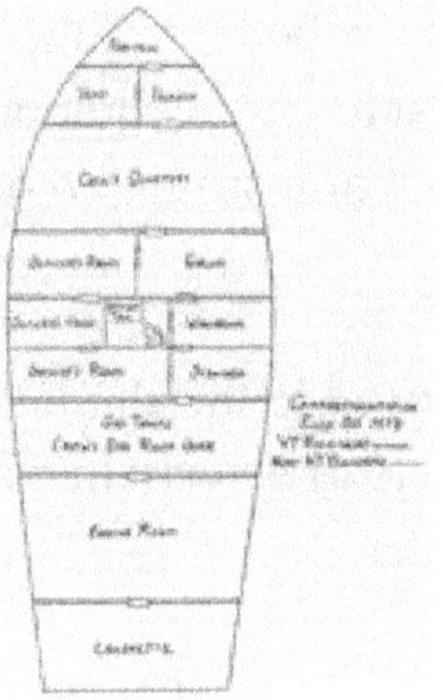

Figure 56.

deck and planking are bolted to a single continuous wooden member the entire length of the hull. The construction appears to be very strong and should give no difficulty. The deck is of double-planked mahogany, 3/8-inch upper and $^5/16$-inch lower, with marine glue and airplane fabric between the plank layers. The planks are laid fore and aft, each lower plank acting as a batten for the upper planks and fastened throughout, with brass screws.

(B)The planking is double diagonal mahogany laid in the same manner as on the 77-foot MTB's. The total thickness of the topside planking is $^3/4$-inch, inner $^5/16$-inch, outer $^7/16$-inch. The bottom planking totals $1^5/16$-inch; inner, $^7/16$-inch; outer, $^1/2$-inch. The fastenings to the main frames are Monel screws below the waterline and brass screws above and copper rivets or clinched nails are used for secondary fastenings. Due to the war requirements of copper, brass, and Monel, it is certain that, in production completed after the summer of 1942, all fastenings will be galvanized steel.

(C) The deck houses are built of spruce frames with curved mahogany corners and covered on both sides with light plywood. The space between the frames in the superstructure is insulated with cork and the whole house is covered with airplane fabric, doped and painted. Hatches are provided to remove gas tanks and engines.

Potable water is carried in a single 200-gallon tank located in the bilge under the chart room. The CO_2 tanks are also installed in the same location with manual releases on the port side aft of the bridge and outside of the engine room hatch. No automatic discharge for the fire extinguisher system is provided.

(D) The engineering installation is almost the same as the 77-foot MTB's. The heat exchanger, oil tank, and expansion tank for the center engine are in the port side of the engine room: those for the wing engines are in the conventional location. A seat for the engineer is provided on the starboard engine from which he can start the engines, observe the instrument panel, control the spark and scoops, and shift clutches. A square hatch with hold-down bolts may be lifted off to remove engines.

Chapter3. HULL REPAIRS

(A) One of the most common hull casualties is a crack in the superstructure or canopy. Such damage has little effect on the structure of the boat itself but does cause leaks. Unless the canopy frame itself is broken, covering the crack with a patch of aircraft fabric, doped and painted, is sufficient to stop the leak. If the framing is damaged, corrosion resisting steel patches not more than 0.060-inch thick should be put on both inside and outside of the canopy. White lead and canvas should be laid under the patches to make it watertight. In canopy, as well as other repairs to the boats, care must be taken to keep the bonding system intact and, if new material is installed, it should be connected to the boats' bonding system.

(B) Small gouges in the hull, if not through the outer planking, can best be repaired by putting on several thin layers of plastic wood and sanding it off flush with the planking. More serious cuts or cracks require the replacement of planks, although

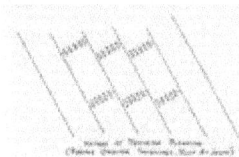

Figure 57.

it is usually necessary to replace only the outer layer. It is generally considered advisable to replace entire planks but if the damage is slight, sections of planks may be installed. When installing only sections of planks, the seams where the new patches butt against the old planking must not be in a straight line but should be staggered.

Care should be taken in the removal of damaged planks from Elco MTB's to damage as little as possible the aircraft fabric between the planks. If the fabric is not seriously damaged, a coat of marine glue should be applied and the new planking installed over the old fabric. If it is damaged considerably, the fabric must be removed and now fabric installed. All screw holes should be plugged with wooden pegs and the old fastenings duplicated as nearly as possible. The new planks must be very carefully fitted but if a slightly open seam is unavoidable, it should be filled with plastic wood. The new planking, when completed, must be sanded down to a very smooth finish.

(C) Main frames break occasionally and, being almost impossible to remove, they must be repaired in the boat. The most

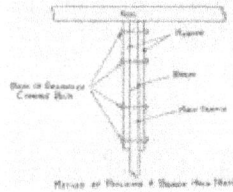

Figure 58.

effective frame repair is the installation of two heavy plywood "sister frames" extending on both sides of the break as far as possible. The two plywood pieces are cut to the shape of the frame, placed on both sides of it at the break and through-bolted with brass or galvanized bolts. It is advisable to use fairly large bolts and few of them because the fewer holes drilled in the frame, the less the chances are of the break recurring.

Cracked battens do not materially weaken the construction of the boat unless there are several of them cracked. A successful method of patching such casualties is to place a similar sized batten over the damaged member and secure it to the main frames with metal angles. The new batten should also be screwed down to the damaged one.

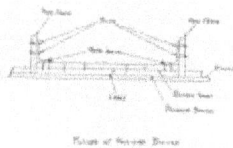

Figure 59.

The rub strake and chine cap are put on the boat to prevent damage to vital parts of its construction when the boat makes contact with the dock or floating objects. Because of their purpose both members require fairly frequent replacement. The damaged pieces should be taken out in entire sections as they were built on the boat, the screw holes plugged, and new sections installed. In the shaping of a new chine cap, particular care must be taken to have the bottom of the chine extend at least

1/8 inch below the bottom of the cap to prevent the force of the water from ripping the cap off.

(D) MTB's frequently suffer casualties to their struts, shafts, and propellers due to contact with the bottom or a floating object. A bent shaft can be corrected only by replacing it with a new shaft. Monel shafts are somewhat flexible but a shaft should never be reinstalled unless it is tested with a dial indicator or some other accurate method and determined to be true.

A bent strut must be removed and straightened or replaced with a new one. To replace a strut, it must first be determined whether the shaft is bent and if it is, it must be replaced. The after part of the shaft must be blocked up so it is perfectly straight. This can be checked with a dial indicator. The new strut is then placed on the shaft and the wooden strut pad planed down until the shaft has the same "pinch" all around the rubber bearing when the strut is tightly held against the pad. The strut bolts should then be installed, tightened and the whole job tested again for accuracy of alignment.

(E) To remove a damaged propeller, the cotter key and lock nut should be removed and the shaft nut backed off about $1/2$ inch. The propeller puller should be put on and tightened up to the point where it puts a strain on the propeller. Further tightening will break the puller. The blades of the propeller should then be struck sharp blows with a hammer which will "shiver" the propeller loose from the shaft. The shaft nut and propeller may then be removed.

To install a new propeller, the brass key should be removed from the shaft and the propeller pushed "home" on the taper. Mark the forward end of the propeller hub on the shaft and remove the propeller. Insert the key in the keyway on the shaft and put the propeller on. The propeller must come up to its previous position on the shaft or it is "riding" the key, thus unbalancing the propeller and perhaps shearing off the key. When the propeller is in the proper position, the shaft nut, lock nut, and cotter key should be installed on the shaft.

(F) Rubber strut bearings have a long life but they will eventually wear out and should be replaced when they do because a worn strut bearing causes a great deal of vibration. Merely because the shaft compresses the bottom of the bearing and does not

--373--

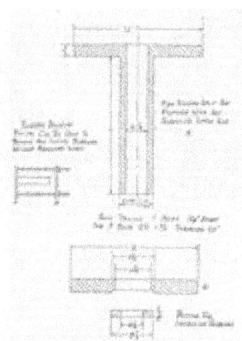

Figure 60.

--374--

touch the top when examined out of water does not mean that the bearing is worn out. The weight and flexibility of the shaft will cause that. The shaft should be blocked up until it is straight and the bearing examined. If the shaft does not "pinch" the rubber slightly around its entire circumference, the bearing should be replaced. The rubber bearing is vulcanized to a bronze bushing which is a push fit in the strut and secured with set screws, and therefore considerable pressure is required to remove it. A bearing puller has been designed which permits the removal of the old bearing and the installation of the new one without removing the shaft. (See illustration.)

MTB RON Form No. 11

U. S. S. PT _____　　　　　　　　　　Date _____

HULL CHECK OFF LIST

The following inspections will be made weekly under the supervision of the boat captain and "OK" put in the "Condition" column if satisfactory and "NG" if unsatisfactory. In any item marked "NG," give reasons in the "Remarks" column. These lists will be kept in each boat available for inspection by the squadron commander or first lieutenant.

	Condition	Remarks
1. Bilges (cleanliness and dryness).		
2. Self-bailer shut-off.		
3. Self-bailer intake strainer		
4. Self-bailer anti-siphon hole.		
5. Hand bilge pumps		
6. Weigh fire extinguishers		
7. Weigh Lux tanks		
8. Check Lux release valves		
9. Fresh-water tanks and piping.		
10. Fresh-water pumps		
11. Steering chain and sprocket lubrication.		
12. Gemmler gear lubrication		
13. Tiller bar lubrication		
14. Main and secondary frames		
15. Planking		
16. Deck		
17. Superstructure		
18. Girders and deck longitudinals.		
19. Paint (topside)		
20. Paint (below decks)		
21. Deck fittings (cleats, chocks, etc.)		
22. Stowage and condition of ground tackle.		
23. Stowage of ammunition and ordnance gear.		

	Condition	Remarks
24. Stowage of gear in lazarette.		

	Condition	Remarks
25. Tightness of all hatches, ports, etc.		
26.Rub strake		
27.Lines and fenders		
28. 20 m/m. and torpedo tube deck pads and framing.		
29.Blackout system		
30.Bonding system		

WHEN BOAT IS HAULED

1.Propellers		
2. Rudders		
3. Shafts		
4. Struts		
5. Rubber bearings		
6. Scoops		
7. Planking		
8. Chine cap and chine		

THE LAWS OF THE NAVY

Now these are laws of the Navy,
   Unwritten and varied they be;
And he that is wise will observe them,
   Going down in his ship to the sea;
As naught may outrun the destroyer,
   Even so with the law and its grip,
For the strength of the ship is the Service,
   And the strength of the Service, the ship.

Take heed what ye say of your seniors,
   Be your words spoken softly or plain,
Lest a bird of the air tell the matter,

And so ye shall hear it again.

If ye labour from morn until even'
    And meet with reproof for your toil,
It is well that the guns be humbled,
    The compressor must check the recoil.

On the strength of one link in the cable,
    Dependeth the might of the chain.
Who knows when thou mayest be tested?
    So live that thou bearest the strain!

When the ship that is tired returneth,
    With the signs of the sea showing plain,
Men place her in dock for a season,
    And her speed she reneweth again.

So shalt thou, lest perchance thou grow weary
    In the uttermost parts of the sea,
Pray for leave, for the good of the Service,
    As much and as oft as may be.

Count not upon certain promotion,
    But rather to gain it aspire;
Though the sight-line end on the target,
    There cometh, perchance, a misfire.

If ye win through an Arctic ice floe,
    Unmentioned at home in the Press,
Heed it not, no man seeth the piston,
    But it driveth the ship none the less.

Can'st follow the track of the dolphin
    Or tell where the sea swallows roam;
Where Leviathan taketh his pastime;
    What ocean he calleth his home?
Even so with the words of thy seniors,
    And the orders those words shall convey.
Every law is as naught beside this one--
    "Thou shalt not criticize, but obey!"

Saith the wise, "How may I know their purpose?"
    Then acts without wherefore or why.

Stays the fool but one moment to question.
  And the chance of his life passeth by.

Do they growl? It is well: Be thou silent,
  So that work goeth forward amain;
Lo, the gun throws her shot to a hair's breadth
  And shouteth, yet none shall complain.
Do they growl and the work be retarded?
  It is ill, speak, whatever their rank;
The half-loaded gun also shouteth,
  But can she pierce armor with blank?

Doth the funnels make war with the paintwork?
  Do the decks to the cannon complain?
Nay, they know that some soap or a scraper
  Unites them as brothers again.
So ye, being Heads of Departments,
  Do your growl with a smile on your lip,
Lest ye strive and in anger be parted,
  And lessen the might of your ship.

Dost think, in a moment of anger,
  'Tis well with thy seniors to fight?
They prosper, who burn in the morning,
  The letters they wrote overnight;

For some there be, shelved and forgotten,
  With nothing to thank for their fate,
Save that (on a half-sheet of foolscap),
  Which a fool "Had the honor to state--."

Dost deem that thy vessel needs gilding,
  And the dockyard forbear to supply;
Place thy hand in thy pocket and gild her,
  There be those who have risen thereby.

If the fairway be crowded with shipping,
  Beating homeward the harbour to win,
It is meet that, lest any should suffer,
  The steamers pass cautiously in;
So thou, when thou nearest promotion,
  And the peak that is gilded is nigh,
Give heed to thy words and thine actions,

Lest others be wearied thereby.
It is ill for the winners to worry,
    Take thy fate as it comes with a smile,
And when thou art safe in the harbour
    They will envy, but may not revile.

Uncharted the rocks that surround thee,
    Take heed that the channels thou learn,
Lest thy name serve to buoy for another
    That shoal, the Courts-Martial Return.
Though Armour, the belt that protects her,
    The ship bears the scar on her side;
It is well if the court acquit thee;
    It were best hadst thou never been tried.

Now these are laws of the Navy,
    Unwritten and varied they be;
And he that is wise will observe them,
    Going down in his ship to the sea.
As the wave rises clear to the hawse pipe,
    Washes aft, and is lost in the wake,
So shall ye drop astern, all unheeded,
    Such time as the law ye forsake.

Now these are the Laws of the Navy
    And many and mighty are they.
But the hull and the deck and the keel
    And the truck of the law is--OBEY.

--By Captain Hopwood, R. N.

Transcribed and formatted for HTML by Larry Jewell & Patrick Clancey, Hyperwar Foundation

www.ingramcontent.com/pod-product-compliance
Lightning Source LLC
Chambersburg PA
CBHW050618110426
42813CB00010B/2605